MW00805377

DEATH'S SHOWCASE

THE MIT PRESS   CAMBRIDGE, MASSACHUSETTS   LONDON, ENGLAND

THE POWER OF IMAGE IN CONTEMPORARY DEMOCRACY

ARIELLA AZOULAY

Translated by Ruvik Danieli

DEATH'S SHOWCASE

© 2001 Massachusetts Institute of Technology

All rights reserved. No part of this book may be reproduced in any form by any electronic or mechanical means (including photocopying, recording, or information storage and retrieval) without permission in writing from the publisher.

This book was set in Janson Text by Graphic Composition, Inc.
Printed and bound in the United States of America.

Library of Congress Cataloging-in-Publication Data

Azoulay, Ariella.
  Death's showcase / Ariella Azoulay; translated by Ruvik Danieli.
    p. cm.
  Collection of works previously published chiefly in Hebrew. With new works and introduction.
  Includes bibliographical references and index.
  ISBN 0-262-01182-4 (hc.: alk. paper)
  1. Death in art.   2. Photography, Artistic.   3. Artists and museums.   4. Arts, Israeli—20th century.   5. Death—Psychological aspects.   6. Postmodernism.   I. Title.
NX650.D4 .A99 2001
306.9′09′04—dc21

                                                        00-064600

CONTENTS

In course of writing this book I have benefited from the enlightening remarks and encouragement of Etienne Balibar, Michal Ben Naftali, Roger Conover, Eda Cufer, Eyal Dotan, Yaron Ezrahi, Hanan Hever, Adi Ophir, and Irit Rogoff.

Translated by Ruvik Danieli in association with Michal Ben Naftali (part of chapter 2), Vivianne Barsky (chapter 6), and Maya Landau (part of chapter 9).

"[Death's] Display Showcase" was supported by a grant from the Rosenzweig Center at the Hebrew University in Jerusalem.

"The [Spectator's] Place" was published in Hebrew in *Theoria ve Bikoret*, no. 15 (1999).

"The [Blind] Gesture" was published in Hebrew in *Plastica*, no. 3 (1999).

"[Critical] Image" was published in *D'Israel*, a catalogue of Israeli art, Dominique Abensour, curator, Musée Le Quartier, Quimper, France.

"The Simulated City" is based on a lecture given at the Bellagio conference "Visions of Jerusalem."

"The Floodlit Arena [of Murder]" was published in Hebrew in *Theoria ve Bikoret*, no. 9 (1996).

"Save as JerusalemS" was published in English in *Urbanism and Propinquity*, edited by Joan Copjec (London: Verso 1999). An earlier, shorter Hebrew version appeared in *Reading*, no. 3 (1995).

Most of the interviews in chapter 10, "The Picture [of the Battlefield]" were published in Hebrew in Ariella Azoulay, *How Does It Look to You?* (Tel-Aviv: Babbel, 1999).

"[Art] Museum" was first published in Hebrew in *Iyunim Bachinuch*, vol. 2 (1997).

ACKNOWLEDGMENTS

DEATH'S SHOWCASE

CHAPTER 1

INTRODUCTION:

ON THE WORK OF DEATH
IN THE AGE OF MECHANICAL REPRODUCTION

The museum, the muteness (of the work of art), the instrument (a camera, a gun), the spectator, the body of horror (Hitler), the simulated city (Jerusalem), the erased city (Hiroshima), the battlefield, the arena of murder (Yitzhak Rabin), the postmortem showcase (television): these are the heroes of this book. It is a book about the visual work of death in the age of mechanical reproduction. In each case, similar questions are raised and discussed. Who sees? Who is capable of seeing, what, and from where? Who is authorized to look? How is this authorization given or acquired? In whose name does one look? What is the structure of the field of vision? To whom should or can one report what one sees? In each case, the questions are framed through the scopic regime associated with photography, with the museum, or with both. The two are cultural sites that authorize the aesthetic view of death, in which it is permissible, sometimes even desirable, to publicly display death. Between the museum and photography, the authorized display of death oscillates between a spectacle and an exhibit. The following book seeks to understand the conditions that make such display possible.

This is a book about the public display of death in contemporary culture. It deals with three formations of display enclosed within three typically modern sites: the psychoanalyst's clinic, the white cube of the modern museum of art, and the television screen. These three seemingly neutral spaces allow three kinds of images to appear: imaginary, tangible, and virtual. The images on display in each of these sites constantly refer to a lost or an absent image, an image of loss and death that gives sense and direction to the ongoing act of display. In the psychoanalyst's clinic the missing image is the image of the traumatic moment. The museum, which is usually crowded with images, always seeks an image (that is still missing) of the next genius, style, or fashion, yet unheard of, that will transcend and outlive all previous ones. And within the television set, the missing image is the image of death itself, of the very presence of death, which would somehow transcend the flux of its representations constantly projected on the screen. No matter how differently these three sites are organized, they share a similar motivation: to help the apparition of the lost image. But in fact they all produce the conditions for an unfinished work of mourning.

The several drafts of "The Work of Art in the Age of Mechanical Reproduction," written by Walter Benjamin in the second half of the 1930s, were an attempt to clear a space for a discussion of visual culture as a *sui generis* domain. The contours of his discussion still prevail today:[1] his discussion of the transformation of

---

1. My references to the artwork essay are to the third (French) and fourth editions (Benjamin, 1978, Benjamin, 1991).

the ontological and social status of the work of art as well as the transformation of the entire sphere of the visible in modernity. Toward the end of the essay Benjamin points to the inherent relations between the modern material conditions of the re-production of the visible and the condition of the display of death in modern society:

Mankind, which in Homer's time was an object of contemplation for the Olympian gods, now is one for itself. Its self-alienation has reached such a degree that it can experience its own destruction as an aesthetic pleasure of the first order. (Benjamin, 1978, 242)

Benjamin did not elaborate on this passage, which, like many of his insights, has remained enigmatic. In attempting to interpret this passage, I have engaged in a close reading of "The Work of Art," devoting special attention to Benjamin's in-sights about the representation and place of loss and death in modern visual cul-ture. This essay, together with some other Benjaminian texts in which the imagery of death is invoked, help me reconstruct a mosaic of relations between visibility and death. Although the explicit reading of Benjamin comprises only two of the book's eleven chapters, these uncanny and sometimes thrilling relations inform the book in its entirety.

In the second chapter, where Benjamin's insights are explicitly invoked and in-terpreted, the question of the aura is inverted. Benjamin's essay, which seemingly describes the loss of the aura, is shown—from both philosophical and historical perspectives—to produce the aura by the very description of its loss. The third chapter examines the relation between Benjamin and Heidegger, who each wrote an essay about art, loss, and death in the second half of the 1930s. I demonstrate that despite the clear and acknowledged differences between the two thinkers, a certain important common ground, which the chapter articulates, throws new light on both of them and on the fundamental relation between the modern gaze and death.

From the fourth chapter on, the book consists of a series of essays dedicated to different case studies in visual culture in which death is displayed through museum and photographic practices. The museum and photography are two distinct, yet closely related cultural practices that have had great impact on the modern con-struction of the visual in general and on the public display of death in particular. In different ways, the museum and the photographic image perform a similar func-tion as an interface through which individuals are interpellated to look at framed segments of an inaccessible visual world and to relate the sayable (*dicible*) and the visible. It is in and through these two kinds of interface that death is most commonly confronted in modern and postmodern culture. Along with other image showcases (mainly television), these two clusters of visual practices play a crucial role in the formation of the postmodern subject as a spectator of death.

Chapter 4 examines a unique exhibition of the Israeli artist Roee Rosen at the Israel Museum, in which the spectator is invited to "live and die as Eva Braun" (Adolf Hitler's mistress), in relation to the public debate stirred by this provocative invitation. It is shown how, at one stroke, the artist's gesture problematizes the limits of Holocaust discourse, the culture of memory in Israeli society, and the traditional role of the museum spectator as the one who commands the discourse about art and is rarely commanded by it.

Rosen's exhibition is associated with *Hiroshima Mon Amour*, the 1959 film directed by Alain Renais and written by Marguerite Duras, to bring out the political meaning of the conventional dissociation of three proper names—World War II, the Holocaust, and Hiroshima. Thus the fifth chapter focuses directly on Hiroshima and examines the possibility of a nonrepressive work of remembrance that will not turn the survivors into its victims. A special project, *Hiroshima Collection*, by the French artist Marie Ange Guilleminot, serves here as a point of reference. The project is shown to be an attempt to deconstruct the concept of a community of gaze and replace it with an intimate, bodily, and invisible gesture of commemoration that has no presence in the public space.

The sixth chapter deals with the conditions of possibility of the photographic image through the works of five Israeli artists—Michal Heiman, Barry Frydlender, Efrat Shvily, and Dana and Boaz Zonshine—who experiment in different modes of production of images and their display. This chapter, which introduces the question that comes up several times in the course of the book—What makes an image critical?—deploys the theoretical, cultural, and political context for the next three chapters (chapters 7–9), dealing with the simulated city and the scene of murder. Chapter 7 analyzes the place the city of Jerusalem occupies in the symbolic order and the Israeli occupation of the West Bank. The city is presented as multilayered, an object of projection for many individuals and institutions, nations and regimes, each of which strives and some of which succeed in incarnating their fantasies in the city's physical texture. Jerusalem is presented as the repressed side of both the Oslo Accords, which sought to end the Israeli occupation, and of the assassination of Yitzhak Rabin, Israel's prime minister, who sought to implement the Oslo Accords.

Chapter 8 is a study of Rabin's assassination in Tel Aviv's floodlit city plaza. The assassin wanted to change the course of history, and so did his victim. They both were critical of their fellow citizens and tried to translate their criticism into action. A third actor at the scene was an amateur photographer who happened to be at the site, who foresaw, so it seems, the forthcoming eruption of violence, and who documented it with his video camera. A fateful, contingent series of events and two fatal instruments, the camera and the gun, relate these three figures—the assassin, his victim, and the photographer. Through an analysis of these relations this chapter seeks to question the limits and conditions of critique in the domain of the visible.

The ninth chapter examines a special cluster of relations between subjectivity and citizenship, conceptualized and exemplified by two projects by Israeli artists who work in Jerusalem, Sigalit Landau and Aya & Gal. The two projects deal with a common theme in highly original though quite different ways. They both show how differences of status between native inhabitants and formal citizens in Jerusalem are inscribed in the urban and virtual spaces of the sacred, divided, terror-ridden city, are embodied in its inner and outer boundaries, and are reproduced through the different scopic regimes established within it.

The tenth chapter focuses on the image of the battlefield through a series of interviews with photographers who have photographed battle scenes and a close look at their contacts. Death is displayed in a space created by the gap between the visible (what the photographers show) and the sayable (what they say when they talk about what they saw, what they photographed, and how they show what they saw).

The eleventh chapter raises the analogy between photography and the museum and examines the role of the museum in the formation of individuals as subjects and citizens. In the museum the individual learns how to speak about, and for, the mute visible and how to take a stance toward the visible—a stance that may be at one and the same time critical and yet anticipated by the social order that has made it possible through the museum apparatus.

The disposition and skills of the spectator are essential for the constitution of the modern citizen as a sovereign subject capable of judgment and critique. The book examines the existing continuity between the practice of "looking at" acquired in the museum by a detached spectator looking from a safe distance at pictures in showcases (which he or she is not allowed to touch or manipulate) and the way one learns to look at the display of death and dying during the modern era.

The theoretical framework of this book draws freely on contemporary French thought, especially on the works of Michel Foucault, Gilles Deleuze, Jean-François Lyotard, Jean-Luc Nancy, and Jean Baudrillard. The book critically engages their analyses of social space and modern and postmodern regimes of vision. It also makes selective use of some of these thinkers' understandings with respect to the cultural, logical, and political implications of different modes of representation, their production, and their dissemination in social space. Even more important, however, is the debt this book owes to the pertinent cultural insights of Walter Benjamin, mainly those scattered in his essays "The Theses on History" (1983), "A Short History of Photography" (1980, 1996a), "The Passagen Werke" (1989), and, above all, "The Work of Art in the Age of Mechanical Reproduction" (1978, 1991).

CHAPTER 2   [DEATH'S] DISPLAY SHOWCASE:

WALTER BENJAMIN

That which withers in the age of mechanical reproduction is the aura of the work of art. This is a symptomatic process whose significance points beyond the realm of art. One might generalize by saying the technique of reproduction detaches the reproduced object from the domain of tradition. By making many reproductions it substitutes a plurality of copies for a unique existence. And in permitting the reproduction to meet the beholder or listener in his own particular situation, it reactivates the object reproduced.

—BENJAMIN (1978, 221)[1]

1

The title of Walter Benjamin's essay—"The Work of Art in the Age of Mechanical Reproduction"—is misleading. One might assume that the essay is concerned with works of art and the changes they undergo in this era, and thus it is commonly interpreted. This interpretation of the essay, as dealing with an object termed a "work of art," can be misleading. It may lead one to understand the text as a nostalgic discussion of the loss of the work of art that existed in the period before the era of technical reproduction. I here offer a different frame of reference for Benjamin's essay, emphasizing certain passages in the text. I try to isolate these passages[2] from the narrative framework in which they are embedded—a framework that relates the history of the "work of art"—and cast them in a new light. Two of these passages are "This is a symptomatic process whose significance points beyond the realm of art" (221) and "Photography freed the hand of the most important artistic functions, which henceforth devolved only upon the eye looking into a lens" (219).

The significance of the process, says Benjamin, extends beyond the field of art. In other words, it is not typical solely of the development of the field of art. For this reason I contend that this process cannot be interpreted as being evident in the diachronic history of the work of art. Rather, it must be located in the synchronic dimension in the coexistence of different forms of spatial organization, exchange of objects, and structures of subjectivity. To search for traces of the process in the history of the work of art is mistaken because this must assume that the object termed a "work of art" is stable over hundreds of years and that the process has brought about a transmission of that very same object.

---

1. All citations in this chapter are from "The Work of Art in the Age of Mechanical Reproduction" and are taken from Benjamin (1978). Further citations refer only to the page number.

2. These passages are usually left undeveloped within "The Work of Art." Some of them appear in various versions in other of Benjamin's essays, particularly "Theses on History," (1983), "A Short History of Photography" (1980), "The Author as Producer" (1979), and "Baudelaire" (1983).

2

The object termed a "work of art" and the central characteristic Benjamin ascribes to it—the aura—are modern products that did not exist prior to the age of capitalism, which is characterized by certain production conditions that Benjamin, following Marx, seeks to examine.

3

The aura is lost by a process that is symptomatic of how the human body is spatialized in the age of capitalism, especially how various limbs and organs are dispersed in space and how a "class of 'hands'" is created. Benjamin speaks of the liberation of the hand. Marx and Engels spoke of the freeing of the hand with the invention of the first tools. The transformation of flint into a knife enabled man to produce to supply his needs "in universal fashion."[3] The hand, they continue, was freed from the body—from its needs—and reached high levels of sophistication (muscles, tendons, and bones) that enabled it to create Raphael's paintings and Paganini's music. In Benjamin's essay, he implies from the start that he is attempting to analyze the state of culture to provide an analysis that will conform with Marx's prophecy.[4] The hand described by Marx and Engels became both free and subservient to the machine at the same time. Free or subservient, this hand remained identifiable as a hand belonging to its owner and bearing his mark. Yet the hand that appears at the beginning of Benjamin's essay appears in two guises. It is present in its absence, a sort of invisible hand hiding behind the traces of its action, or else it branches off from the human body and becomes a new type of limb, which is no longer subservient solely to its owner. The invisible hand is the one that—starting from the nineteenth century, the period to which Benjamin devoted most of his research—brings the light into our homes and channels the water through the pipes to the tap of the individual user: "Just as water, gas, and electricity are brought into our houses from far off to satisfy our needs in response to a minimal effort, so we shall be supplied with visual or auditory images, which will appear and disappear at a simple movement of the hand, hardly more than a sign" (219).[5] However, this is also the invisible hand, the

---

3. The discussion on the hand appeared in Engel's 1876 article "The Role of Labor in Anthropomorphizing the Monkey" (Marx and Engels, 1951).

4. The transformation of the superstructure, analyzed by Benjamin, "takes place far more slowly than that of the substructure, has taken more than half a century to manifest in all areas of culture the change in the conditions of production" (1978, 217–218).

5. In 1859, the paraffin oil lamp was invented, enabling a light to shine without an individual clipping the wick or adding oil every few minutes. In 1889, a toilet bowl with flowing water was introduced. Both

protagonist of Adam Smith, a metaphor that stands for an explanation of market phenomena that cannot account for the results of the interplay between intentions and fulfillments (Smith, 1976). At best we may speak of an invisible hand that orchestrates a large number of activities that have not been connected together and that no one specifically intended to bring together. Modern working conditions have led to the gradual loss of the aura of the unique hand of a king, warrior, or artist and the anonymous hand that generates phenomena. The marked hand of the specific individual multiplied and was reproduced by the hand of every individual in the mass, so that it has become impossible to locate it and find the source from which it stems and acts.[6]

4

A short history of the artist's hand demonstrates a few of the changes it has undergone. The artist's hand—since the Renaissance, at least—has been marked by (and has marked in its turn) the specific function and profession of its owner (its subject). The artist's hand—to which a magic touch is attributed—is also the unique location in which his (and the artist was virtually always male) most authentic subjectivity was supposed to reside, the emblem and conduit of his creativity. Throughout the annals of art, the hand—when it was the hand of a great artist—was the place from which his greatness issued forth, traced like a birthmark in the work of art itself.[7] The artist's hand was supposed to have a unique touch, impressing its traces on the painter's canvas or the sculptor's marble. Traces of the artist, his greatness, style, mood, and soul, were present beyond the traces left by his hand. The hand was the mediator between the artist's subjectivity and the objective product of his work, as it was also the place (in the body) where his creation took form. The hand was a conduit of originality and authenticity from the subject of art to its object—the work of art. This regime of subjectivity assumed an ideal synthesis of view, speech, and action—a place wherein the contemplative eye, speaking mind, and active hand have all been integrated.[8] The locus of this integration was the threshold of the phenom-

---

these inventions—just a sample of the hundreds introduced during the nineteenth century—express the magic of the hidden hand: the water flowing from inside a wall to appear in the toilet bowl, the light glowing in the lamp without requiring work.

6. See Marx's (1936) descriptions of the laborer's hand in *Capital*. Regarding the warrior, see the discussion on the primacy of the technological gaze over the hand in Virilio (1989).

7. See the essays of Israeli artist Michal Ne'eman, which address the relationship between the creation of work and a birthmark, as well as Ne'eman's lecture on the subject in Tel Aviv, in 1996.

8. Feminist writing on art taking the hand as its subject should genderize the ostensibly neutral hand that appears in the history of art. In practice, this hand always already appears in gender-specific terms. Un-

enal world. The world was external to this disembodied, immaterial subject who was contemplating it, speaking about it, and acting on it. The eye functioned as an organ of interiorization, making it possible to assimilate the world into the subject's internal space. The tongue and hand became organs that served to exteriorize this interiority, linking it anew to the external world. The organs were defined by this internal space, not as part of this world but as agents acting on it from outside.

5

These internal and external relations break down in Benjamin's essay. The hand may be part of a real body, but it is also an organ floating in the world to which the individual is extending a hand, responding to its interpellation.

6

The hand in Benjamin's essay is the hand of the individual in the mass. This notion of the hand presupposes Marx's "class of 'hands'" exploited by a class of masters. But by placing the hand in the mass, Benjamin deconstructs the distinction between the hands of the master class and the hands of the "class of 'hands.'" Benjamin begins to delineate a portrait of a hand that has disappeared behind the individual's back, which has been buttoned to his shirt in a way that constrains its movement by a sleeve: "For the first time in the process of pictorial reproduction, photography freed the hand of the most important artistic functions which henceforth devolved only upon the eye looking into a lens" (219). The "liberated" hand makes it possible to pose the individual's eye as his sole weapon—an eye contemplating dreams that have been packed for it inside display showcases. When the hand is buttoned back, free of duties, it responds to the principle of action and instruction inscribed inside the display showcase ever since the creation of the modern concept and institution of display—the museum: "Look, but don't touch."[9] The display showcase is a void

---

til the 1960s, this hand was always that of the male artist, while women's hands formed a preferred object for pictorial or sculptural representation. In the context of the degenderism exhibition held in the Stagaya Museum in Tokyo (1996), I attempted to genderize a number of hands (including those of the artists Marie Ange Guilleminot, Aya & Gal, and Sigalit Landau) and later to problematize this genderization. Sections from the text relating to Marie Ange Guilleminot were published in French (Azoulay, 1997c).

9. In her article "Aesthetics and Anaesthetics: A Re-examination of Walter Benjamin's Essay 'Reproduction'," Susan Buck-Morss (1992) develops the theme of sleep-anesthetization and awakening-shock in Benjamin. She claims that the revolution Benjamin generated lies in the return of the concept of aesthetics to its etymological root in the Greek *aisthisis*—"sensory experience of perception." In the context of Benjamin, on the one hand, and medical discourse, on the other, Buck-Morss analyzes the sensorial system as a synesthetic system blending sensation, motoric response, and expression. In a technological environment,

inside which lies an object, a commodity—in fact, an image of commodity. The showcase is resplendent in its beauty—a wondrous beauty, like that of a Medusa who paralyzes any onlooker around her or in front of her, including everyone desirous of her. Thus the eye of the onlooker—whether desirous or repelled—is also locked on the object. The spectator's eye becomes an object of a gaze reflected on by the eye of the object that enchants and hypnotizes it.[10] Is this what is meant by the evil eye? Benjamin described this enchantment as a state of deep dormancy that falls on the mass and that sinks into the phantasmagoric sights of commodity as the embodiment of an exchange value and the loss of the use value.

7

Several times in the text Benjamin assumes the work of art as a fixed point of reference and examines its forms of reproduction. Before the invention of the camera, these forms included casting, stamping, and printing, which made it possible to copy (reproduce) a work of art. Later came means of technical reproduction. Actually, both practices of copying and reproduction made it possible for a work to appear outside the *place* of its *presence*. Benjamin posits photography as something that makes it possible for a work to appear *without being present anywhere*. With the in-

---

this system protects against shock (the quintessential modern experience, according to Benjamin) and protects the body against trauma or concussion. Thus the sensorial system is subject simultaneously to intensified stimulation and to desensitization. In effect, "the cognitive system of sinaesthetics has become, rather, one of *an*esthetics" (Buck-Morss, 1992, 18). As the general anesthetic takes effect, claims Buck-Morss, the experience breaks down into three factors—the surgeon, the operated object, and the observer. Regarding the social body, the same breakdown may be noted: "labor specialization, rationalization and integration of social functions, created a techno-body of society, and it was imagined to be as insensate to pain as the individual body under general anesthetics, so that any number of operations could be performed upon the social body without needing to concern oneself lest the patient—society itself—utter piteous cries and moans" (Buck-Morss, 1992, 30). Following Benjamin, Buck-Morss analyzes the use made of this experience by fascism, quoting Goebbels, who in 1933 depicted the Nazi leadership as artists charged with formalizing the raw material of the masses. She claims that "this is the technologized version of the myth of autogenesis, with its division between the agent (here, the fascist leaders) and the mass (the undifferentiated hyle [undifferentiated 'brute' matter], acted *upon*). We will remember that this division is tripartite. There is as well the observer, who 'knows' through observation. It was the genius of fascist propaganda to give to the masses a double role, to be observer as well as the inert mass being formed and shaped."

The conception of the force that is capable of creating form that emerges from Buck-Morss's comments in this passage is pyramidal and monodirectional, presenting the masses as clay in the potter's hands. Buck-Morss's analysis of the motif of anesthetization in Benjamin is brilliant, but in addressing a no less central motif—reproduction—her analysis ignores the spatial ramifications of the concept and thus the role of the masses in the new power relations that develop thanks to the inherent potential of reproduction. This chapter attempts to address this motif.

10. See Taylor's analysis of Heidegger's "thing" and Lacan's "Freudian thing." Taylor quotes the jellyfish as an example of the classic evil eye (Taylor, 1987, 96–103).

vention of photography the ontology of the work of art is transformed. Previous forms of reproduction (which were executed manually to one degree or another) were based on the hierarchical difference between the reproduced original and its copies and assisted in creating and preserving this difference. The invention of photography (and later the cinema) led to the change that Benjamin discusses. Technical reproduction makes it possible to produce many copies of "original works," just as it makes it possible to produce many copies that do not refer to an original. The work of art appears outside its distinctive place, outside any distinctive place of its own, in which case it can appear anywhere. I later deal more extensively with the link that arises, then, between origin and place.

8

Benjamin identifies the question of the original as the decisive difference between ancient and modern forms of reproduction. However, his identification of the ancient forms of reproduction—casting and stamping—permits the definition of an additional difference and one that may prove to be decisive. This difference relates to the transition from the three-dimensional reproduction of a three-dimensional object to the two-dimensional reproduction of any object, regardless of its number of dimensions. With modern technical reproduction, the world becomes a surface of a picture, or as Heidegger puts it, we are living in an era of "the conquest of the world as a picture."

9

Benjamin assumes the work to be an essence that he defines by negation. He points to the lacking dimension in the new product generated as a result of technical reproduction: "Even the most perfect reproduction of a work of art is lacking in one element: its presence in time and space, its unique existence at the place where it happens to be" (220). The real work of art—which is unblemished and lacks nothing, the complete work—has the "here and now" that the new one lacks. Benjamin identifies the "here and now" with the authenticity of the work, and their loss signifies the work's loss of authenticity.[11] Is Benjamin lamenting the loss of authenticity or the loss of the aura?

---

11. In an article written for the exhibition *The Artist Facing History*, Hal Foster describes the artist of the 1980s and 1990s as an anthropologist who addresses what lies beyond the "here and now," in another place, in other identities, in otherness of any type. One might extend Foster's point, arguing that the "here and now" lost by the artist was—according to Benjamin—lost by art with the invention of photography. Today, when the "here" encounters the "now" through various communication networks, might it be accurate to speak of their loss in terms of the act of the artist, or might one claim that in Foster's context as well, he produces or formulates the object of loss? This discussion is outside the scope of this essay (Foster, 1996b).

10

It is customary to portray Benjamin's essay as an historical story describing the loss of aura of the work of art. This reading misses Benjamin's melancholy attitude toward the work of art. Melancholia, writes Giorgio Agamben, following Freud, "offers the paradox of an intention to mourn that precedes and anticipates the loss of the object" (Agamben, 1997, 20). Benjamin's essay, I attempt to show, is a preparation for mourning that precedes the loss because the object of the loss, the work of art possessing an aura, is produced during the course of that mourning itself. Furthermore, the aura does not belong to the object; rather, it is a description of the new relation created in modernity between the gaze and the possibility of action. The aura, says Benjamin, is a unique manifestation of distance, close as it may be. Could there be a more accurate description of television than Benjamin's description of the aura?

11

In the 1930s, the period during which Benjamin wrote his essay, the work of art still lacked a clear, commonly accepted institutional identity and definition, as is implied by some of his descriptions.[12] The main institutions that dealt with the display of art in the 1930s—the "museum," "salon," and "great exhibition"[13]—placed side by side types of objects and images that current classifications would differentiate between: engines, paintings, jewelry, photographs, sewing machines, stereoscopes, movies, railroad cars, and panoramas. "Art"—whatever that may be—was regularly presented in the popular context of fairs and salons, which did not permit the display (and the production) of its aura. It should be noted that at this time the distinctive and sanctified museal venue for modern art had not yet been institutionalized. There had not yet been institutionalized that neutral white space that is entirely devoted to hosting the work of art so that its aura may be seen. Art institutions did not at that time sanctify works of art as original, bestowing on them the aura, the loss of which Benjamin describes (at the same time as he constitutes it).[14]

---

12. In this context, it is interesting to examine Benjamin Buchloh's article on the development of the identity of the Museum of Modern Art in New York (Buchloh, 1988).

13. I include in the concept of the "great exhibition" the universal exhibitions, international exhibitions, and the various salons (see Crow, 1985).

14. His contemporaries also spoke of authenticity and the original, though in slightly different senses. See, for example, Rosalind Krauss's article on Duchamp, Picasso, and the zootrop (Krauss, 1988) and Crary's book on the observer (Crary, 1992).

1 2

In Benjamin's essay, the aura turns into a definition of the essence of a work of art, and the story of its loss serves as the pivot for the writing of the progressive history of the work of art.[15] This avenue of loss that Benjamin chooses to pursue enables him to isolate one of the expressions of art—"manual art"—and turn it into a point of departure—the source, the genesis from which all else ensues. The change undergone by the work is depicted as a change in values due to the blurring of the distinction between two different axes of description: the chronological axis, describing the transition from old to new, and the hierarchical axis, describing the transition from being to nonbeing, from authentic to deficient, from an object possessing an aura to an object bereft of one. The identification of these two axes with one another obscures the fact that by Benjamin's time, photography was already a long-established and institutionalized practice.[16] Indeed, it was in fact the "work of art" that was just making its start, which had just begun acquiring its aura and was about to establish shrines for itself to put itself on display. Only with the establishment of those shrines—museums devoted to modern art—was the work of art institutionalized as a consistently identifiable point of reference whose sequential history could be written in a positive manner. It is only then that the art museum became the display showcase of the work of art.

1 3

By the same token, consider Duchamp's urinal—the conceptual framing of a common object—which was presented as new and deviant with regard to art such as painting. Contrasting it with the panorama—the framing of nature—could actually cast it as a variant of the framing activity—of the putting of something into a display showcase.[17]

1 4

In the context of the aura, it should be recalled that the urinal—a serial object transferred by Duchamp from its utilitarian, mundane, industrial, and commercial

---

15. This suggests a simplistic and linear conception of history that is completely at odds with the perspective Benjamin develops in two other places: in his Passages (1989) and "Theses on History," (1983) Benjamin proposes an alternative notion of history based on a dialectical image bringing together the actual moment and the moment of "then."

16. Merely by way of example, see Dominic Baqué's book, which brings together hundreds of articles on photography from the professional and popular press during the interwar period (Baqué, 1993).

17. In Benjamin's article "Paris, the Capital of the Nineteenth Century" (1935 lecture), he describes the liberation of painting following the panorama (Benjamin, 1989, 37). On Duchamp's urinal, see Azoulay (1997a).

context to the artistic context—was shown exclusively as an image.[18] The "original" object ("original" in what sense?) was rejected by the Society of Independent Artists' Exhibition in 1917 and lost, though not before it had been conserved on a negative by the photographer Alfred Stiglitz. The copies of the urinal—from the first one in the form of Stiglitz's photograph and through to the replicas produced by Yannis, Linda, and Duchamp himself—are those that created the aura of the urinal and its distance, however proximate it may be through its reproductions.

15

Benjamin's description of the relation between a work of art possessing an aura and a reproduced work lacking an aura conceals two fundamental discrepancies. The first discrepancy is between (1) the set of relations between a work of art and its manual reproduction and (2) the set of relations between a work of art possessing an aura and a work of art that has been technically reproduced. Benjamin projects the first set of relations on the latter. Such a projection posits the technically reproduced work of art as constantly falling short of the work of art that possesses an aura. This is the lack—the loss of the aura—that Benjamin laments. The second discrepancy appears in Benjamin's discussion of the material dimension of a work, which is responsible for its standing as authentic and as bearing the traces of the "here and now." These traces, Benjamin claims, can be discovered by means of scientific practices; in other words, they aren't merely impressed on the object but are revealed to the eyes of the expert who knows how to extract them. These traces, Benjamin continues, are not evident in technical reproduction. He does not explain this statement, and it may be assumed that in the spirit of his discussion of photography in that period, he takes it as self-evident: after all, photographs are flat, two-dimensional, devoid of thickness, and serial—a consistent medium for transmitting a picture. As such, photographs cannot accumulate physical changes. But is this really so? Does photographic paper not deteriorate and crumble? Does the image always retain its consistency? Is it always printed in the same fashion from the negative? Is the photograph only a reproduced image and not a material object? This discrepancy in Benjamin's text stems from his attribution of the discovery of the traces of the "here and now" (which he claims are embedded in a work possessing an aura) to established procedures for identifying, analyzing, and prompting those traces (procedures that have been developed especially to deal with objects of this type). When Benjamin

18. It might also be asked why the majority of Duchamp's works exist only through the photographs that document them, following the loss of the original.

discusses the reproduced work, he switches levels of discussion and begins discussing the essence of the object itself, determining that physical and chemical analyses are "impossible to perform on a reproduction" (220) or, to be more precise, on the image transmitted by means of the object itself—the photograph. This discrepancy in the text is one of many that make it possible to read the essay both as a conservative essay in the field of art history and as a radical essay on visual practices.

16

Benjamin places spatial and temporal distance as a condition for the existence of the aura but does not clarify whether this distance existed prior to the desire to overcome and reduce it or whether this distance is merely a product of the desire to span and eliminate it. Prior to the appearance of the modern desire to draw near what is far, I argue, one could not have spoken of aura.

17

Benjamin's eulogy for the aura—one of the most famous and widely quoted essays in the literature about art since the 1930s—made a key contribution to the creation and shaping of the aura[19] (the loss of which the eulogy could not have bemoaned, for at the time it was written the aura had not yet been created). The essay, I contend, is a eulogy to something else—the loss of place. The loss of place means a transition from a unique place in which one must be present to experience it to a place that can be experienced without necessarily being there, due to the various technologies of reproduction.[20] Or as may be implied by Paul Valery's remarks, as quoted by Benjamin: "Just as water, gas, and electricity are brought into our houses from far off to satisfy our needs in response to a minimal effort, so we shall be supplied with visual or auditory images, which will appear and disappear at a simple movement of the hand, hardly more than a sign" (219).

18

Art, faced with an accelerating process of loss of place—the loss of a necessary link between place and presence (and not necessarily an original)—denied this loss by establishing certain unique places in which the drama of the loss of aura (which makes

---

19. See Jeannene Przyblyski's (1998) article, which reviews the numerous studies of Benjamin written in recent years.

20. The conquest of space has intensified in recent years, but even in Benjamin's time colonization of space through optics and transport had reached impressive proportions.

it possible for the mourning to continue)[21] is reenacted anew with each viewing. When the work of art loses its anchor in any particular place and does not need a place of presence to be, museums—clear spaces, retrospective exhibitions, art galleries—are constituted as its proper place. The establishment of unique shrines in effect sentenced art to the production of original objects that would justify the existence and the claim of the museum space. From the moment art was limited almost entirely to a single mode of activity—the production of original objects—it was sentenced to building unique shrines for itself. Either way, it was doomed each time to experience anew the loss of the aura of these objects.

19

I shall extract the connection between original and place from Benjamin's essay itself: "Secondly, technical reproduction can put the copy of the original into situations which would be out of reach for the original itself. Above all, it enables the original to meet the beholder halfway, be it in the form of a photograph or a phonograph record" (220–221). The copy is not committed to any specific, unique place and may therefore appear anywhere. The original, in contrast, is linked to a place and is therefore barred in principle from appearing outside it. The original must be present in a place, a certain here and now, at which the beholder must arrive to confirm it as an original. The detachment from the unique place means the loss of the here and now, as well as the loss of a work's standing as original. In other words, the original's loss of standing is not the result of technical reproduction (a means of production) but is the result of its detachment from a single, specific, and unique place. It follows that the loss of the here and now, of which Benjamin speaks, has not been undergone by the work of art but by the place that displays it.

20

The museum has no exclusive prerogative over the act of display. The public arena is replete with an increasing number of display showcases.[22] Many years after the invention of photography, the art museum absorbed photography and now even de-

---

21. In the 1980s, the largest wave of the working through mourning of art occurred in the museological space. Numerous exhibitions throughout the world addressed the subject.

22. During the first decades following the invention of photography, "events" first occur that are institutionalized over the course of the nineteenth century and become key characteristics of the practice of art—the retrospective, the individual exhibition, and so on. The universal exhibitions were a catalyst for the emergence of such institutions, effectively integrating art within the idea of progress and development through its very inclusion in the format of display.

votes a separate department to it. Thus, the museum has managed to perpetuate the distinction between work that may be reproduced manually and work that may be reproduced technically, while continuing to act as if art work is the hub around which the world and world history revolve. The museum—the place of art—acts as an institution charged with preserving the aura and restoring the loss origin. It acts through denying its role in creating the aura while enjoying a privileged status relative to other "display showcases" scattered in the public arena in which images and artistic objects may be seen.

21

The museum gains this privilege by acquiring the status of an original: a place that is original, a place elevated above and more qualified than any other place. Thus the museum is not merely a domicile that displays original works but also a unique place that allows these works to be present and not to be re-presented. The museum enables the social practice of creating and disseminating art to be reproduced in such a manner that the approach to the work of art (including what, in principle, may be indefinitely reproduced) remains unchanged.

22

Benjamin claims that the new means of production do not permit the continued preservation of the value of the original, which the previous means of production allowed. But is he really speaking about the means of production of works of art? In two passages in the text, Benjamin directly states his understanding that what is involved is a revolution that extends beyond the narrow context of art and its means of production: "We must expect great innovations to transform the entire technique of arts, thereby affecting artistic invention itself, and perhaps even bringing about an amazing change in our very notion of art" (217); and "Today, by the absolute emphasis on its exhibition value, the work of art becomes a creation with entirely new functions, among which the one we are conscious of, the artistic function, may later be recognized as incidental" (225). In this essay, through a variety of formulas, Benjamin generates a Copernican revolution in the visual sphere. He transfers the center of gravity from the work of art—which he abandons as the linchpin of the discussion of art—to the economics of images in the modern era. This Copernican revolution, which Benjamin describes (generates), remained obscured for a long time behind the sanctifying institutions of the field of art, which strove to mask it. Benjamin observed this revolution and described it succinctly and prophetically, as if seeking to force his way through the sacred values thrust forward by the field of art—"creativity, genius, eternal values, and mystery"—and to liberate a different space for the visual. Instead, however, of seeing modern visual space as including the ritual space of the field of art, making the latter a subactivity within the former, he once again succumbed to a chronological historical perspective that ignores the simultaneous character of phenomena and orders them as sequential, so that one usurps the other.

2 3

Benjamin's working hypothesis, presented at the start of his essay, is that a work of art can always be reproduced. This assumption is supported by another: "Man-made artifacts could always be imitated by men." Hence, art is made by human hands. Its ritual value or display value is determined within the framework of the social exchange relations in which it is embedded. It follows that what has changed in the transition from art having ritual value to art having display value is not derived from the object itself but from the exchange relations. Moreover, in this transition from ritual to exhibition, the object—what Benjamin refers to as the work of art—also changes: "The existence of the work of art with reference to its aura is never entirely separated from its ritual function . . . the unique value of the "authentic" work of art has its basis in ritual, the location of its original use value" (223–224). The use value of an object placed in a ritual function is always concerned with presence and with place. To consume the object and use it, the individual must approach it without claiming ownership—that is, not through its reappropriation (the object belongs to the place where it is located and is not part of a commercial process) and not through its interpretation (the practice of interpretation did not exist with regard to ritual objects). Under the conditions of exhibition, the object's value and patterns of use change and may be seen as a critique of previous conditions—critique of the sanctity of place (any space, provided that it is a "white cube," may contain the object) and critique of the distancing of the object (the object becomes an object for infinite interpretation, at each viewing being usurped anew from the authoritative hands that sought to grasp and distance it).[23] Yet even as part of these new conditions, the object is not completely conquered: it must remain only partially accessible in order for the spectator or critic to continue to long for it. Thus, for example, the interpreta-

---

23. In his article "Qu'est-ce que la critique?" Foucault (1978) locates the beginning of the modern era in the interpretation of the holy texts. One may also extend this description regarding the approach to objects subject to gaze (Foucault, 1978, 35–63).

tion must miss the object to prevent the object from becoming completely transparent to interpretation, as if it has yielded its secret. In any case, the work of art as an object worthy of conquest, as an object to be secured, is born with the birth of its use value—its interpretation.

24

The whole of Benjamin's essay constitutes a rereading of Marx. Marx characterized the change in the form of exchange relations in the capitalistic period by analyzing the commodity and its fetishistic nature. Instead of speaking about commodity in general, Benjamin speaks about reproduction, which he uses to render an accounting of the new form of exchange relations in the age of capitalism. The work, the object, the thing—stripped of its materiality and subject to scientific scrutiny "with the help of physical or chemical analyses"—has been flattened into a two-dimensional object, a reflection, a picture, an image. The object flattened in the process of reproduction is equivalent to any other object that has been flattened in the process of reproduction. Between one and another flattened object, a new market of exchange relations has opened. The reproduced image develops a mark from within itself, a sort of birthmark that identifies it as exchangeable. This mark is not a sticker pasted on it from the moment it enters the world of display and exchange but is a part of its essence and therefore ineradicable. I use this essentialist language deliberately.

25

In a short essay on "Painting, or Signs and Marks," Benjamin (1996b) formulates the difference between a sign and a mark.[24] A sign is impressed on an object from outside, whereas a mark emerges from a body (usually a living one), from which it follows that a mark is a "medium." Benjamin's distinction here echoes his distinction between manual reproduction and technical reproduction. Manual reproduction assumes the perfection of the reproduced object (the original), to which it is external and inferior. Technical reproduction has no need of the object it is supposed to reproduce. Rather, the reproduction appears in advance as lacking an original. It is not an index of the original within relations of representation but a symptom of relations of reproduction.

---

24. In this same essay, Benjamin also develops the connection between these two concepts (sign and mark) and painting (Benjamin, 1996b).

2 6

This flattening of the object—its having become an exchangeable commodity—is the mark of the order of things (or the way in which they are seen): the subsistence of a "universal equality" between them.[25]

2 7

By "universal equality" Benjamin refers to things and also to human beings: "At any moment the reader is ready to turn into a writer. . . . Literary license is now founded on polytechnic rather than specialized training and thus becomes common property" (232). "Universal equality" refers to places, as well. "The cathedral leaves its locale to be received in the studio of a lover of art; the choral production, performed in an auditorium or in the open air, resounds in the drawing room" (220–221). "Universal equality" means that, in principle, anything can turn into an image, anyone is entitled to have his image taken, and any image can be subject to the gaze of anyone. But although this universal equality refers to the source or place of power, it contradicts the actual property relations of the masses. To maintain the conditions of ritual the source or place of power must be invisible. Once the source or place of power has been revealed, when anyone may demand its appearance, the conditions—those of art as well—change from conditions of ritual to conditions of display, of exchange, and of politics. "But the instant the criterion of authenticity ceases to be applicable to artistic production, the total function of art is reversed. Instead of being based on ritual, it begins to be based on another practice—politics" (224). Authenticity is nothing other than the criterion of power, whose source or place cannot be challenged.

2 8

Throughout his essay, Benjamin speaks about a transition from the value and conditions of ritual (for images) to new conditions that he designates successively by display, exchange, and politics. Are these three terms equivalent to one another? All three are opposed to the value of ritual. On the one hand, "being-present" in a specific place or origin characterizes the value of ritual. This "presence" is limited, administered, and supervised: to use Benjamin's example, "Certain Madonnas remain covered nearly all year round" (225). On the other hand, "being-present-anywhere-but-nowhere-in-particular" and "anything-being-exchangeable-for-any-other-thing" are

---

25. Destroying its aura is the mark of a perception whose "sense of the universal equality of things has increased" (Benjamin, 1978, 223).

characteristic of display, exchange, and politics. Here are two sets of rules for two different games. The aestheticization of the political, of which Benjamin speaks at the end of the essay, may therefore be interpreted as the subjection of the rules of the game of politics to those of ritual. But instead of preserving a single hidden source of power, the source of power becomes exposed and is nothing other than an intensified reflection of the mass: "Mankind, which in Homer's time was an object of contemplation for the Olympian gods, now is one for itself" (242). Under fascism or during war, display, exchange, and politics are transformed into a ritual of the people, the state, or the nation: "War and war only can set a goal for mass movements on the largest scale while respecting the traditional property system" (241).

29

The aura is "a unique phenomenon of a distance, however close it may be" (222), and its loss is effectively the elimination of that distance. Benjamin claims that there are two reasons for the loss of aura which are in fact one and the same: the passion that the masses have developed "to bring things 'closer' spatially and humanly" and the passion to overcome "the uniqueness of every reality by accepting its reproduction" (223). Thus, the passion to draw close refers to both making something similar, close, and familiar and eliminating the one-timeness of each reality by making each occurrence similar to others. In other words, the degeneration of the aura results from the need to transform the world into statistical data, on the one hand, and into pictures appearing in display showcases, on the other. Both instances relate to the control of phenomena and their transformation into currency that may be placed in ethical or aesthetic statistical tables: "Thus is manifested in the field of perception what in the theoretical sphere is noticeable in the increasing importance of statistics" (223).

30

The subject of Benjamin's Copernican revolution in the visual sphere (the transference of the center of gravity from the work of art to the economics of images) is none other than the masses, who through new and intensive consciousness of their actions demand that the world become more "accessible" for them: "The adjustment of reality to the masses and of the masses to reality is a process of unlimited scope, as much for thinking as for perception" (223). In the past, the work of art was connected to ritual, and its force lay in its mere presence as an original in the one-time place of ritual. In the age of technical reproduction, the work has been replaced by a work whose value and status are derived from exhibition—from its existence as a subject of contemplation. Contemplation of the work of art that was associated with ritual was not available to all or at all times. Benjamin illustrates this point by referring to the paintings of the Madonna that remain hidden behind screens for almost the entire year. In the age of technical reproduction, by contrast, any thing may in principle be presented to any person: "With the emancipation of the various art practices from ritual go increasing opportunities for the exhibition of their products" (225). Throughout Benjamin's essay we meet a host of products, a host of opportunities for display, a host of displayers, and a host of observers. Each of these has the right to produce (to display), to see (not to touch), to be displayed (to be placed in a political context), to be reproduced (to take the place of a work of art as the object of observation)—"modern man's legitimate claim to being reproduced" (232).

31

During the 1930s, when Benjamin wrote his essay, television was a fantasy. Although John Logie Baird first displayed an early television that used a revolving disk in 1926, the establishment of a television communication network that broadcasts one-time pictures on a "real-time" basis could not have been part of Benjamin's world. Benjamin identifies the need of people to draw "things" nearer, although he confuses this need with the ability to satisfy or realize it. The different patterns identified by Benjamin as intended to overcome distance (and thus destroy the aura) succeed in creating distance as something that cannot be reduced. Accordingly, not only do they produce the aura, but they also produce an indestructible aura. Television is a quintessential expression of this paradox: television shows what is happening "there"— draws it closer, makes it similar, overcomes difference—and yet it illustrates the unbridgeable distance between the viewer and what is happening "there." In other words, television embodies the modern distinction between physical space and the space of appearance (in which intervention may take place).

32

Television is the ultimate display showcase: it allows viewers to approach ever closer and yet never arrive, to observe and yet to be unable to touch. Television cameras are present in nearly every place, as if no one-time moment shall remain alone. Cameras would lurk in anticipation of capturing the ultimate one-time moment—death—at its moment of occurrence. Already, the television camera, an accessory serving the secular practice of breaking distance and overcoming the different and the one-time, brings its prey to the ultimate display showcase, in which ritual takes place within display. This is death's display showcase.

3 3

Benjamin claims that "for the first time in the process of pictorial reproduction, photography freed the hand of the most important artistic functions, which henceforth devolved only upon the eye looking into a lens" (219). Taken at face value, this argument credits photography with enabling artistic tasks to be implemented untouched by the human hand. Over time, this position came to be used by art discourse to delegitimize photography as art. This interpretation trivializes Benjamin's argument. Thus presented, it may easily be refuted due to its invalid distinction between an action requiring the use of the hand (painting, for example) and an action not requiring such use (photography). Benjamin's argument may usefully be read alongside the writings of Marx and Engels on the unfettered hand—that is, the hand motivated by a subject who has acquired technical skills that are inherited from previous generations. For Benjamin, however, the unfettered hand has freed itself from the subject and overthrown his or her yoke. Freed from its tasks, the hand is no more than one side of an equation that reverses the functions of hand and eye in implementing the artistic task. Eye and hand exchange functions and yet remain intertwined in a manner that Benjamin (1989)—in his unfinished book *The Passages*—argues is emblematic of modernity. Nineteenth-century cities—of which Benjamin's passages (arcades) are but one example, alongside museums, shopping centers, winter gardens, and panoramas—became splendid, illuminated showcases. The eye is invited to contemplate the sight that faces it from within these display showcases, while the hand acquiesces to the demand "do not touch"—to maintain its distance and not to intervene. Contemplation and distance are unequivocally reflected in the very act of display and thereby enable the viewer to enjoy the show.

3 4

Two elements in Benjamin's remark about photography freeing the hand from artistic functions that were taken on by the eye deserve particular emphasis. The first relates to the characterization of artistic tasks as those relating to the "process of pictorial reproduction," while the second relates to the focus on the act of observation—"the eye looking into the lens." The process of reproducing the picture is a process whereby the picture exists and must be reproduced through photography. In most cases, however, the process of reproduction of the picture also includes the framing of the world as a picture and only thereafter the reproduction of this framing. This is actually the double process of photography: first framing the world and thereafter fixing it through the engraving of light on a negative (and later on photographic paper). The contemplating eye through the lens uses the framework supplied by the camera to generate the process of reproduction. Whatever is in front of the camera—whether an art picture or a world—also enters the display showcase that is the camera and is observed by the photographer. This display showcase, the camera, is not merely an instrument—a means of production enabling reproduction of the world that is in any case "out there"—but also a device that frames this world and delivers it to the eye of the person holding the camera. The camera—a metal "showcase" with a hole in its front facing the world and a hole in its rear facing the photographer—is to the museum as the photograph is to the painting. If photography marks the loss of the original, relative to painting, then the camera—relative to the museum—marks the loss of place. Photography marks the loss of the here-and-now as a one-time place in which the original appears, while the camera marks the loss of the here-and-now as a one-time event at which the original exists.

35

The camera is not merely a lens that the photographer uses to view and produce a picture that will later be printed in the darkroom. It is itself a display showcase that invites the viewer-photographer to view the world in the present, right now, while tying his hands behind his back. Thus he is invited to look at but not to touch— Bosnia, Rwanda, Baghdad, Kosovo.

36

"For example, in photography, process reproduction can bring out those aspects of the original that are unattainable to the naked eye yet accessible to the lens, which is adjustable and chooses its angles at will" (220). Photography is capable of seeing what the eye cannot see, and the camera is not capable of seeing what the eye does see. Benjamin is actually formulating the unbridgeable gulf between the picture revealed to the naked eye and the picture revealed to the eye of the camera: "Evidently a different nature opens itself to the camera than opens to the naked eye" (236). Thus Benjamin's comment may be interpreted as a general argument relating to photography: the camera is perceived no longer as a tool enabling the documentation of that which the eye sees but rather as a display showcase in its own right—as a mobile museum. Observer-photographers in this mobile museum tie their hands behind their backs to suspend and remove their actions from the world. To see what is revealed in the display showcase, observer-photographers must detach themselves from the surrounding world and forget their existence within the world. They must devote their hands exclusively to actions relating to the operation of the camera as display showcase. If the eye is diverted from the viewfinder or the hands are allowed to perform other actions, the picture will disappear from the showcase, never to return. Inserting a film into the display showcase and engraving the image thereon is a double-edged ancillary action: it connects the individual to a network that places an exchange value on the revealed picture and that compares the picture to other pictures, and it connects the action of viewing to the capitalist system of exchange relations of products and rentability.

37

Through the camera, Benjamin claims, "The camera introduces us to unconscious optics as does psychoanalysis to unconscious impulses" (237). The camera enables us to isolate details, disconnect them from the whole, enlarge them, show their points of contact with other things, and illuminate them in a new light. Benjamin compares what is captured by the lens to what escapes consciousness—to the unconscious. In psychoanalysis, the unconscious belongs to the individual and is connected solely to him or her. Photography disconnects the unconscious from the individual by framing a visual space that is not limited to the photographer's conscious gaze. This unconscious transcends the sum total of all the conscious actions and gestures of the photographer that may be subsumed to his or her desires and intentions. The function of art, argues Benjamin, is to imbue the person with the dimension of reality that eludes the instrument—that has not undergone instrumentalization and commodification. Paradoxically, the act of photography capable of supplying this aspect (the visual unconscious) cannot take place without the assistance of instruments (the camera). To extend Benjamin's line of thought, one might emphasize the paradoxical dimension inherent in the camera itself. The camera teaches us about the visual unconscious and successfully reveals it, yet the visual unconscious is not there when the camera is not present: only when the camera opens its eye on the world does it produce the visual unconscious.

38

On the eve of World War II, the period when the essay was written, Benjamin identifies the manner in which fascism "attempts to organize the newly created proletarian masses without affecting the property structure which the masses strive to eliminate" (241). Under fascism, the actions of the masses are channeled into war: "War and war only can set a goal for mass movements on the largest scale while respecting the traditional property system" (241). War is an event of disorder that the individual member of the masses takes part in to restore order—which is actually inequality in the property system. Men participate in war through patterns of generality (they are recruited into military service to protect the homeland) and through patterns of publicness (the operation of technological force, not of governmental force, becomes overt in the technology that soldiers run). War is no longer confined to the place in which it occurs as a one-time event—the battlefield, for example—but is reproduced and broadcast as a picture in display showcases: "Mankind, which in Homer's time was an object of contemplation for the Olympian gods, has now become one for itself" (242).

39

In its early days, claims Benjamin, the display value of photography threatened to marginalize its ritual value: "But cult value does not give way without resistance. It retires into an ultimate retrenchment: the human countenance. It is no accident that the portrait was the focal point of early photography" (225–226). Here, too, Benjamin illuminates the ultimate emblem of modernity: the secularized portrait of death, of each individual member of the masses, which restores its unique and one-time status.[26] "Polished lenses" are ubiquitous; they transform the camera into a useful weapon in the efforts to control death and to prevent or delay its onset. The photographer—"descendant of augurers" (Benjamin, 1980, 215)—uses his camera to locate the coming death. Thus death is trapped and perpetuated in a portrait, its display showcase.

40

In "The Short History of Photography" Benjamin writes:

. . . in that fishwife from Newhaven who looks at the ground with such relaxed and seductive shame something remains that does not testify merely to the art of the photographer Hill, something that is not to be silenced, something demanding the name of the person who lived then, who even now is still real and will never entirely perish into *art*. (Benjamin, 1980, 202)

The photographic image is not only the last refuge of the cult value, as Benjamin writes in his essay on art; it is also that which enables the recuperation of the ethical stance and a certain resistance to the threat of aestheticization. This, I believe, is what the above citation from the essay on photography implies. Benjamin is not re-

---

26. Though once again, in so doing, he presents a strictly chronological Weltanschauung according to which the display value usurps the ritual, ignoring their simultaneous existence.

ally interested in the name of the person photographed,[27] her specific testimony, or the traumatic event that has given birth to her portrait. He is interested in photography—and in looking at photographs—as practices that make possible the recuperation of experience and its transmission, which make possible in turn the recuperation of an ethical stance in the age of mechanical reproduction.[28]

41

The distinction between cult value and exhibition value, between auratic art and non-auratic art, collapses throughout the essay on art. The "here and now" that Benjamin ascribes to auratic art are also ascribed to photography. The differentiation of photography from auratic arts cannot be grounded in the presence of the aura—defined that way—and the aura cannot be ascribed to pre-modern forms of art alone. In conclusion: The aura is an effect of tradition, and tradition is a practice of transmission. In the essay on art Benjamin juxtaposes in fact two coexisting, rival traditions, not two successive artistic practices. The first tradition is capable of transmitting the unique and the one-timeness; the second—which includes founding, stamping, woodcutting, lithography, and photography—transmits reproducibility. The threat of fascism hovers over the former, as it is prone to aestheticization; the latter contains a force capable of resisting fascism, hence one should spell out its ethical stance. Some of the artists whose works this book has discussed—Marie Ange Guilleminot, Michal Heiman, Sigalit Landau, Roee Rosen—work within the latter tradition and in their art they are striving to recuperate an ethical stance, to impose it on the aesthetic.

---

27. In his essay, Benjamin doesn't indicate her name: Mrs. Elizabeth (Johnstone) Hall (taken from the annotated French translation—Benjamin, 1996, 31).

28. On the loss of experience see "The Storyteller" (Benjamin, 1978).

CHAPTER 3

THE [AESTHETIC] DISTANCE:

BENJAMIN AND HEIDEGGER

In his essay "A Short History of Photography," Walter Benjamin (1980) analyzes a photograph of Karl Dauthendey and his wife. Dauthendey was one of the pioneers of daguerreotype photography in Germany. On viewing the photograph, Benjamin writes, the viewer feels an irrepressible urge to identify in it "the tiny spark of accident, the here and now . . . burned through the person in the image with reality" (Benjamin, 1980, 202). Looking at the photograph is an occasion for capturing the present moment—that split second of the act of photography during which physical reality was imprinted on the negative, leaving the seal of the camera's optical unconscious beside the bare facts. In other words, Benjamin is seeking what the photograph at once exposes and conceals, discloses and encrypts, opens and closes. Benjamin seeks out an almost unmediated intimacy with the moment, the "here and now" of the photograph. He contemplates the photograph mentioned above and describes it as follows: Karl Dauthendey supports his wife, who appears aloof, her gaze directed past him, as if mesmerized by approaching death. Benjamin, who is familiar with the particulars of Frau Dauthendey's suicide, describes death hovering over the photograph in the same factual terms as he describes the presence of the man and woman. Both descriptions are posited as stemming from what is seen in the photograph. However, in a note to the recent French translation of this essay, translator André Gunthert (Benjamin, 1996a) notes Benjamin's mistaken identification of the woman in the photograph beside Dauthendey: she is not his first wife, who committed suicide, but his second wife. The traces of death hovering above her, which Benjamin sees in the photograph as an expression of an articulation of reality and the photographic moment, are only his own projection about a death that he'd read about in the biography of Karl Dauthendey written by his son, the poet Max Dauthendey.

In his essay "The Origin of the Work of Art," Heidegger (1977) analyzes Vincent van Gogh's 1886 painting *Shoes*. Heidegger seeks an unmediated intimacy with the truth of the work of art—with the way in which it simultaneously reveals and conceals a world. Within this intimacy the painting speaks, and the viewer merely serves as its mouthpiece.[1] Heidegger would like to extricate that world out of van Gogh's painting. He offers his readers a dry and factual description of what's seen in

---

1. Heidegger speaks about the unmediated quality of bestowal, which lies at the basis of the work's grounding: "Bestowing and grounding have in themselves the unmediated character of what we call a beginning" (Heidegger, 1971, 76). Unmediated intimacy with the truth of the work also arises when he speaks about preservation: "Preserving the works means: standing within the openness of beings that happens in the work. This standing-within of preservation, however, is a knowing. Yet knowing does not consist in mere information and notions about something" (Heidegger, 1971, 67).

Karl Dauthendey, *Self-Portrait with His Fiancée*,
St. Petersburg, September 1, 1857.
Courtesy Société Française de Photographie.

the painting: "A pair of peasant shoes and nothing more. And yet—From the dark
opening of the worn insides of the shoes . . . ," and so on (Heidegger, 1971, 33). Out
of the darkness looming within the gaping orifices of the shoes, the darkness that discloses a world—out of this equipment he extrapolates the bread that is lacking, the
uncomplaining worry of the woman who owns the shoes, the anxiety, the shudder
before a child's sickbed, the terror of death that hovers menacingly above. All this,
Heidegger repeatedly emphasizes, is revealed by the painting itself: "This painting
spoke," as he himself writes. But are the shoes in the painting indeed those of a
woman rather than a man? Does Heidegger really see what he sees in the painting
itself, a result of unmediated intimacy with the painting and attentiveness to the
painting's words (as we already know, the painting spoke), or are his comments a

THE [AESTHETIC] DISTANCE: BENJAMIN AND HEIDEGGER

projection of his peasant grandmother's life, over which death constantly hovered and with which he'd been familiar since childhood, or perhaps a projection of some other image of the peasantry?

Whatever Benjamin sees, he does not see it in the photograph. Whatever Heidegger sees, he does not see it in the painting. They both look at pictures and see death in them, traces of its presence and absence. Death subsists in the image that becomes its locus—its showcase.[2] They are not really concerned with the status of the visible in the pictures they're looking at, and in their essays the picture functions as visual facts, which are transmitted through descriptions. Both pretentiously claim to be enabling "the visible thing" to appear, so far as is possible, in unmediated fashion—to speak itself and for itself (as Heidegger might say) or to burn itself into the negative and leave an indexical seal in it (as Benjamin might say). This oversight by each of them, as expressed in their readings of the two images mentioned above, is common to them both and serves as the point of departure for my discussion of two thinkers who are often represented as having absolutely nothing in common.[3] Heidegger was a member of the National Socialist Party and saw art as the nation's gateway to its historical mission,[4] whereas Benjamin bitterly opposed fascism and saw art as a tool for fighting it. Despite these differences, I attempt to show that these two thinkers are located within the boundaries of the same discourse: they share the same field of vision, refer to similar objects, and make similar assumptions, even if they develop them in distinctive directions or come to distinctive conclusions that are sometimes completely contradictory.[5] My discussion focuses on their essays dealing with art or with the visual, written in the latter half of the 1930s.[6]

---

2. On photography as the locus of death, see Barthes (1980).

3. In this framework I do not discuss the differences between the two images respectively chosen by Heidegger and Benjamin—the former out of what he terms "great art" (Heidegger, 1971, 40) and the latter out of a popular culture that is interdependent with the economic sphere. For Heidegger (1971, 29) a work of art expresses self-sufficiency, which resembles a later reincarnation of Kant's "disinterestedness," a distinction that Benjamin rejected by his willingness to discuss works of art belonging to what is termed "culture industry."

4. "Whenever art happens—that is, whenever there is a beginning—a thrust enters history, history either begins or starts over again. . . . History is the transporting of a people into its appointed task as entrance into that people's endowment" (Heidegger, 1971, 77).

5. I have been able to find only two systematic discussions of the two and no full-scale treatment of the connection between these two thinkers, both of whom devoted a great deal of attention to art during much the same period (see Ziarek, 1997, 199–208; Caygill, 1994).

6. Benjamin: "The Work of Art in the Age of Technical Reproduction" (1978), "A Short History of Photography" (1980); Heidegger: "The Origin of the Work of Art" (1977), "The Age of the World Picture" (1996), "What Are Poets For?" (1971).

THE MATTER CALLED ART

Heidegger is seeking the origin of the work of art. Benjamin is seeking the contemporary conditions for the production of art. These statements derive from the titles of their essays and describe the differences between them. But is the one really searching for the unhistorical essence and the other for a concrete historical expression? Although both are trying to understand what a work of art is, they are actually trying to understand something else through art. Benjamin discusses art from an aesthetic aspect, in the original sense of the Greek term *aisthitikos*—"whatever is grasped by means of the senses and feelings" (see Buck-Morss, 1992). Heidegger discusses art as a mode of connection to a world or to being.[7] Both of them deal little with concrete works: they have only a scant interest in "works of art." They are interested in "art" itself or, to be more precise, the conditions for its appearance and the historicity of these conditions. In his essay on art, Heidegger barely discusses the historical conditions of art and suffices with a general statement on the relation between art and history: "Art, as founding, is essentially historical. . . . Art is history in the essential sense that it grounds history" (Heidegger, 1971, 77). In his essay "The Age of World Picture," which was written in the same period, Heidegger (1996) explores the relation between art and history. There he contends that with the advent of modernity, the world appears as a picture—as an object that is "set in place" and that can be represented.[8] It is an anthropocentric world picture: pictures are made by human beings, who are located within them, at their center: "we are in the picture," Heidegger says.[9] People posit what is in front of them so that it is grasped as a picture. The world as a picture is one of the modern conditions for the appearance of history, sciences, and the arts. "Nature, in being calculated in advance, and history, in being historiographically verified as past, become, as it were, 'set in place' [*gestallt*]" (Heidegger, 1996, 54). In modernity the being of everything is grasped as an object. Science is a mode of investigation, which levels everything to a single plane and compares each thing to

---

7. To emphasize what is common to both thinkers, I abandon the concept of art and speak in what follows about pictures (Heidegger), images (Benjamin) and their conditions of production in modernity.

8. When Heidegger speaks about the picture—"the conquest of the world as a picture"—he is not in any way referring to a picture as a product of art but to the modern conditions of art.

9. "'Picture' here does not mean some initiation, but rather what sounds forth in the colloquial expression, 'we get the picture' [literally, we are in the picture] concerning something. This means the matter stands before us exactly as it stands with it for us. 'To get into the picture' [literally, to put oneself into the picture] with respect to something means to set whatever is, itself, in place before oneself just in the way that it stands with it, and to have it fixedly before oneself as set up in this way" (Heidegger, 1977, 129).

everything else. Truth undergoes a reduction and turns into the certainty of representation, while man turns into the "relational center of that which is as such."

In his essay "On the Work of Art," Benjamin (1978) also discusses the transformation of the world into a picture. Here we can pinpoint a difference between Heidegger and Benjamin: Heidegger sees art as having the possibility of deviating from the conditions that limit it to create works that are neither picture nor object but that enable the truth to appear, whereas Benjamin sees the latent potential in these limiting conditions and thinks that art's purpose is to make virtue out of necessity and to act within the logic of the picture, the image, the photograph. However, such a reading misses the complexity of the step taken by both thinkers, just as it misses the powerful connection between them in regard to this point. As opposed to such a reading, I believe that both Heidegger and Benjamin are trying to ascribe a similar essence (Heidegger) or purpose (Benjamin) to art. Truth, Heidegger contends, appears through the work of art, which enables the work to be exposed in all its complexity, as both revelation and concealment. Western civilization has repudiated this essence of art and created instrumental conditions for the exposure of the truth.[10] Art is the possibility of deviation from these historical conditions: it exposes the concealment of truth at the same time that it makes possible the extraction of the truth out of the darkness. Deviation from these conditions by means of art doesn't mean their complete elimination, for if the naked truth were to appear, it would lose its essence.[11] The work doesn't expose any contingent moment, nor does it fix a form for any length of time. Its opening up is a momentary event. It captures the moment, so to speak, as a witness to the essence of what is and at the same time a witness to its partialness, to the transitoriness of this appearance, to its appearance as a moment of renewed encounter with the world and never as the entrenchment of an old concept of the world. Benjamin describes the loss of the aura as the loss of "uniqueness and permanence" in opposition to the "transitoriness and repetition" characteristic of art that is devoid of an aura. But careful reading of the essay on art will show that this opposition crumbles: "transitoriness and repetition" are not opposed to

---

10. "Nevertheless, the clearing is pervaded by a constant concealment in the double form of refusal and dissembling. . . . The nature of truth, that is, of unconcealedness, is dominated throughout by a denial. Yet this denial is not a defect or a fault, as though truth were an unalloyed unconcealedness that has rid itself of everything concealed. If truth accomplish this, it would no longer be itself" (Heidegger, 1971, 54).

11. We should understand in a similar manner, the relation that Heidegger posits between the essential and the historical or between permanent and transitory existence, as expressed, for example, in the following: "The work, therefore, is not the reproduction of some particular entity that happens to be present at any given time; it is, on the contrary, the reproduction of the thing's general essence" (Heidegger, 1971, 37).

"uniqueness." On the contrary, they appear as its intensification, as a search after the temporary, the eventuation, after the difference that is not subjected to a concept, after what seeks to repeat itself anew each time and thus enables the difference to appear (see Deleuze, 1968). In Heidegger, just as in Benjamin, "transitoriness and repetition" stem from the opening up to a world that in principle happens differently each time. Benjamin speaks about the instrument, the camera, that makes it possible; Heidegger does not mention the camera but will speak about the flash (*blitzen*) and the gaze, which manage to penetrate being for a split second.[12]

In his essay "On the Work of Art," Benjamin describes the conditions of modernity in terms similar to those used by Heidegger. He speaks about the transformation of the world (and art too, of course) into a picture—into a two-dimensional image, reproducible and exchangeable: "the desire of contemporary masses to bring things 'closer' spatially and humanly, which is just as ardent as their bent toward overcoming the uniqueness of every reality by accepting its reproduction" (Benjamin, 1978, 223). This is an anthropocentric world picture in Benjamin too, or to be more precise, a mass-centric world picture: "The adjustment of reality to the masses and of the masses to reality is a process of unlimited scope, as much for thinking as for perception" (Benjamin, 1978, 223). In the age of technical reproduction, we are speaking about masses—of spectators, of producers, of pictures, and of means. This multiplicity, in all its various aspects, is described by Benjamin as the tension between the fragmentary (which repeats itself like ornamental units, like a beat striking remorselessly, a repetitive shock, a disruption) and the fantasy of the whole (a generalized image whose purpose is to disguise this fragmentation). Benjamin identifies in fascism an intent to suppress this duality between fragment and whole and to produce false images in which the intermittent appears as a whole and the dismembered as one weld. Inside the arena in which fascism is the great enemy, Benjamin has assigned a key role to art: to emphasize and empower this duality through explicit and exaggerated use of intermittence, disruption, and shock as weapons.

A CRITIQUE OF THE ANTHROPOCENTRIC WORLD PICTURE

For both Heidegger and Benjamin, the transformation of the world into a picture stems from the anthropocentric course of modernity. Both of them criticize idealistic, neo-Kantian aesthetics, in whose framework genius and creativity are central

---

12. See Heidegger's (1977) discussion of the flash in his essay "The Turning."

concepts. Instead of these concepts and instead of the concept of subject in general, Benjamin suggests a framework of discussion in which an antisubject stands at the center intertwined in the new conditions of production. This framework requires an antisubject in two senses—first, as a part of the mass of individuals, undifferentiated and devoid of sovereignty, and second, as part of the new material conditions leading to a spatialization of the individual's body and its fragmented deployment in space as an incoherent concatenation of limbs, instruments, and senses. Heidegger too speaks out against modern subjectivity, which mistakenly assumes that creativity is an expression of self-sovereignty and genius, just as it assumes that technique is an agency at the artist's disposal when it is the artist who is at the service of technique (see Heidegger, 1977). Heidegger analyzes different modes of attempting to account for the thing or the equipment, all of which he defines as a "thing-concept"—the violence of the concept regarding the thing as an assault on the thing by the explanatory, clarifying, interpretive concept. Idealistic aesthetics assumes that only the thing is objective, a sort of infrastructure that can uphold values, which makes it possible for aesthetics to appear as a metastructure, as a value that has been ostensibly added.

From Heidegger's viewpoint, this is ontological superstition. He begins his analysis of van Gogh's *Shoes* with a discussion about the thing and then about the equipment, gradually rejecting both as a point of departure for a discussion of the work of art. Nevertheless, Heidegger doesn't wholly reject the thingly characteristic of the work but contends that the discussion must proceed in the contrary direction—not from the thing to the work but from the work to the thing (see Heidegger, 1971, 38–39). The work doesn't conform to the material matrix of the thing but posits a world in its own right: "To be a work means to set up a world" (Heidegger, 1971, 44). Thus, through van Gogh's *Shoes* a world is exposed—the world of the peasantry. The work is like the place where the world appears. A work of art, contends Heidegger, is an entity that stands in its own right; in standing in its own right not only does it belong to its world, but its world is present in it. A work of art opens up its world, and the more it stands in its own right and cuts all ties to human beings, the better its truth is able to rise to the surface (66).

In his essay on art, Benjamin (1978) also criticizes the dichotomous distinction between infrastructure and metastructure. At the start of his essay he makes it clear that he doesn't see the relation between conditions of production and art as one between an infrastructure and a metastructure, which it upholds, and doesn't see art as a ground that upholds "proletarian art" as a value, as a representation. Benjamin proposes to think of art in the age of technical reproduction as part of the change in the sensory apparatus of the individual stemming from the condition of the object (as an image that can be reproduced or exchanged), the condition of the subject (as a dismembered and discontinuous body), and the correlation between the two. Both Heidegger and Benjamin are analyzing the continuity that extends from the subject's condition to that of the object, and both attribute this continuity to a desire (on the part of the "masses," Benjamin might say) to conquer the world as a picture, to be in the picture as an object. This desire reaches a peak, contends Benjamin, when the masses finally appear as a spectacle to themselves in the center of the picture that they themselves would like to produce: humanity's "self-alienation has reached such a degree that it can experience its own destruction as an aesthetic pleasure of the first order" (Benjamin, 1978, 242). Benjamin derives this description from the new conditions of art analyzed by him as the loss of aura. Heidegger speaks not of the loss of aura but of the loss of the thing or being: "Where anything that is has become the object of representing, it first incurs in a certain manner a loss of being" (Heidegger, 1977, 142).

Benjamin attempts to find in art different ways to undermine the simulated unity of the picture and to use the model of shock, which characterizes industrialized modernity as an instrument for liberating the masses from fascism or, to be more precise, for calling them to arms against fascism. Heidegger too seeks to undermine the picture. He seeks to liberate it from the human being who clings to it and would like to use it as a means of representation. But whereas Benjamin's approach might be termed a fight against fascism, a politicization of the aesthetical, Heidegger's might be termed a fight in behalf of the thing, of being, of truth, of art, as an aestheticization of the political.[13] In his essay "The Thing," which was written shortly after World War II, Heidegger (1971) expresses what Benjamin had already warned against in 1936, on the eve of the war: "Man stares at what the explosion of the atom bomb could bring with it. He does not see that the atom bomb and its explosion are the mere final emission of what has long since taken place, has already happened" (Heidegger, 1971, 166).

PHOTOGRAPHY

The aura, writes Benjamin (1978), is "the unique phenomenon of a distance, however close it may be." The desire to approach, overcome, and conquer negates the

---

13. In Heidegger's discussion of the artist, Benjamin would have recognized what he called "the aestheticization of the political." In great art, writes Heidegger, the artist is a corridor that destroys itself in the creative process so that the work might appear. Art, the picture, turns into an object of human sacrifice, in which humanity can contemplate its own destruction.

necessary distance, which the aura must have in order to exist. Benjamin doesn't attribute this negation of distance to the essence of the object. He contends that it stems from a change in the conditions of production, appearance, perception, distribution, and consumption of the thing. These changes preclude any further regard to the work as having a specific value, a ritual value, and reduce the work to having only an exchange value, which means that it can in principle circulate in various exchange networks. These changes apply to the work as an origine/al and also to the place—the work's space of appearance. The place loses its specific and distinctive connection to the work, undergoes secularization, and turns into a neutral, industrialized, and undistinguished exhibition space that is called the white cube—a space intended to house exhibits, articles that have lost their ritual value and are now being traded in various exchange networks that endow them with new value. Heidegger also lingers over the changes in the work of art and in the place of exhibition, which reduce the work into an object: "World-withdrawal and world-decay can never be undone. The works are no longer the same as they once were.... The whole art industry, even if carried to the extreme and exercised in every way for the sake of works themselves, extends only to the object-being of the works. But this does not constitute their work-being" (Heidegger, 1971, 41).

Heidegger associates this condition with a state of constant motion and mobility, with the loss of connection to a specific place, and with the conditions of homelessness that art must overcome. But overcoming these conditions or restoring the former conditions isn't something that can be taken simply at face value. We can't return from the present to the former conditions and effect a transition from one form of existence to another, from one environment to another. This overcoming or restoration is a struggle—an eventuation, an event, a becoming—that constitutes the becoming of the work: "Art then is the becoming and happening of truth" (Heidegger, 1971, 71). The loss of home, shrine, or place shouldn't lead to a renewed fixing of being in a place, under a defined, distinctive, and designated form. A work of art is an event that consists of opening up, creating a world, exposing the truth, bestowing, and overflowing: "The nature of art is poetry. The nature of poetry, in turn, is the founding of truth.... Founding is an overflow, an endowing, a bestowal" (Heidegger, 1971, 75). Overflow, conflict, strife, and rift constitute the eventuation of the work. They don't allow it to become fixed or to turn into an object.

For these to subsist in a work—"This letting the work be a work" (Heidegger, 1971, 66)—the work needs not only artists but preservers as well. When Heidegger discusses the preserver, he might seem to be referring to a human agent as someone who serves as a mouthpiece for the work and who helps the work disclose itself.[14] But this assumption is easily refuted by Heidegger's text itself. First of all, Heidegger explicitly writes that through the conservational actions done by all those who deal with the work—critics, connoisseurs, historians—we do not meet the work itself but at most the work as information, as data.[15] The preservation act, as described by Heidegger, is essential to the work and independent of a specific preserver. Just as the work has a creator, so it also has a preserver. The preserver is bidden to preserve not what he or she may think worthy of preservation but the historic truth that has been opened up through the work. Human beings, as we have already seen in Heidegger's discussion, mistakenly interpret creativity as self-sovereignty. They might mistakenly interpret their task by attempting to ascertain what is worthy of preservation and thus eliminate the overflow opened up in the work. The general context of this essay by Heidegger, at the center of which stands a critique of anthropocentrism, supports the possibility that the preservation act is not a matter of human agency. Who or what, then, is that preserver? I believe it is a preservation activity that takes place unknowingly, involuntarily, and unconsciously and that enables art to become an opening for history without human mediation or guidance: "art is by nature an origin: a distinctive way in which truth comes into being, that is, becomes historical" (Heidegger, 1971, 78).[16] Art, says Heidegger, has always and will always take place in the saying.[17] He strengthens the assumption with respect to a preserved unconscious or to an unconscious preservation: "Projective saying is saying which, in preparing the sayable, simultaneously brings the unsayable as such into a world" (Heidegger, 1971, 74). The parallel to Heidegger's linguistic unconscious in Benjamin would be the optical

---

14. See, for example, the chapter on art in Abraham Mansbach's (1998) book.

15. In another place in "The Thing" essay, Heidegger (1971) claims that only poetry or philosophy can endow the work with a linguistic dimension. But this possibility is also refuted through Heidegger's discussion of the preserver.

16. The historical is part of the preservation: "Art is historical, and as historical it is the creative preserving of truth in the work" (Heidegger, 1971, 77)—that is, preservation is the writing of "the here and now" in the work rather than the writing of a particular event.

17. Apart from determining that a necessary relation subsists between art and language, Heidegger doesn't thematicize this relation, nor does he analyze the nature of the relation between what is spoken and what is seen. After describing van Gogh's *Shoes*, Heidegger (1971) writes that it would be self-delusion of the worst kind to contend that as a viewer he'd first thought what he'd thought and only later projected it onto the painting. Near the end of the essay, Heidegger contends that the the work's encounter with language makes it possible for being to appear and that language also summons up the linguistic unconscious—the unsayable. But Heidegger never develops the discussion of the linguistic unconscious or the unsayable and consistently ignores his own linguistic unconscious—everything he himself unwittingly projects onto the painting (35–36).

unconscious—what the human eye is unable to see without the mediation of the instrument (camera). Although Heidegger doesn't refer directly to the camera, if we accept the assumption that the preserver is not an agent with intention and consciousness, the act of preservation can clearly be seen as part of the metaphors that Heidegger uses to describe being and truth, thing and work—metaphors that are largely taken from the same world, the world of writing with light, of photo-graphy.[18]

The nonhuman, unintentional preservation that is carried out by means of the instrument in principle preserves something else that could not have been exposed to the human eye, that could not have been immediately deciphered, that exceeds any name.[19] The work of art in Heidegger's description functions like the camera described by Benjamin.[20] They both open up to the world, and the world opens up in them;[21] they frame what appears in front of them,[22] through them, and by means of them. They bring closer, and they distance, expose, and frame what the human eye cannot see. They conceal some of the details, bring what lies deep in the field of vision to the surface of the picture, create the illusion of depth inside the surface, and function like a dark room through which the being flashes. The image is trapped inside the dark room, burnt into the surface of the negative, which never will be exposed in its entirety. Never will there be found the positive that can safeguard it out of conformance or agreement with the negative. When Heidegger's discussion of the work of art as a camera is thus juxtaposed with Benjamin's discussion of the photograph as a work of art, it is difficult to continue maintaining in simple fashion that the photograph eliminates any and all distance, that it negates the aura (the "unique phenomenon of distance, however close it may be"), that it levels everything, or that it is a disembodied image that flattens the world into a two-dimensional plane.[23]

---

18. "In the work of art the truth of an entity has set itself to work. 'To set' means here: to bring to a stand. Some particular entity, a pair of peasant shoes, comes in the work to stand in the light of its being. The Being of the being comes into the steadiness of its shining" (Heidegger, 1971, 36).

19. "In photography, process reproduction can bring out those aspects of the original that are unattainable to the naked eye yet accessible to the lens, which is adjustable and chooses its angle at will" (Benjamin, 1978, 220).

20. Heidegger's questions about distance and nearness could not have been posed prior to the conceptual and technical possibilities of reducing distance as evinced by modern technology in general and photography in particular. Three of his essays—"The Thing" (1971), "The Origin of the Work of Art" (1971), and "The age of World Picture" (1996)—deal with the question concerning distance and nearness.

21. "The art work opens up in its own way the Being of beings. This opening up, this revealing, the truth of beings, happens in the work" (Heidegger, 1977, 166).

22. Heidegger uses the term *Gestalt* (Heidegger, 1971, 84).

23. Consequently, the distinctions they make between art that has an aura and art that doesn't have an aura or between great art and nonart (which is what Heidegger called cinema, which they felt caused the loss of vision) are invalid.

Heidegger (1971) opens his essay "The Thing" with a description of a man contemplating the atomic bomb and asking himself what it could bring with it. Looking after being, after truth, after art preoccupied this man. This man does not see, contends Heidegger, that the bomb is nothing other than "the mere final emission of what has long since taken place, has already happened" (Heidegger, 1971, 166). In this essay Heidegger associates the elimination of sight and hearing in the wake of technology—the elimination of distance and the conquest of the world as a two-dimensional picture—with the eradication of humanity by its own hands.[24] Heidegger doesn't explicate his choice of the atomic bomb as an example, nor does he develop it. Nonetheless, it is hard to ignore the chilling connection between the atomic bomb and the action of the camera that formed Heidegger's way of thinking. The bomb is like a literal realization of the photograph—the conquest of the world as a picture, the leveling of the world, and its inscription in light. In Hiroshima and Nagasaki, the necessary distance for maintaining the view was eliminated. From the pilot's cockpit, the object of the view is enframed and conquered so that nothing is left of it except for a two-dimensional picture, a disembodied image. The flattened image left of these two cities is ostensibly a distinctive example of the eradication of the distance between the world and the picture, testimony to the eradication of the aura. But in paradoxical fashion, the only thing that wasn't eradicated in Hiroshima and Nagasaki was the aura: the aura of an object that will never be able to appear again, that will always remain an absence, that is no longer, that will always preserve its aura, the "unique phenomenon of distance, however close it may be." Nearness, as Heidegger contends in "The Thing," always preserves farness (Heidegger, 1971, 178). The destruction of the two cities is like an overexposed photography. The blazing light of the bomb burned and scorched each city and made it two-dimensional. The bomb turned the city into a gigantic camera, the bottom of which—the surface of the city, its earth—functioned like a negative on which the city's destruction was written.

---

24. The worst thing that happened before the bomb was dropped, in Heidegger's words, was the uprooting of everything from its place and the conquest of all distances, which nonetheless leave the near or nearness out of bounds.

THE [AESTHETIC] DISTANCE: BENJAMIN AND HEIDEGGER

CHAPTER 4   THE [SPECTATOR'S] PLACE:

ADOLF HITLER AND EVA BRAUN

Dear customer: As soon as you put on the state-of-the-art headgear, body suit, and electronic sensors, you find yourself in the bunker's livingroom. Late April 1945. The subterranean quarters are comfortable and opulent, if somewhat morose. The noise of exploding bombs is dimmed by soundproof walls, but you sense the blasts by the shudders sent through rooms and up your body. Your lover is about to arrive. You head to the bathroom to tidy yourself up. You look into the mirror, leaning forward, and your own image is revealed to you for the first time. You are blond, your face is still young, your complexion pinkish-pure, your bosom ample. You seem truly good-natured. Anyone would be thrilled to be you, but for you it should merely be a given—you are Eva Braun. . . . Excitement jolts through your body when you hear the steps outside. When he opens the door, you gasp at the sight of his small mustache. Because you are not only Eva, it seems menacing, almost monstrous. But everything around the moustache is so congenial. He comes toward you with such warmth, his smile tired, his arms open to embrace you. Remember—you are Eva. When Hitler closes his arms around you, the view darkens, and you are surrounded by his presence. You are almost overwhelmed with titillation when you feel the whiskers of that famous little facial tuft tickle your ear and the back of your neck. . . . You realize, with some pride that you are the sanctuary of this special man, your lover.

—ROSEN, *Live and Die as Eva Braun*

RESISTANCE TO MEMORY

Who is the "dear customer" who appears in this appeal, which was posted at the entrance to Roee Rosen's 1997 exhibition? The Hebrew text addresses the customer first in the masculine—"but you [m.] sense the blasts by the shudders sent through the rooms and your body"—and then in the feminine—"Anyone would be happy to be you [f.]." The customer turns into someone else, who is no longer he himself but who is not yet who he is to become. Ostensibly there is a tension here between the generalized identity of a "customer" (a sort of neutral position that, in principle, anyone is invited to occupy) and the specific identity of "Eva Braun" (Adolf Hitler's beloved). However, the tension between masculine and feminine as well as generalized and specific obscures a more complex set of identities—a system in which the specific, fixed identity loses its rigid boundaries and can be described only in terms of becoming, of transforming, of changing.[1] The Eva Braun identity that is offered to the customer in the exhibition is already, as can be gleaned from this short text, part of the customer's identity. The text doesn't leave the customer the option of not

---

1. On the concept of becoming (*devenir*), see Deleuze and Guattari (1980).

Roee Rosen, *Live and Die as Eva Braun*, details, 1997

always being Eva Braun. The text doesn't refer to two separate and distinct characters that, by some process of transformation (disguise, identification, makeup, simulation), turn one into the other but refers instead to a sequence of becoming. The mirror, the distinctive place of the self-portrait, appears in this short text as the place in which one watches oneself becoming someone else: "You look in the mirror, leaning forward, and your own image is revealed to you for the first time. You are blond." Is Eva Braun always and already part of the customer's identity? Is the customer's yearning toward Eva Braun also—necessarily—a yearning toward the object of her desire, Adolf Hitler? Is the yearning—toward someone, to be someone, to see how he appears in his intimacy, to see out of his intimacy, to yearn from inside of him— necessarily a betrayal of (personal) identity, (societal) belonging, (museum) function, and (civilian—the work of memory and remembrance) destiny? Is it clear that the customer's personal identity distinguishes between himself and the set of identities offered to him at the exhibition? What is this identity that is supposed to function like a suit of armor in the face of the temptations offered to him? Does the exhibition even ask the customer whether he wants to be Eva Braun?

THE [SPECTATOR'S] PLACE: ADOLF HITLER AND EVA BRAUN

Roee Rosen, *Live and Die as Eva Braun*, details, 1997

Rosen's exhibition places the museum spectator in the intimacy of the bed-room—and not just any bedroom but the bedroom of the Berlin bunker that belonged to Eva Braun and Adolf Hitler. A small two- or three-year-old boy looks down from the bunker's wall. A dotted barber's apron lies across the boy's shoulders; two pairs of gigantic scissors fence above his hair. The child's black eyes are open wide and blazingly intense, his lips are rounded like a button, and Hitler's mus-tache—a relatively small black rectangle, an abstract and ostensibly meaningless form, but nonetheless one that cannot be mistaken—adorns his face. The face is that of Roee Rosen as a child; its reflection that of Adolf Hitler. The boy has seemingly succeeded in his Oedipal mission. He has murdered the father and penetrated into the mother's bedroom in the guise of the father. But he doesn't suffice with that. He wants to produce more and more of the mother figure, of Eva Braun—an abun-dance, a proliferation, and a flowering of Eva Braun.

You, dear customer, are invited to be Eva Braun: the surplus value, the interest, the profit. "I" (Roee Rosen) am Adolf Hitler. Come hither, look in the mirror. Two monkeys with their weapons drawn will hold up the mirror for you. You need to look into it until your image appears, is revealed out of its own splendor, coalesces with the instruments, images, and symbols that have already passed through this image-producing mirror. These things, images, and symbols have passed through the mirror and yet remain forever, impossible to be erased completely. It remains impossible to create a portrait out of nothing or one that doesn't bear the traces of other portraits. Look into the mirror that is being held up to you for another moment. That little mustache may insinuate itself between your own nose and upper lip. Or desire may lead you to contemplate the skin of your beloved, who is managing Europe's destiny from your bedroom.

Sacrilege? What is sacrilege in your eyes, dear spectator—the reenactment of the Oedipus story, the fact that Hitler plays the father's role? Or maybe it's the image of Roee Rosen, a three-year-old boy festively wearing Hitler's mustache. Is it the boy's presence in your bedroom, or maybe your presence in Hitler's and Eva Braun's bedroom, with you taking the place of the latter? Indeed, are these all the possibilities? Maybe the sacrilege lies in the mutual presence of you and Roee Rosen on "this" side of memory (and why should we immediately divide memory into sides; is it not everyone's duty to remember the same thing?). Maybe it's your surprise at discovering that this exercise doesn't concern remembrance at all or any connection between an experienced event and its recall in memory but that it does concern a game of fantasies and desires, the fabrication of pictures and scenes, roleplaying, the staging of situations, the realization of anxieties. However, the fabrication of images and memories (and this you must have felt as soon as you stepped inside the exhibition) is not part of the familiar and reassuring game of Holocaust remembrance. But who said anything here about the Holocaust or the work of commemoration, which is a framework that provides each person with a predefined role and makes clear-cut distinctions—of profession, generation, ethnic, and class—between the various functionaries?

Dear customer, if this exhibition is a sacrilege in your eyes, do not expect this text to rehabilitate the sanctity. The above questions are not in the nature of open questions to which this text is meant as a reply. They appear sequentially, in a series, to outline the range of discussion. These questions seek to strengthen the oppressiveness, annoyance, uncertainty, discontent, and discomfiture elicited by Rosen's exhibition—from its appeal to the museum spectator as a customer, through its intimate treatment of the "Nazi" body, and until its conclusion as an allegory for the state of painting. The exhibition—and this is the only merchandise that this text attempts to serve to its customers in a wrapping—seeks to arouse a scandal and to profane, not as a purposeful action in its own right but only to reemphasize that "the real sacrilege, if at all, is Hiroshima itself." The sacrilege doesn't lie in a sentence that interjects "Hiroshima" into a discussion that is supposed to concern "the Holocaust."[2] The sacrilege doesn't lie in the discussion of the horror in a bedroom or the link this text posits between two events, over the separation of which an army of gatekeepers is appointed (despite the connection between them derived from the event that encompasses them both and is known as "World War II"), but the real sacrilege is "Hiroshima," "extermination of the gypsies," "extermination of the Jews," "extermination of the ill," or in the words of Marguerite Duras (1961, 9) in the introduction to her screenplay for the movie *Hiroshima Mon Amour*:

This beginning, this official parade of already well-known horrors from Hiroshima, recalled a hotel bed, this *sacrilegious* recollection, is voluntary. One can talk about Hiroshima anywhere, even in a hotel bed, during a chance, and adulterous, love affair. The bodies of both protagonists, who are really in love with each other, will remind us of this. What is really sacrilegious, if anything is, is Hiroshima itself. There's no point of being hypocritical and avoiding that issue.

The bite of the name in the living flesh of events—like the boundary between "World War II" and "Hiroshima"—plays a central role in director Alain Renais's movie *Hiroshima Mon Amour*. The movie begins with a close-up of two naked bodies intertwined. The bodies appear limbless, and for several seconds they are separated from one another by layers of sweat, dust, dew, ointment, rash, burn. If not for these layers, which alternately replace one another, the bodies would merge into each other completely and become a single undifferentiated pile of body. From out of this wounded, unifying, rehabilitating, caressing, incisive, doting intimacy, from

---

2. Quite a few works, books, and films made since *Hiroshima Mon Amour* propose new possibilities of speech deviating beyond the boundaries posed by private names (such as "Hiroshima," "Auschwitz," or "Rwanda") or by the names of the events that are part of them ("Holocaust," "World War I," "World War II," or "ethnic cleansing"). By deviating beyond the boundaries posed by the name itself, these works seek a way out of the economy that turns the name into a resource—of which more and more can be produced, indeed, but only within permitted boundaries that are determined not according to the essence of the resource itself but according to the cultural context of its exploitation. Events close together in time and place (such as the "Holocaust," "Hiroshima," and "World War II") remain closed loops that refuse to open up and become linked together in certain parallel stories for fear of losing their unique identity. Thus, we find some who would posit World War II as the primary event, place the Holocaust as just a marginal addendum to it, and maintain this hierarchical relation between the two events. Others would present World War II from the perspective of the Holocaust and posit the latter as the reason for, and essence of, the former. Some would prefer to remove Hiroshima from the arena in order to preserve World War II as a European event and continue associating the concept of extermination solely with the Jewish Holocaust, while others would present the annihilation of Hiroshima as the end of the war or as the beginning of a new era after the war and thus obliterate its significance.

out of this complete loss of boundaries and identities, one of them emerges, relocates outside, attempts to testify to his identity and express it. Considering the matter, he states in reproof: "You didn't see anything in Hiroshima." "I saw everything in Hiroshima," replies the woman. "Everything." "You didn't see anything in Hiroshima," he insists. As opposed to his "nothing," she sticks to her "everything." After a few more such lines, she concedes and retreats. It only then becomes clear to the spectators that the man is Japanese, the woman French. He can be identified by gaze, she by voice. When their national identities are disclosed onscreen and the geographical distance between them with all its attendant historical ramifications becomes clear, she begins to withdraw from her adamant position and to detail exactly what she did see: museum, hospital, news reports. "Four times in the museum," she tells him repeatedly. At this point the equilibrium that obtained between the declarations of the two, between his "nothing" and her "everything," is disrupted. As soon as the equilibrium is disrupted, the dialogue between them becomes focused on the specificity of each one's point of view—Japanese versus French. You, a French woman who celebrated the victory at the end of World War II, "didn't see anything in Hiroshima." How could you have seen anything? All you could see in France was victory, he seems to be saying to her.

At this point in the movie, the woman contrives a change in the dialogue between them. At the start of the dialogue, she had posed her gaze as equal to his. Afterward, when he negated her point of view and berated her pretension to have seen something in Hiroshima, she was pushed into the position of justifying herself as if she had something to prove: I saw the horror, I understand, I know, I remember, I consecrate. He refuses to be persuaded. And then—and this is the turning point of the movie—she gives up any pretension to prove or demonstrate or even any pretension to see. She addresses his words at their face value, ignoring the context of remonstration, negation, and exclusion—you, as a French woman, didn't see anything—and simply tries to correct his mistake. France celebrated the victory, I didn't celebrate any victory.[3] I didn't celebrate the victory because I identified with the victims of Hiroshima, who had been wiped from the face of the earth. Simply, France isn't me. Unlike the Japanese man, who would like to consecrate the memory of Hiroshima and place it on the level of the sublime, the French woman is trying to do the exact opposite—to desublimate the memory. From here on, throughout the entire movie, she tells the story of her love for a German soldier who was shot on the

3. "Victory" here refers to the end of World War II rather than the liberation of France.

THE [SPECTATOR'S] PLACE: ADOLF HITLER AND EVA BRAUN

day of France's liberation. The enemy that France exterminated was her lover. On the day that France exterminated her enemy—the woman's lover—she herself became an outcast, became the enemy of France.

In effect, as soon as the Japanese man attempts to proscribe her from a certain community of gaze, as soon as he tries to deprive her point of view of its legitimacy, she returns or is returned to the trauma of being ostracized by her family and townsfolk. She returns to the day on which France was liberated, her lover was shot to death and she was exposed as the German officer's beloved. She returns to the day on which her head was shaved and she was incarcerated in a cellar. And she is trying to get him back to the first shot of the movie, to the moment in which their bodies are melded together and memory doesn't function as an instrument of exclusion. Unlike the regime of gaze that he would like to impose (the nationalist gaze that constitutes its subjects and draws the boundaries of their field of vision), she is trying to rehabilitate contact, both her lost contact with the German officer's body and the contact that just now she and her Japanese lover had been a part of and that has been erased beneath the crush of the gaze. When she recalls in his ears her meeting with her dying lover, she doesn't merely pose the Japanese man as an eyewitness to her story as an addressee; she poses him as her dying German lover and demands that he impersonate him with his body. She appeals to him as if she were there right now, on the railroad platform, and he, the Japanese man, was lying and dying on the platform like the German. She makes it impossible for him to be outside the story that she is now enacting, in the act of remembrance, and thus she manages to resist memory as a fixed picture, a museum image on a wall, which he or she can look at, process, and interpret.

In *Hiroshima Mon Amour*, Renais resists the traditional roles of gaze, testimony, and proof in the economy of memory, while trying to remove memory out of the territory of gaze and nationality into the territory of physical contact and the personal. But he also proposes new boundaries for the narrative of the horror: Hiroshima without "Hiroshima." The movie proposes a secularization of memory and its intertwinement in the individual's—any individual's—daily work of mourning, without examining the extent of his proximity to the "Trauma" with a capital T. The price (in other words, forgetfulness) is clear, and in the 1950s Renais already found it a worthwhile price to pay. In the early fifties, a few years before he shot *Hiroshima Mon Amour*, Renais had shot a short documentary film, *Night and Fog*, about the Nazi extermination apparatus, in which he used footage from period newsreels (Caruth, 1994, 128):

If one doesn't forget, one can neither live nor act. The problem was posed for me when I made *Night and Fog*. It wasn't a matter of making another monument to destruction but to think of the present and the future. Forgetting must become constructive. It is necessary, on the individual plane just as on the collective plane. What is always necessary is to act. Despair is inaction, the withdrawal into the self. The danger is to stop moving forward.

After *Night and Fog*, Renais was commissioned to direct a documentary film about "Hiroshima." A long time after working on the archives relating to the destruction of Hiroshima, he decided to devote a feature film to the catastrophe, fearing that if he did make a documentary film about Hiroshima, it would look too much like the movie he'd made about the Holocaust. Renais in effect came out against the pretension and injunction to document, remember, and propagate and posed forgetfulness as the condition, the basis, for exchange relations with the present and future. In a certain sense, Renais's response resembles that of Claude Lantzman, the director of the 1985 movie *Holocaust*. Where Renais insists on making manifest forgetfulness, Lantzman tries to make manifest incomprehension. Forgetfulness, like incomprehension, is presented as a condition for the work of memory (Lantzman, quoted in Rothman, 1997):

It is enough to formulate the question in the simplest terms, to ask, "Why were the Jews killed?" The question immediately reveals its obscenity in the project of understanding. Not to understand was my iron law during all the years of the elaboration and production of Shoa. I had clung to this refusal of understanding as the only possible ethical and at the same time the only operative, attitude. This blindness was for me the vital condition for creation.

Both Renais and Lantzman are opposed to memory as a purposeful activity whose role is to understand the past or to transmit its lessons to the future. Both of them come out against economies of memory centered on the practice of gaze—the investigative gaze or the incisive gaze—whose aim is to present to the spectator a meaningful story, which features causal development and a teleological structure, a readable story based on conventions amenable to decipherment, a story that ostensibly evokes an identification with it, a tangible story that provides visual evidence. Serge Daney (1997, 615), the French cinema critic, spoke in this context of a visual story that demands "optical confirmation" of the spectator, confirmation that what is seen does indeed exist, a "reception perfect" signal like the technical confirmation provided by a fax machine after the transmission of information has been successfully concluded.

THE [SPECTATOR'S] PLACE: ADOLF HITLER AND EVA BRAUN

At the beginning of *Hiroshima Mon Amour*, when confronted with the Japanese man's remonstrance, the French woman is obliged to provide such optical confirmation. But quickly she draws herself together and challenges the very rules of the memory game. Confirmation of the seen in the framework of such an optical procedure in effect erases the field of vision and its spectrum of contingent possibilities, demarcating it in the framework of a closed exchange economy that produces and manages subjects, data, and merchandise. Within this closed economy, memory is presented as a separate activity, isolated from mundane routine and from economic, political, and personal life, which is managed as an activity with independent patterns of looking at, solemnizing, and sanctifying the "exhibits" of memory.[4] This activity makes possible both the transformation of memory into an exhibit worthy of interpretation and the constitution of the spectator as an interpreting subject who is called on to look at the horror, confirm it, take part in the nationalist story in which it is intertwined, and become a subject of the transmitted lesson. The game of mutual recognition between memory (as an exhibit meant for interpretation) and subjects (who are invited to interpret it) is conducted within institutional boundaries that seek to preserve the memory, preserve the modes of its preservation, and thus impose restrictions on the intertextual network inside which an exhibit may be interpreted. For example, restrictions arise that stem from the constitution of the Holocaust as a unique and incomparable event.

Renais and Lantzman would like to deviate from the economies of memory described above. They propose an open and diffusive economy whose products cannot be determined in advance and may be determined anew at any time, just as the economy can move from one area of meaning to another. This is an economy based on recognizing the limitation of profit ("the legacy of the Holocaust") or loss ("Hiroshima forgotten"), which can be prognosticated, managed and controlled. It seeks to leave an opening for gaze, contact, and speech, which are not predicated on purpose and intentions. Lantzman, Renais, and Duras are actually speaking about an economy predicated on resistance to memory as sanctifier, a productive resistance that leaves its traces out of and around which more and more resistance activity can be strung together. This resistance engenders—by happenstance, without benefit of guidance or management—contingent traces of memory. They do not propose eliminating memory but eliminating the management of memory. They propose re-

---

4. A distinctive example of such patterns are the remembrance rooms in Holocaust museums, which adopt modernist architecture and art (a bare white space and monochromatic abstract painting) to create a shrine to the view as the locus of memory (see the Holocaust Museum in Washington, D.C.).

sistance to memory as guide, memory with purpose, and memory managed by agents who claim a monopoly because of their greater proximity to the truth of the event or because they are worthier representatives of the event and its victims. Resistance to memory as sanctifier means resistance to memory that presents itself as worthy. Memory, then, is an act of resistance—fragmentary in nature, eluding agreement, incomplete, qualified, unclosed, indeterminate.

THE MUSEUM MERCHANDISE

In the context of the museum space, resistance to memory takes on additional dimensions manifested by the museum object and its relationship to the spectator. Two recent projects challenge these dimensions from cultural, historical, and economic aspects. French artist Marie Ange Guilleminot dealt with Hiroshima and the trauma of obliteration—of the city, of life, of memory. Roee Rosen dealt with the memory of Hitler and the trauma of this memory. In relation to the official remembrance activity of the Holocaust or Hiroshima, both these projects (to paraphrase Duras) are concerned with the intentional profanation of memory. Both projects would like to be subsumed within established modes and patterns of consumption (such as buying and selling) and to come out against the introspective silence of commemoration, against the role of gaze and contemplation, against the vacuum of what cannot be represented, and to divert exchange relations with the spectator to other areas. Guilleminot's project begins with an item for sale in the museum gift shop; Rosen's begins with an appeal to the museum spectator as a customer and with the display of Rosen's art as merchandise offered to satisfy the customer's needs. Both projects take as their point of departure the immediate language and practice of consumption, without benefit of disguise or camouflage. Both refuse to adopt capitalistic exchange relations as is but seek to emphasize and to problematize the exchange relations between the producer of memory and the consumer of memory. Both projects are searching for a specific and unique exchange economy that doesn't abide by the rules of the game of capitalist economics or by the rules of the game of the museum economy, which sanctify the visible and manufacture the conditions for its sanctified appearance.

What is the museal economy? The museum, whether of history or art, exhibits and preserves the different, the deviant, the unique, the rare. This has been the museum's historic purpose ever since it was established in the late eighteenth century. Actually, the museum was established as a shrine of negation: what's collected inside is distinguished by the negation of everything that came before it and constitutes an incomparable uniqueness. The museum must find objects in their purest state and preserve them. This is the social and cultural logic underlying the museum as an institution that provides preservation services to society through a team of experts. However, the museum isn't just an agent of preservation. Its portrayal from this viewpoint obscures another aspect of museum activity that is anchored in the economic logic of capitalist society, of which the museum is a part. The museum owns capital and merchandise, and it participates in a complex network of cultural, political, social, and economic exchange relations.

The object exhibited in the museum is also merchandise. It has use value and exchange value in each of the aforementioned spheres—cultural, economic, and political. The unique structure of museum merchandise expresses itself in both its use value and its exchange value. First, this merchandise is a sign. Consumption of the sign (use of it) is manifested by the act of interpretation. The consumption of museum merchandise—its interpretation—is embedded in the framework of a story. Out of this use emerges a unique exchange system that supports the economic system but is not identical to it. In the framework of this exchange system, something of the exhibit is exchanged but the work remains in the possession of its owner. The institution, the owner or representative by proxy of the exhibit, is always offering the use of the work to the next spectator in line. Spectators purchase tickets that entitle them to view the exhibit, to add to their accumulated experiential capital the fact that they "have seen it," and to be among those who recognize both the exhibit and its value. In the framework of the exchange relations that the museum makes possible between the spectator and the work, between the spectator and the interpreter or critic, and between one spectator and the next, the merchandise is exchanged, and recognition and interpretation are accumulated as virtual property.

The use value and exchange value of museum merchandise pull in different directions. The use value, which is determined in the act of interpretation, points to the particularity and uniqueness of the exhibit; otherwise the exhibit would be unworthy of consumption (interpretation). The use value of Marcel Duchamps's *Fountain*, for instance, is supposed to be derived from the particularity of its form and content as an object; otherwise, there would be no point to collecting it inside the museum. The exchange value points in the other direction, toward the exchangeability of the exhibit; otherwise, it would not be found worthy of traveling through the museal exchange networks. The exchange value of the same *Fountain* is to be derived from its difference and distinctiveness from all prior works; otherwise, there would be no point to collecting it inside the museum. The exhibit's use value obscures the fact that the meaning that must be interpreted from within the exhibit is not contained within it at all but actually stems from a place in the exchange network of other merchandise. Its exchange value obscures its particularity, which imposes restrictions on virtual exchange relations in a way that prevents its simple exchange by any other merchandise. The museum exhibit is the point of contact between these two values: use value, (from which we may infer that the source of the capital lies in the exhibit itself and its specific weight) and exchange value (from which we may infer that capital is produced, increased, and accumulated in the very act of exchange). Use value suggests an attempt to preserve the exhibit as it is—entangled in its original exchange networks, accumulating layers of age and authenticity. On the other hand, exchange value suggests an attempt to mobilize the exhibit as much as possible—to transport it from one exchange network to another (for example, to exhibit it at the Museum of Modern Art in New York and at the Museum of Contemporary Art in California) so that it will circulate inside them and accumulate layers of capital simply by virtue of its movement in the framework of these networks and among them.

The museum exhibit—whether belonging to the museum of art, science, history, or the Holocaust—is subject, to varying degrees, to the twofold logic of merchandise (use value and exchange value) I have described above. Nevertheless, the exhibit usually, though not always, benefits from an image that is preserved because of its rarity, uniqueness, and worthiness of being preserved. Against the background of this contention concerning the twofold nature of the museum exhibit, I would like to examine the encounter between the rules of museum discourse and those of discourse concerning the Holocaust.

At the center of discourse concerning the Holocaust stands a deviant, unique, rare, and extraordinary event comparable to none other. On examination, the encounter between museum discourse and discourse concerning the Holocaust would seem to be the ultimate encounter between two discourses, at the basis of which stands the category of uniqueness, regulating their logic of action. However, the unique has a different standing in each of these discourses. The purpose of the discourse concerning the Holocaust is to preserve the unique in its uniqueness and to protect it from any other unique event—to expurgate any event that threatens to challenge this uniqueness and share the position of unique horror that the Holocaust occupies.[5] In the discourse concerning the Holocaust, the unique is derived from the

---

5. One of the more hair-raising cases of an encounter between the Holocaust and the logic of the museum occurred in real time in Prague during World War II, while the Holocaust was still an ongoing process of extermination. Nazis and Jews began a museum to commemorate the vanishing Jewish race, which demonstrated the Nazis' use of the museum institution and discourse as well as a manifestation of the

"use value" of the signifier "Holocaust"—the restrictions imposed on interpretations of the object called the Holocaust or of the Holocaust as object. The uniqueness of the Holocaust will not be allowed to concede ground before the uniqueness
of any other event. In museum discourse, on the other hand, uniqueness is derived
from the "exchange value" of the exhibit—from the fact that each exhibit is distinguished anew from all the other exhibits being transmuted at the same time in the
exchange network. In other words, the purpose of museum discourse is to exhibit
and preserve the unique but also to replace one instance of the unique with another
each time and to always preserve a place for the new instance of the unique that is
bound to follow. In this sense, a museum of contemporary art is based on the existence of a space intended for the unique—an empty space that functions on the principle of alternately being filled and emptied.

THE EXHIBITION

The contrary proclivity of the rules of these two discourse systems of the museum
and the Holocaust (which I pointed to above) can be of assistance in analyzing the
patterns of viewing, reception, and distribution of Roee Rosen's exhibition. The appeal to the spectator that Rosen's exhibition proposes shatters the network of relations that has been customary in the museum ever since its establishment: a silent,
dumb object faced by an interpreting subject who knows how to make the visible
speak out.[6] Instead of this network of relations, Rosen's exhibition posits the spectator as an attentive, speechless, nonsovereign subject, a recidivous consumer who is
exposed to new possibilities and temptations, enchanted by the wonders of virtual
reality, and embroiled from the start of the exhibition in a mimetic vortex inviting
him or her to become anyone or anything that is met along the way. The exhibition
is built as a walkway to be negotiated at reading or viewing pace, consisting of ten

---

possibility contained in the institution itself. Nazis and Jews joined together in common purpose to preserve
the unique and the authentic, which would soon become rare and immediately thereafter turn into a memory of something that had been annihilated. The Nazis made use of museum logic to establish a museum that
would participate in the extermination of the Jewish race and also in the purification and preservation of authentic Jewishness. The only thing left after the war would be the rarest and most unique memory that could
be extracted from it: the Jew whose actuality had become abstract. Extermination as the condition for the
preservation of the unique and authentic was a concept that underlay the extermination of everything that
didn't suit the authentically German. With the establishment of the museum for the vanishing Jewish race,
a link was extended between the nation-state and the museum that had formerly been hidden from view.

6. It should be noted that at this stage the interpreting subject knows how to make the visible speak out
but he is requested to do so outside the museum space. In other words, in the exhibition space he's invited to
be just as mute as the object. The only voices heard in the exhibition space are those that are authorized by
the museum in the guise of its exhibition guides.

Roee Rosen, *Live and Die as Eva Braun,* general view of
the exhibition, 1997

stations (ten chapters laid out along ten placards of text) and sixty black-and-white
paintings of various size but all relatively small (see photo above). The viewing
course is elucidated by the placards. The text appeals to the spectator and describes—as in a running voice-over commentary—how the customer becomes Eva
Braun as she awaits Adolf Hitler's arrival, gets into bed with him, sheds a tear, commits suicide, and turns into a wax statue or a two-dimensional figure in hell. In this
exhibition, speech emanates not from the interpreting subject but from the wall.
This speech is precedent to the subject. It interprets the subject, describes the subject's actions, offers him or her a way—but also remains attentive to the conflict in
which the subject is embroiled. For instance, in the concluding statement of the first
station's placard: "Who would have believed it! In fact, you read German even if you
don't understand a word. After all, it's your mother tongue—since you are Eva
Braun." The exhibition preserves the pole of muteness, but, contrary to the usual
structure (the mute object), it's on the spectator's side.

This is a radical inversion proposed by Rosen's exhibition because it strikes at
the ostensible sovereignty of the spectator-citizen in the museum. The latter has internalized the rules of the discourse and knows what behavior is expected of a spectator who comes to a museum. This radical inversion clearly deviates from the rules
of museum discourse, from the rules of discourse concerning the Holocaust, and

THE [SPECTATOR'S] PLACE: ADOLF HITLER AND EVA BRAUN

from the usual encounter between the two as well. The machinery of museum discourse has been delegated to preserve the pole of muteness on the side of the object and consequently to preserve its own standing and that of the spectators as interpreting subjects who know who they are, where they are coming from, what's hanging on the wall in front of them, and where they are going. Ever since its establishment over two centuries ago, the museum has been one of the primary arenas for the interpreting subject who knows how to make the mute object speak out—how to place the object in the framework of a story—"art," "Holocaust," "Israeli art," or "art concerned with the Holocaust." Both the producer and the consumer of art are educated to become subjects of art who know how to make it speak out.[7] The museum is the main site for acquiring the technique of making an object speak out. It resembles a huge concert hall where people gather to listen—through and beyond the works of art—to the transcendent law of art. Everyone who takes an active part in the field of art agrees that a worthy object is a mute object, an object that mustn't appear arbitrary (so as to justify the interpretative effort) but that mustn't appear too bespoken or too outspoken either (also to justify the interpretative effort).[8] This intermediate situation—neither arbitrary nor able to speak for itself—is essential not to the object but to the exchange relations subsisting among the different agents looking at, speaking about, and exhibiting it. Spectators, critics and interpreters are all dedicated to preserving and rehabilitating—if need should arise—the exhibit's space of meanings and intertwinement in the traditional exchange system each time. In the case of Rosen's exhibition, the overturning of the traditional relation between exhibit and spectator precipitated a surfeit of activity, the purpose of which was the rehabilitation of the exhibit's space of meanings and its incorporation into the familiar pattern. This activity actually required turning a blind eye to the visible and the bespoken from the walls, so that the exhibition could be embedded in a sort of security zone in which rages an ostensibly furious controversy on the lines of "Israeli art and the Holocaust." The polemics, vigorous and vociferous as they may be, actually function as an apparatus that reaffirms the customary distinctions, the traditional relations, and the consensual divisions of labor by successfully jump-starting the museal engine—the engine of differentiation.

---

7. For more on the way in which the museum takes part in constituting interpreting subjects who acknowledge the transcendent value of art, see the last chapter.

8. In my book *TRAining for ART: A Critique of the Museal Economy* (Azoulay, 1999a), I described the patterns of behavior and exchange relations displayed in the home of artist Rafi Lavi and how the individuals who trained and visited this place of knowledge (the Lavi home) learned how to see art, speak about art, speak like artists, and behave like artists (Azoulay, 1999a).

THE POLEMICS

The controversy surrounding Rosen's Eva Braun and Adolf Hitler exhibition was characterized by a polarization of opinion between those who castigated it, believing that it did not belong inside a museum, and those who crowned it as one of the important exhibitions ever seen in Israel. Detractors and enthusiasts alike used identical categories, pointing to the exhibition as a turning point, a boundary marker, the crossing of a border: "his excellent, stimulating, undermining exhibition"; "there's a limit to everything and the limit is pornographic exploitation of the Holocaust"; "an important document in the annals of sensationalism"; "one of the most moving exhibitions ever seen in Israel"; "a profane transgression."[9]

Spectators at Rosen's exhibition, then, can be divided into those who were for it and thought it was *deviant, unusual, and disturbing* and those who were against it and thought it was *deviant, unusual, and disturbing*. Detractors thought that these characteristics were exactly the reason that the exhibit should be removed from the museum walls, while supporters thought that for the same reason the exhibition's run should be extended so that more people could see it. Both positions served a polemical function for each other and also a confirmatory function as well. The fact that detractors sought to silence the exhibition was grasped by supporters as proof that the exhibition was indeed disturbing and worthy of being exhibited, while the fact that supporters considered the exhibition to be a stimulating and disturbing event convinced detractors that the supporters' only interest was in sensationalism—in "getting attention at any cost."

This mirror-image response stems from the connection between museum discourse and discourse concerning the Holocaust. Besides the relation to the unique that I discussed earlier, a dimension of universality characterizes them both. Anyone is entitled—and even obliged—to partake in the memory of the Holocaust because it bears a universal message. Anyone is entitled to take part in the act of viewing what's inside the museum because what's exhibited there is presumed to have universal value. Both discourses are custodial and preservative, and the speaker-spectators in them have proved their ability to listen to (and, of course, interpret) the objects that need to be preserved. Both involve an unbiased subject (spectator or speaker) who is capable of clearing the museal arena pending the appearance of nonmediated knowledge (museum knowledge or knowledge concerning the Holocaust). The speakers in the framework of these discourses are supposed to serve

---

9. See Breitberg-Semel (1997), Gladman (1997), Green (1997), Gurevich (1997), Riegler and Trebelisi-Chadad (1997), Rosen and Yahav (1997), Samet (1997), Sheffy (1997), Shragay (1997), Tsippor (1997), Yosi-fon (1997).

S

knowledge, worship it, and be subject to it. The "anyone" who is invited to be a spectator at the exhibits of these two discourses is supposed to constitute himself in the image of the "expert"—a universal, unbiased subject of knowledge. In principle, anyone is entitled to adopt this persona, but in practice, the only ones who are entitled are those who are already part of the formal or symbolic community that apportions entitlement and takes part in the transformation of "anyone" into an entitled person. The rejection of Arafat's request to visit the Holocaust Museum in Washington a few years ago exposed the inner workings of the entitlement machinery. That machine cranks out entry permits only to those subjects who have already been acknowledged as entitled and as capable of listening to the museum exhibit of the Holocaust and extrapolating from it the universal lesson of the memory of the Holocaust. In prevalent Jewish and Israeli discourse, that lesson is nothing other than the uniqueness of the Jewish victims, the uniqueness of the event, the Jewish and Israeli monopoly over the representation of the event, and the acceptance of these conclusions as universal principles that everyone is supposed to acknowledge and agree to (see Elkana, 1988; Zuckerman, 1993; Ophir, 1987). This entitlement apparatus is managed by a team of experts who have been delegated to interpret the exhibits and make them speak out. They are its ideal consumers, according to the logic of merchandise described above. In practice, their role is to preserve the exchange value of the exhibit—to guard the boundaries of the exchange relations and the restrictions attached to them so that the consumption of the object will be conducted by all who enter into the exchange relations in exactly the same manner.[10]

SEEING HOLOCAUST

Immediately after Rosen's exhibition *Live and Die as Eva Braun* opened, it was labeled as dealing with the "Holocaust." The argument that accompanied the exhibition's reception revolved naturally—so thought curators and art critics—around the relationship between art and the Holocaust because Rosen's exhibition deals with the Holocaust. The artist is the son of Holocaust survivors. The museum—the authoritative voice in this debate—presented the exhibition to its spectators as one that deals with the Holocaust: "In his works, the Holocaust is made visible from a tem-

---

10. In 1998, the administration of Yad Vashem (the Holocaust Martyrs and Heroes Remembrance Authority) reneged on its decision to award a prize to controversial leftist Israeli sculptor Yigal Tumarkin. This expressed Yad Vashem's commitment to its delegated mandate—the safeguarding of knowledge of the Holocaust and its memory from the "nationalistic," which paradoxically means the elevation of "nationalism" into the organizing pattern to which everything, including interpretation of the Holocaust, is subservient and the purpose of which everything is supposed to serve.

poral and spatial distance, and is thus transformed from a fresh, vivid traumatic experience into a traumatic memory" (Perry-Lehman, 1997).[11] It was presented as part of the "museum's continuing commitment to allow younger artists in Israel to grapple with the difficult subject of the Holocaust—particularly as their contemporary experience becomes increasingly remote from the actual experience of the Holocaust itself" (Perry-Lehman, 1997). The museum's declared commitment expresses the demarcation of the "Holocaust" square on the chessboard of Israeli art, an examination of its status, whether occupied or vacant, as well as an examination of various Holocaust-related exhibitions to determine whether they are qualified to occupy this square. Several articles published in recent years have examined this square and have almost unanimously determined that it is on the whole vacant.[12]

Articles written about Rosen's exhibition, however, have determined that it occupies the vacant square. Many of these articles have dealt with the question of why the trauma of the Holocaust is unseen in Israeli art. Prevalent explanations have pointed to the inadequacy of the Muses in the face of the trauma and the systematic instrumentalization of the Holocaust by the Zionist state. These explanations may be largely satisfactory with regard to the specific question—the attitude of Israeli art toward the Holocaust—but they obscure the limitations of the question. Where is the discussion of the connections between artistic and museal practices and the practices of memory and commemoration of the Holocaust? Why is there such disregard for the factors that enable the instrumentalization, reification, and fetishization of the Holocaust, the aim of which is to determine the Holocaust's standing once and for all as a singular and unique object that must be preserved outside the exchange economies of the discourse concerning the horrors of the twentieth century.[13] In other words, what's involved here is the dogmatic acceptance of an axiom on the lines of "one can't compare the slaughter of the Armenians to the Holocaust." It is not surprising that the Holocaust has been disregarded by artists and has remained unrepresented, for this is possible only if the Holocaust turns into a fixed object outside the exchange economies of the horrors of the twentieth century. Thus any treatment of World War II is enfolded into the framework of "art and war," while any

---

11. From the foreword to the exhibition catalogue, which was written by the acting head curator of the museum.

12. These articles were written by various people in the Israeli art world, including Roee Rosen himself, who wrote about other artists (see Rosen, 1996).

13. Such a discourse merely strengthens the Holocaust's fixed standing as an "object" and in effect forestalls the undermining action of an exhibition such as Rosen's, which claims to be acting in several additional fields of discourse.

THE [SPECTATOR'S] PLACE: ADOLF HITLER AND EVA BRAUN

Roee Rosen, *Live and Die as Eva Braun*, details, 1997

discussion of Hiroshima falls into the category of treatment of the Other, and all this safeguards the differentiation of the object called the "Holocaust." Such action to preserve and safeguard the differentiation of the discourse is carried out in various fields of activity, of which the museum is but the tip of the iceberg.[14]

For a long time I too subscribed to the diagnosis that Rosen's exhibition deals with the "Holocaust." That's how the museum presented it: "Combined with his own

---

14. The educational system is the primary watchdog institution for this fetishization, and a small personal anecdote may serve to demonstrate. When my daughter was in the second grade, she was requested to bring something connected with the Holocaust to class. I suggested that she take a photograph of my father from the period when he served in the French army during World War II. My daughter refused my offer, saying: "Mom, the teacher asked us for something connected with the Holocaust, not with World War II."

Roee Rosen, *Live and Die as Eva Braun*, details, 1997

personal iconography, the images, symbols and other elements in his works deal directly with the Holocaust" (Perry-Lehman, 1997). But after devoting several weeks of thought to the exhibition, I realized that my view had also been blinded as a result of this assumption, which seemed self-evident. Renewed examination of the exhibition and its works showed me that not one of its images or symbols could be viewed as customary Holocaust iconography. The public discourse concerning the "Holocaust" deals with the Jewish victims and the Nazi regime almost solely through the prism of the genocide of the Jews. Rosen's exhibition doesn't deal with Jews, genocide, or the "Jewish" motif in the Nazi regime. The "Holocaust," then, has no presence in Rosen's exhibition.[15] The exhibition throws spectators into a maze of intricate systems of noncausal, nonrational, and unmanaged relations of representation. They encounter different possibilities of being the subject (of a museum, of

---

15. Rosen also shattered the narrative space (space of fantasy) of the Holocaust by dragging into it the one person who's not supposed to be there—Adolf Hitler. Hitler's presence inside the space of fantasy, rather than as its condition of possibility, in effect topples the possibility of a fantasy world called the Holocaust existing in isolation from the holocaust of gypsies, homosexuals, mentally ill people, and abnormal people in general. But it doesn't negate or deny—only challenges the manner of its dissection and delineation as an object of knowledge and memory.

THE [SPECTATOR'S] PLACE: ADOLF HITLER AND EVA BRAUN

control, of representation, of evil, of sexuality, of passion, of rejection, of will, of resistance, and of loss) but also of being an object (shoe, sexual organ, arm, tree, puddle, monster, flag). It is an unbounded mishmash of becoming something or someone else—Rosen, who turns into Hitler, who turns into Eva Braun, who turns into moonlight, which turns into a puddle, which turns into a stain, which turns into a tongue, which turns into a mountain. Confronted by this outflow, the spectator can only simulate his sovereignty as interpreter. He can only disregard the swirling morass and try to isolate and establish certain segments of it as exhibits for his sovereign interpretation. He then becomes a part of the machinery of discourse that would like to traffic in the object called the "Holocaust" and at the same time to maintain sole control of the rules of exchange governing this object.

THE IMPERATIVE

But there's another option beyond the simulation of sovereignty. Viewers can acknowledge the imperative "live and die as Eva Braun," which completely shatters the exchange systems that the spectator usually takes part in within the framework of the museum, and see where it leads to. Let's begin with a question: what exactly am I being enjoined to do by the wall, by the picture, by the imperative "live and die as Eva Braun"? I am being enjoined to renounce my universal identity, my being "anyone" just like anyone else—the position that the principle of universal citizenship, of which the museum is a distinct representative, has prepared for me, the position of "anyone" regardless of their name, social status, religion, gender, or race. Suddenly I am being enjoined to become someone else with a name, status, religion, gender, and race who is called Eva Braun. I can refuse, of course. But this refusal cannot obliterate the other renunciation that preceded it and that the present imperative made manifest—my renunciation of my own name, status, religion, gender, and race to occupy the vacant position of the universal spectator, the "anyone" of the museum who is also the universal subject of democracy. This imperative makes manifest the previous imperative, which enjoined me to put myself into brackets and postpone my actuality to be entitled to become the unbiased subject of an object that has universal value. This renunciation has actually created a situation in which spectators are completely exposed: their only armor is that of one who has renounced most of the elements of personal identity to claim the vacant place of "anyone." When this vacant place is filled by someone concrete—Eva Braun—its vulnerability is exposed. It is capable of becoming anyone, of resembling any proposed model, of losing control, of whirling out of control among the proposed models.

THE RETURN OF THE REPRESSED [BODY]

At the end of the exhibition's course I found myself accompanying Hitler to his death and taking part—with, through, by means of, and following Rosen—in the formulation of another version of Hitler's death.

Hitler's death. On May 1, 1945, at 9:45 A.M., German radio interrupted its broadcasts to announce that in several minutes there would be an important and bitter announcement. After a short while the voice of Grand-Admiral Karl Dönitz, who presented himself as the successor to the Reich, informed the nation of Hitler's death while "fighting at the head of his troops" (Petrova and Watson, 1996). This announcement signaled the start of the war of versions concerning Hitler's death—a plethora of contradictory, complementary, scientific, fantastic, substantiated, and farfetched versions. For many years versions were propagated that cast doubt on Hitler's death and claimed that he was hiding in a cave in Germany, living inside a bunker in England, or roving free in Argentina.[16] The version of Hitler's death by suicide was made public only a few months after the end of the war by Hugh Trevor-Roper.[17] Each version sought to rewrite the death, and to conclude the story differently—in a more proper, precise, scientific, justified, and poetic manner.[18] In 1995, when the Russian archives were opened, a new scientific version was published laying claim to be the definitive one: *The Death of Hitler: The Full Story with New Evidence from Secret Russian Archives* (Petrova and Watson, 1996).

But these versions didn't begin after his death. How Hitler would die, what would cause his death, what the setting would be, who would take part in the spectacle, what remains would be left: these and other details concerning his death preoccupied Hitler himself throughout the last several months of his life, which he spent in the Berlin bunker (January to late April 1945). At the end of January, reported his associates, he had declared that he "has no intention of falling into the hands of the enemy" and that he "doesn't want a Jew or Communist to march his body in a procession."[19] He wanted to manage his own death no less than he'd managed the death of others. From the moment he concluded that Germany was

---

16. The sources of these versions were different people, variously aligned with or against the Nazi regime. Some versions prompted intelligence agents to conduct lengthy searches; others were instantly refuted.

17. Trevor-Roper's version came out in 1947 in dozens of editions. Other versions appeared in various ways—rumor, information forwarded to the relevant government agencies, newspaper reports, books, articles, and films.

18. Especially interesting, in this context, is the version written by George Steiner, which is interspersed with doubts as to how to end Hitler's life, one proposal being to send him to Israel to mingle among the people, who all know who he is but are prohibited from killing him (Steiner, 1981).

19. Hitler's own remarks, as cited in *The Death of Hitler* (Petrova and Watson, 1996, 25).

Roee Rosen, *Live and Die as Eva Braun*, details, 1997

approaching defeat, he began staging his death with careful attention to the details of the production.[20] A few days before his death he legally married Eva Braun, wrote his political will and testament, and gave away the paintings that were dear to him. Then he poisoned Eva Braun, who'd become Frau Hitler, and shot himself in the mouth, but not before ensuring that their bodies would be burnt.[21]

---

20. Eva was poisoned first, and after her death Hitler shot himself using a Walther 7.65 caliber pistol. Both bodies were incinerated, and a part of Hitler's skull was preserved. The Russians, who were first to enter the bunker, found isolated remains of Hitler's burnt body and gathered them into their archives, completely suppressing any knowledge of them until 1995.

21. Hitler's management of his death included his marriage to Eva Braun, the bequest of his possessions to the nation and the party, the writing of a will and its removal outside the bunker, and the order to publish the will

Roee Rosen, *Live and Die as Eva Braun*, details, 1997

To this staging of his death Hitler had covert partners who joined forces unwittingly, each in his own behalf, to achieve a goal that was similar to Hitler's own—the disappearance of his body. They eliminated any possibility of his body being interred in a place that might become identified with his absent presence or his present absence. Hitler's commemorative passion reached its peak with his complete disappearance and transformation into a ghost, a repressed figure who would in the future preoccupy many and return again and again.[22] In the way he managed his death,

when Hitler should command it or immediately after the confirmation of his death. The contents of the will were an attempt to have the last word, with Hitler reclaiming responsibility for the extermination of the Jews: if the Jews should fail to be exterminated so that the extermination can't testify to itself, or if the Jews should try to appear as testimony to its noncompletion, at least Hitler's testimony would confront the extermination and as the last word would summarize what has come before. The will and order to publish it fell into Russian hands.

22. Hitler's passion for the management of commemoration expressed itself in the final hours of his life in the bunker, which were devoted to conversations about art, commemoration, and museums. His conversation with his pilot Baur concerned the portrait of Friedrich the Great, which Hitler wanted to give him. Baur agreed to accept it only if he could donate it to a gallery or museum. Hitler explained that it was a personal gift to Baur of prominent historical value, which he was interested in passing on to the future.

THE [SPECTATOR'S] PLACE: ADOLF HITLER AND EVA BRAUN

Hitler in effect determined the range of options of his continued existence among the living. Those options range from cooperating with him and his wishes so that his body won't appear (in a wax museum, a monument, or a grave site) to refusing to cooperate with him (and thus in effect cooperating in the transformation of his body into a fetish, an object of pilgrimage to both supporters and detractors).

I contend that Roee Rosen's exhibition marks out a third option: attentiveness to Hitler's requests—"I just hope they don't put me in a wax museum" or "I just hope not to fall into the hands of a Jew"—and a literal manifestation of this anxiety in the museum's exhibition space by means of a consummate mise-en-scène, which puts it up for display inside the museum, and which in effect invites the spectator not only to become Eva Braun but to intimately confront and deal with Hitler's body.

The journey through Rosen's exhibition at the Israel Museum at Jerusalem begins with a picture in which spectators are offered a pair of hands—the gloves that they (the Jewish spectators, of course) can use to handle Hitler's body marching backward toward its death. The "play" button has been pressed, and the journey begins. The "Jew" is invited to handle Hitler's death and cheat Hitler of his control of his death.

As for the question "Why do the dead return?" we might have recourse to Lacan's reply: "because they haven't been buried properly" (Zizek, 1992, 23).

CHAPTER 5   THE [BLIND] GESTURE:

HIROSHIMA

For us, a language game always and first of all means somebody speaking. But there are language games in which listening is the important thing, in which the rule applies to the listener: this is the game of justice. And we speak in it to the extent that we hear. In other words: speak as hearers, if one may put it like this, and not as authors at all. It is a game without an author.
—LYOTARD ("The Fourth Day," 1985)

A spatial attitude toward horror stands at the basis of the ethics of the modern gaze. The body—wounded, mutilated, shot, beaten, disfigured, dying—is the very heart of the spectacle in the public sphere.[1] It is the object of a desire to see, to see more, to blow up the body, to open it to the gaze, to penetrate into the body (corpse) and allow it to appear, to invite interiority to the surface of the screen (the screen as body and the body as screen), to let the survivor (of an accident, of the Holocaust, of a massacre, of a conflagration) transform the "being there" into spectacle. The spectators desire to see. There is no superfluous testimony. There is no limit to testifying. There is no end to it. This seeing brings the spectator permanently close to the event so that the distance between the spectator and "what happened there" will be maintained forever and feed the spectacle of the body on display. This spectacle is a "singular phenomenon of distance, close as it may be."[2] On the threshold of the event, the spectator is very close but also far away enough so that the sentence "You didn't see anything in Hiroshima," the opening sentence of the film *Hiroshima Mon Amour*, can continue to be said.

Is it possible to remember outside the regime of the gaze? Is it possible to create a commemorative community that doesn't have a common public space in which the horror and the body that bears its traces must appear as spectacle? I would like to present Marie Ange Guilleminot's 1998 project *Hiroshima Collection* as just such a possibility of remembering.

Why didn't you see anything in Hiroshima? Because *you* cannot see, because there is *nothing* to see in Hiroshima. This sentence expresses a state of "*différend*," an unbridgeable gap between two language games: on the one hand, the game of testimony is played by whoever was there, and on the other hand, the game of art[3] is played by whoever wasn't there but wants to see and show, to say something about

---

1. Mark Zeltzer terms this public sphere pathological (see Zeltzer, 1998).

2. In his essay "The Work of Art in the Age of Technical Reproduction," Benjamin (1978) discusses the loss of the work of art's aura and its retreat to the portrait. Further to Benjamin's discussion of the aura, I suggest considering the spectacle of the survivor's body as the site in which the aura is reconstituted.

3. The "game of art" in the traditional sense displays an object to the spectator's view. In this sense, the game of art also approaches other discursive games, such as the game of historical discourse, which employs a factual language of sight, or the language of statistics, which quantifies and formalizes.

the event, to put it in a different light, to manufacture an event in which "the event" is endowed with a different visibility. You can visit the Hiroshima Peace Memorial Museum, become familiar with every item inside it, get to the bottom of each and every exhibit, see the traces of the horror in body and space—but still, like the heroine of the film, you are distinctively the addressee of the sentence "You didn't see anything in Hiroshima." But this sentence cannot be trapped in the principle of the impossibility of representing horror or in the principle of "*différend*" between whoever was there and whoever wasn't. One cannot help but see in it the traces of destruction as well as traces of the obliteration of the traces of destruction—traces that have been denied the right to appear.

You didn't see anything in Hiroshima. The atom bomb that the Americans dropped on Hiroshima wiped Hiroshima off the face of the earth. What the bomb failed to obliterate was obliterated later, during several years of occupation that silenced the witnesses and rendered the signs mute. This silencing had a clear purpose—to prevent any museumification of the event. There would be no collecting, classifying, and decoding of the signs (testimonies) that could be transformed into information that could be conceptualized, formalized, displayed, and studied, that could teach lessons, and that could be used to draw up an indictment. During the period of U.S. occupation, which lasted from 1945 until 1952, censorship and other control activities prevented the signs from turning into units of meaning and prevented their assimilation into tissues of personal, public, verbal, visual, scientific, or historical story.[4] An effort was made to leave the signs isolated and mute. The only place where some of the signs appeared, as a small number of photographs testify,[5] was in the bodies of the survivors, who were also forced to remain isolated and mute.

During the first few years after the destruction of Hiroshima, the surviving signs and the survivors that signified were prohibited from speaking. It took almost a decade until they were allowed to speak. Time had buried whole series of testimonies about the war's present, but that present had turned into past, and the possibility of intervention and rescue in the present was no longer viable. A body can be healed, a

---

4. This control over information and the restrictions on collecting it contributed in a crucial way to the refusal of assistance to survivors out of concern that this might be construed as an admission that dropping the bomb was an unworthy act. On the implementation of censorship during the American occupation, see (Dower, 1996).

5. During the initial years of occupation, the U.S. army confiscated covertly made films and prohibited the possession of photographic equipment and products. A couple of Japanese painters named Maruki, who painted hundreds of survivors' portraits, described their project as expressing their fear that there might be no visual traces left of the horror of Hiroshima.

THE [BLIND] GESTURE: HIROSHIMA

life can be saved, a memory can be given space: these things do not remain forever frozen in their tracks, awaiting the future. They can turn into an incurably diseased body, a life snuffed out by death, a forgotten memory. "You didn't see anything in Hiroshima" because the gaze and what has been given to it were obliterated in Hiroshima. Several years later, after Hiroshima underwent museumification, "You didn't see anything in Hiroshima" because the image didn't go from an invisible to a visible state but from a visible silenced state to a more visible state (as something spoken). But the visible became spoken within the distinctive framework of an image with a purpose—to disrupt the silence, the cold war, the distribution of power in the world, the construction of a new world order. The new image constitutes packaged information about what happened and conforms to the display showcase awaiting it in the museum of history. The image is nothing other than what the French critic Serge Daney (1997) describes as the optical confirmation of a power procedure—whether technological, political, military, or advertising power: "The visual is a procedure that says 'reception perfect.'"

It is hard not to think of Marie Ange Guilleminot's project in the context of Alain Renals's film *Hiroshima Mon Amour*, with Guilleminot, a French artist, in the role of the French actress who arrives in Hiroshima to take part in the film, and with Hiromi Tsuchida, a Japanese photographer from Hiroshima, in the role of the Japanese architect. But it is also hard not to see the difference between the model of relations that develops between the hero and heroine of the film ("You didn't see anything in Hiroshima") and the model of relations that Marie Ange Guilleminot would like to develop with Hiromi Tsuchida and with Hiroshima (the (im)possibility of seeing something in Hiroshima). Marie Ange Guilleminot's *Hiroshima Collection* testifies to her relinquishment of any pretension to see, to know, to recognize, to enter into the economy of the mangling view that makes memory dependent on the spectacle of the body that bears the traces. It is a relinquishment of the pretension or desire to become an autonomous subject of the view or of knowledge with respect to the object Hiroshima.

Guilleminot's *Hiroshima Collection* project recedes from the arena of public spectacle to propose other modes of memory and of exchange that are not mediated by the (autonomous) gaze. Guilleminot's point of departure is the clothes documented by Hiromi Tsuchida in his book *Hiroshima Collection*. Guilleminot didn't see anything in Hiroshima. That's a fact. She is responding to someone else's gaze, that of the photographer, and only from this point, as the addressee of a different view, statement, or imperative, can she recapture the position of an addresser. She can see only by responding. Her view is directed toward what Tsuchida has made visible for her. Her view has no wish for a white canvas on which to impress its imprint; at the

Hiromi Tsuchida, *Dress,* "Takeyo Hatamura (41 at the
time) was waiting for a train in front of Hiroshima
Station (1,900 meters from the hypocenter). This dress
has thermal radiation burns on its shoulders and chest"
(*Hiroshima Collection*)

most, a white canvas can only reconstruct someone else's statement or garment. Her
view has attached itself to a different view and has assimilated itself to it to divert the
view to new territory—the territory of the gesture. Within the framework of this
territory, the transmission of the seen includes the gesture of transmission, like the
transmission of a story by a storyteller.[6] The territory of the gesture makes it

6. In an essay on the storyteller, Benjamin claims that we have been deprived of the ability "to share experience with others. . . . Didn't they notice at the end of the war that people who came back from the battlefield were mute? Not richer—poorer in experience which can be transmitted" (Benjamin, 1978, "The
Storyteller"). The practice that Marie Ange Guilleminot proposes for Hiroshima reconstructs not only the
garment but the story situation as well. With Guilleminot the story has no storyteller and no words—since
no story can be transmitted any longer in words other than words that are already a "novel" or "journalistic
information," as Benjamin puts it. Yet all the same it preserves the structure of transmitting experience by
motion, gesture, and act.

THE [BLIND] GESTURE: HIROSHIMA

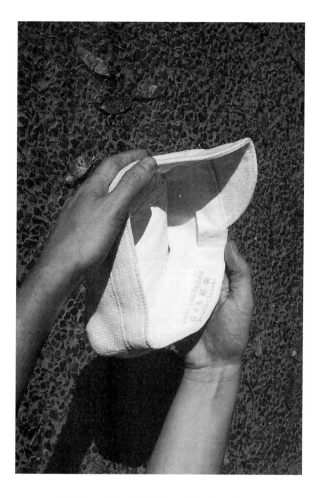

Marie Ange Guilleminot, *Hiroshima Collection 6.8.1998,*
Norihiko Sasaki

possible to interpret Guilleminot's action as one of response—as action that is taken
from the position of an addressee of a call and that becomes addressed only by virtue
of being responsive—for now it turns to you and puts you in the position of an
addressee.

Guilleminot has chosen several articles of clothing out of Hiromi Tsuchida's
book and reconstructed them. She reconstructed the clothes of Norihiko Sasaki,
Tetsuo Kitabayashi, Takeyo Hatamura, and Yukitoshi Masuda and in effect chose to

Marie Ange Guilleminot, *Hiroshima Collection 6.8.1998,*
a project prepared in the framework of
Hiroshima Art Document, Curator Yukiko Ito, 1998

tell their story as it had been told by Tsuchida and as he had heard it from the victims' families. It does not reconstruct the model from which the clothes were sewn but shows their manner of preparation in connection to a hypothetical model that they may or may not have had, utilizing the vestiges of craft as indicators of time and space. *Hiroshima Collection* is a potential collection that was not prepared for display by a specific community (Hiroshima's inhabitants) and has turned into an actual museum collection as a result of its contact with a different community (the United

THE [BLIND] GESTURE: HIROSHIMA

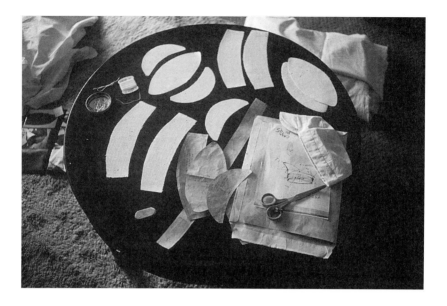

Marie Ange Guilleminot, *Hiroshima Collection 6.8.1998*
preparatory photos, 1998

States) and technology (the atom bomb)—the garment as statement. In the reconstructive act, Guilleminot is not seeking the original author of the garment as statement. She is not erasing from the garment as statement all traces of its acts of enunciation but specifically is reconstructing those acts of enunciation that linked, in a single historic moment, the community that was erased and the community that erased it. She reconstructs the garment, not its original as prepared by a specific tailor or factory but the concrete traces of interpretation of an original, which she has transformed into a type of original pattern.

The pattern is on sale in the museum shop. It is intended for spectators and invites them to reconstruct the garment and to sign it as one would a statement of memory. Spectators are invited to reconstruct an article from the potential collection that became an actual collection, to sign it (rather than to make it as an act of exerting authorship)—in other words, to remanufacture the gap between the pattern and the finished product to which it leads. Thus spectators become speakers (addressers) of the garment as statement, enunciate it, take part in its transmission from one person to the next, from hand to hand, from mouth to ear, from body to body. In effect, they are invited to become part of an invisible community responsible for

Marie Ange Guilleminot, *Hiroshima Collection 6.8.1998,*
preparatory photo, 1998

transmitting the garment as statement, while maintaining its standing as one statement in a vortex of others, which doesn't enable whoever signs the statement to become one with its author (to become the original, to be sanctified). When the signer
becomes the author, the signature seals the statement and prevents the further transmission of the viewing experience, and presents the statement as the authoritative
view or as knowledge. Spectators are invited to preserve this statement from becoming an exhibit in public space in which the desire to see and to be seen turns into
the engine of memory—its only measure, the only testimony to its existence. The
story (as experience, in Benjamin's sense) that Marie Ange Guilleminot is passing on
through her reconstruction of a garment is transmitted in a direct manner that is devoid of words, devoid of a museal gaze of spectators. It is a transmission of savoir-
faire, implemented through an object that is there to be signed, though it is unsigned
and unfinished.

The woman's torn jacket on display in the museum—with a hole in the shoulder
pad, a torn sleeve, a worn collar—appeals to you for confirmation. You will say that
you've been there, that you've seen it; you will say what needs to be said and help

THE [BLIND] GESTURE: HIROSHIMA

inflate the museum's ratings. Guilleminot hasn't only issued an invitation to see. She also invites you to reconstruct the garment from the pattern, to wear it on your body once a year on August 6, the anniversary of Hiroshima's destruction. The manual reconstructive act is not undertaken to restore the aura to the act of manual labor but to resist the transformation of the world into a two-dimensional surface, into a picture which posits the viewers in the position of merely addressees whose only function is to confirm the seen by saying yes or no—"reception perfect."[7] You are invited to wear the garment and display it in the public space outside the museum's, knowing that this space has no mirror, no display showcases. If you wear the white garment outside the museum, you will not obtain the optical confirmation of a display showcase that says, in effect, "reception perfect." Your action is a private a memorial ceremony—a response to the story as experience, a private gesture of response to the imperative to remember, which connects you with a community that is devoid of a gaze and devoid of visibility and that does not display its members in the public sphere.[8] In this silent public sphere, private individuals coalesce into a community that is performing a political act not by means of rational discussion but by means of a blind, intimate, anonymous act meant to evade the political and the instrumental.

"You didn't see anything in Hiroshima." And just because there's nothing to see, Hiroshima is the place you must go to see what "nothing to see" looks like. Even though there's a museum and it's full, there's nothing to see in Hiroshima. Numerous signs scattered about the museum explain to viewers what they're seeing. But the museum is trying to conceal the fact that there's nothing to see, that in Hiroshima the gaze crashed, that in Hiroshima the necessary distance for maintaining the view collapsed in destruction. The signs in the museum seem to express a fear of a state in which the spectator might notice that there's nothing to see. Therefore, they don't prohibit touching the items on display. On the contrary, they explicitly invite spectators to touch, to ascertain that indeed they are standing before eyewitness testimony. A stone that survived lies on a cushion, ostensibly eyewitness testimony to the atom bomb. But more than testifying to the atom bomb, this stone testifies to the eradication of the gaze. When there's nothing left to see, it is permitted to touch.

---

7. In his essay on the work of art, Benjamin (1978) describes the history of technical reproduction. The progression is from reproduction by means of three-dimensional objects (using casting and stamping) to reproduction by means of two-dimensional images (using printing and photography to manufacture a disembodied image projected on paper).

8. In a certain sense Guilleminot's action can be seen as a contemporary echo of the patterns of Christian communion, which makes it possible for people to share bread and wine and thereby intimately exchange thoughts and feelings about their shared faith.

There is no longer any reason to fear that the seen might disclose its unseen side. The stone that survived the atom bomb no longer hides anything. It is the seen and the unseen together. There is no need to protect it from casual passersby or to preserve it like the evidence from a crime scene. It is impervious to every view, to every contact; it has survived everything, including the eradication of testimonies. After it there is nothing. It may be touched. "You didn't see anything in Hiroshima." What is there to see in Hiroshima? In Hiroshima the necessary distance for maintaining the view was completely eliminated. The object of the view has been completely captured from the pilot's cockpit, so that nothing is left of it except, paradoxically, the aura—the aura of an object that can never appear, an object that will always remain an absence, an object that exists no longer.

You are wearing a garment that has touched death and therefore is the reconstructed reflection of death. You are wearing a garment that served sometimes like a barrier against death, which has changed from an external covering for the body (one that may be replaced by another each day) into an accessory that has impressed on the body both the imprint of destruction and the imprint of survival. The body has turned into the image of the garment. The garment functioned like a camera. Through the apertures of this camera—in the form of a décolletage, visor, or sleeve—the blazing light of the bomb penetrated the body and imprinted an image on it by burning it into the skin.[9] This image is the other side of the mushroom cloud image of Hiroshima and cannot be erased. The remnant isn't the spectacle of the horror. It is what cannot be erased or gotten rid of in any event. The obligation to remember is met by transmitting the remnant and by creating the conditions for its appearance. You are invited to wear a garment that has been snatched from death, just as the photographic image has been snatched from its object. Its nearness to death isn't visible, and yet you're aware of it. You don't need any proof. Neither are you invited to reconstruct the garment in its mutilated state to feel its nearness to death. You will reconstruct it in white cloth that gives up any pretense of producing an original and that responds to the experience of reconstruction. You will cut the cloth carefully, immersing yourself in the work. You will join one piece to another until the garment appears out of them. Your body will recoil from contact with it— maybe not suddenly, maybe a few minutes later. This garment—which you have sewn in response to the invitation, from new materials, using a purchased pattern— seems to stink of death. You can't get rid of this smell. It is the remnant that'll never

---

9. Paul Virilio (1989) compares all of Hiroshima to a darkroom in which the Japanese shades were written on the city's walls.

THE [BLIND] GESTURE: HIROSHIMA

leave. You will wear it on your body—knowing that you are not alone in this garment and yet remaining alone in your clothing, like a silenced sign, with no visual recompense, no reflection of yourself in the mirror, in a museum showcase.

The position of being the author of a statement-picture of Hiroshima is renounced not to forget the event but to remember it silenced, lacking a view, as it happened, as it was experienced, as it was reexperienced by being an event transmitted from one person to the next, from mouth to ear, from hand to hand. In the public space horror is usually written in defined formats such as a connection between the interiority of the witnesses and standard models of authenticity into which they are invited to empty their interiority. This pattern of memory is a meeting between a personal story and a historical date, which is effected through the agency of a scarred and burnt body that is exposed in all its intimacy and turns into the carrier of protest.

"You didn't see anything in Hiroshima," says the reproof, but Marie Ange Guilleminot's proposal seemingly rebuts: "I didn't ask to see anything in Hiroshima." I didn't seek to undress witnesses. I didn't look for testimonies. I didn't cast any doubt. I didn't come to interrogate survivors. I didn't collect information. I didn't try to understand. I didn't come to tell Hiroshima about itself. I didn't propose identifying with it. I didn't try to manufacture a statement of my own about Hiroshima. I came to add a signature to Hiroshima as a monument and to give this signature its proper place: a signature that doesn't seal the statement or fix it under its authority but that is at the margins of the statement as a temporary addition. My signature is an identification tag, which by its essence is to be replaced by another signature, which declares the work to be unfinished, which remains an addressee while being an addresser, which transmits someone else's story, which places another in the position of addressee, in the position of one who in turn will be asked to respond, to sign the statement, and transmit it onward.

[CRITICAL] IMAGE

1

The modern museum—arising together with the public sphere at the end of the eighteenth century—is in fact a (spatial) literalization of history writing. The documents (the exhibits) are collected, classified, interpreted, and re-presented. Each new item that's added (or discovered later on) enables the act of rewriting to continue. A unique space, homogenous and delimited, is arranged like a table to absorb the next item. Each new item relates to its predecessor—either directly and purposefully or through the experts entrusted with its integration into the narrative of all the other items. An item for which no place can be allocated within the art history discourse and critique, one of the central institutions of which is the museum, is rejected and remains outside its doors. Photography, appearing in 1839, a few decades after the museum, also offered a new spatial unit—the unique space populated, whether randomly or deliberately if momentarily, by the photographer and the photographed. The main characteristic of this spatial unit is its mobility and its ability to be anywhere. The photographer arriving with a camera outlines the boundaries of the spatial unit for a given length of time, and the moment the camera moves away, that spatial unit disperses. In other words, the space in question is potentially virtual. Technological developments achieved during the past two decades are transforming this potential virtuality of the photographic space into an actual virtuality.

Two distinct forms of subjectivity have an affinity to the modern molds of organizing space—the museum and photography. The museum constitutes the *subject-citizen*—the autonomous, sovereign subject who stands in front of the work of art and is interpellated, as well as authorized to pronounce judgments of taste.[1] The act of photography constitutes the *subject-hostage*, a simulation of a subject who wields the camera as an apparently autonomous and sovereign subject, commands space, documents it, and, in fact, from the moment he wields the camera becomes a captive to the camera's activity. The photographer's actions and the events that he or she participates in occur at a certain point in between photographer and camera.

Museum, camera, and subjectivity: these three axes are essential elements of any reflection on the possibility that the (photographed) image is a critical image. The image is always interwoven into an intertextual network, within which it is interpreted. The image interpreted through this network can also serve as a compass and measure for defining its boundaries. But it also can respond to projections that appear to be extraneous to it and that may transform it, for example, from the status of

---

1. On the relationship between subject, citizen, and culture, see Balibar (1997).

a conventional and banal image to that of a critical and radical one, and vice versa. I do not look to find a contingent answer to that transformation—which can be extricated from the interpretive context of each single image—but rather look to historicize the conditions of the image and the critique in the contemporary context through a discussion of the works of five Israeli artists: Barry Frydlender, Michal Heiman, Efrat Shvily, and Dana and Boaz Zonshine.

2

What is a photographed image? The answer is to be found neither in the ahistoric essence of the image nor in its "origin" (if that term is understood as the historic signpost of the emergence of ahistoric essence). The answer is to be found, rather, in the moment of the historic, contingent appearance of a new structure of relations between the visible and the invisible and between the visible and the sayable, made possible by a new instrument (the camera) and by the crystallization of a new alignment of relations of power in which this instrument found itself involved. The historicization of the essential in the investigated object is nothing but a structural articulation of its supposed origin. Such historicization of the essential in the object is among the distinctive features of genealogic study, of the kind exemplified by Michel Foucault in his essays "What Is an Author?" (1994) and "What Is Critique?" (1978).[2] The latter essay serves me here in a double sense—on the one hand, as a model of genealogical study and, on the other hand, as a model of critique (which I ultimately propose to critique) on the basis of the genealogy of the photographed image and an investigation into the possibility of a critical image.

When was the modern (photographed) image born? All images issue from an act of erasure. Wherever there is erasure, the image aspires to arise. The erasure doesn't precede its appearance; it inheres in it and is the condition of its possibility. For an image to appear, something else has to be erased.[3] Let us for a moment consider the most common modern means of producing images—the camera, which is a black box with a frontal lens that produces images maintaining an indexical relationship with the virtual space outlined by the camera. Everything beyond the frontal, anything that cannot be flattened, is erased and replaced by the single image.[4] This

---

2. The essay was presented (and published) as a lecture (Foucault, 1978, 35–63).

3. This description draws both on Jean-François Lyotard's discussion of the chain mechanism of phrases (*énoncé*) within the discursive framework as developed in his book *The Différend* (Lyotard, 1983) and on Blanchot's (1997) analysis of the image.

4. For a concrete critique of the single focus of the camera, see Aïm Deuelle-Luski's north-west-south-east camera, a camera made of a box perforated on its four sides (see chapter 8 for photos taken with this camera).

image is ready and willing to be transferred to any other box that will host it (a museum, an album, or a screen) and be traded in the various exchange systems that deal with images (artistic, legal, financial, and political systems) and that decide which images are to appear and which are to be erased. The appearance of the image outside of the darkroom is always a moment of visibility within the framework of a field of power relations. And what about the critical image? It arises out of the appearance of an oppressive image, which becomes oppressive from the moment when it seeks to perpetuate the erasure, purports to erase its traces[5] (to become fixed, not to disappear, not to be replaced by another image, the successive image aspiring to appear and to be exchanged within the framework of the museal, political, or cultural economy). An image becomes critical when it contrives not only to oust the previous image and take its place in a perpetual flicker of images but to make the previous image appear oppressive—that is, to make its oppressiveness visible.

Before placing these conditions in an historical context, I dwell on Foucault's answer to the question "What is critique?" and propose a fundamental schema—which he consolidates later in a historical perspective by positing that critique is the other side of governmentality (*gouvernementalité*), Foucault's term for the art of government. Wherever there are forms of control and governing of life, it is, in principle, possible (Foucault claims) to locate critique as "the art of not being governed" (*l'art de ne pas être gouverné*). Given that power does not operate within a vacuum, wherever it is located it is also possible to locate resistance (which Foucault identifies with critique).[6]

Not opposition to but rather consistent intoxication with control and critique leads to an accelerated development of practices of domination that is always accompanied by a series of questions of "how not to be governed in such a manner, by such and such factors, in the name of certain principles, for such and such purposes, or through such and such procedures" (Foucault, 1978, 39). In the face of governmentality—those mechanisms of power that refer to and rely on truth to subordinate (*assujetir*) individuals–critique is "the movement through which the subject assumes the right to investigate the truth about the effects of its power and the power over its discourse on truth" (Foucault, 1978, 39). Critique, according to Foucault, is thus the art of not consenting to be subordinated—that is, resistance.

---

5. It should be noted that the presumption to erase the traces remains and that in most cases the traces of the erasure or repression keep recurring.

6. Foucault doesn't account for other possibilities of power relations, such as submission, integration, or pleasure, which I touch on below.

Foucault establishes a parallel between his definition of critique and Kant's definition of enlightenment.[7] Kant describes humanity as living in a state of minority. The way to overcome this state and turn people into adults, according to Foucault's reading of Kant, is by critique of religion, law (the natural law that limits the authority of power), and (scientific) knowledge. By examining these three axes, Foucault describes both the development of the art of government and the institutionalization of critique. Critique, according to Kant, shows knowledge its limits by indicating to it how much it can know without losing its validity. It's not only what we do with some measure of courage but also the understanding we have of the limits of our knowledge.[8] Thus, the individual can discover the principle of autonomy and establish the limits for heeding the command "obey." Foucault, in effect, turns Kant's concept of critique as the knowledge of the limits of knowledge (by way of negation) into a positive act: "in what is presented to us as universal, necessary, obligatory, what is the part of that which is singular, contingent, and resulting from arbitrary constraints. It is, in sum, a matter of transforming the critique exercised in the form of a necessary limitation into a practical critique in the form of a potential transgression" (Foucault, 1994, 4:574). For both Kant and Foucault, critique demands a subjective point of view and a subject assuming it. Critique is a reflective position—a reflective relation to the present.[9] The practice is defined by Foucault as historical-critical or historical-philosophical. It is not concerned with the legitimization of knowledge but rather investigates its production and institutionalization in different constellations of knowledge and power and reexamines its limits.

Governmentality and critique in effect construct an inter-subjective space of discourse and action. Governmentality produces subjects, whereas critique's role is to resist and to desubjectivize. The concepts of discourse and statement (*énoncé*) enabled Foucault to desubjectivize and "spatialize" the subject equally, annulling the subject's identity as originator and turning him or her into a function of the discourse and the phrase. Notwithstanding Foucault's "spatialization" of the subject, the critical stance and the point of view remain that of an autonomous subject. The subject remains the starting and vanishing point of the critical practice, the outline of which Foucault draws by means of three central questions: how were the subjects

---

7. In addition to the article on critique, two versions of Foucault's essay on enlightenment (Foucault, 1994) specifically thematize the parallel between Foucault's critique and Kant's critique.

8. In the version of his essay on enlightenment published in 1984, Foucault deals with two conceptions of critique in Kant (Foucault, 1994, 562–577).

9. This relationship, Foucault claims, occurs through three axes (of enlightenment): power, truth, and subject.

constituted as subjects of our knowledge (our control of things), as subjects absorbing and using power (our relation to others), and as moral subjects of our acts (the relation to oneself)?

Governmentality and critique are opposite positions within the same system of power relations. The same cultural practices and the same technologies are capable of serving in two directions. Photography is a concrete example of this. From its beginnings to this day, photography has taken part both in the practice of governmentality and in the practice of critique. The camera lens, which since the invention of photography has attempted to replace the eye, is usually presented as an instrument in the hands of the subject activating it. The camera lens alone cannot occupy the critical point of view formulated by Foucault without a subject organizing the seen and investing it with meaning. Only when the camera lens is controlled and directed with an affinity to the logic that characterizes a delimited and controlled site and is activated by a reflective subject can the lens take part in the "critical ontology of ourselves" (*ontologie critique de nous-mêmes*). Only then can we "relate to it not as a theory, a doctrine, or even a permanent body of accumulated knowledge; relate to it as an attitude, an ethos, a philosophical life where the critique of what we are at one and the same time a historical analysis of the limits imposed on us and an examination of their potential transgression" (Foucault, 1994, 4:577).

3

Photography makes a singular and complementary contribution to attempts to regulate the social body and attempts to critique those attempts. At the institutional sites designated for study, healing, or punishment (schools, hospitals, and prisons), workers are preoccupied with taming and domesticating the individual—that is, with rectifying perversions and adjusting them to a standard pattern. Since its beginnings, photography has taken part in these practices.[10] The homology between photography and institutions was made possible by a similar organization and by a mutual intersubjective—a common space. This space constitutes the prerequisite medium for the encounter between therapist and client or between photographer and subject of a specific act of photography.[11] In that sense photography and the dis-

---

10. See three articles by Allan Sekula—on the subject of the police archive (Sekula, 1989, 343–89), on the use of photography in psychiatry, especially in cases of hysteria (Huberman, 1982), and on its uses in the military domain since the early part of this century (Virilio, 1989).

11. Which led to the development of the positivist rhetoric of photography, culminating in Barthes's book and the expression he coined. "It was there" (Barthes, 1980).

ciplinary site fit each other like hand and glove. Photography made it possible to assemble knowledge about the "public body" of the individual. The fixed format of the photograph, the rhetoric of authenticity it rendered possible ("it was there"), the uniformity of the process, its mechanical and standard means of production and reproduction, the camera's availability and virtuosity (which does not require long years of apprenticeship): all these qualities make the task easy and its execution efficient and methodical. These elements made it possible to achieve photographic results that, on the one hand, retained the standard qualities and, on the other hand, preserved the singularity of the individual and the uniqueness of the isolated incidence (Barthes, 1980). The data provided by the camera are easy to sort, classify, and crosscheck, and photography indeed evolved together with its archive. Photography as archive offered central positions of control to administer this body of knowledge. It's as if the police investigator and the physician sit in their control towers in the heart of the archive with all its data available to the hand and the eye or at least are equipped with the means and the authority to obtain the required documents. Here too, as in any other disciplinary site, early knowledge engenders new knowledge. The police investigator can compare profiles, measure, run in filmic sequence all the suspects documented in the archive, and draw the necessary conclusions.

The vantage point from the tower or the "control room" of the photo archive is formed by two modes of disciplining photography. The first touches on photography as resulting from the act of a subject who controls a camera's field of vision and bears witness to that field. The second touches on photography's tendency to produce evidence and assemble it in an archive—an institution and a practice which in their performance essentially resemble other disciplinary sites. Yet from its beginnings, photography concretized both the control and the critique, both the common, one-time space of the position of the direct gaze and its cellular disintegration into private units. This dual signification of photographic practice was countered by the development of two critical practices. The first critical practice aspires to have the camera penetrate into forbidden fields of vision that seek to remain hidden from the public eye and to censure the camera's incursion into their territory. To take an example from the Israeli context, photographs of the Intifada taken by Israeli press photographers often amounted to a critical act, an illegal penetration of photographers into territory defined by the Israeli army as a no-photography area.

The second critical practice aspires to overturn the two central principles of the archive's logic: (1) the single-point view (panoptism) and (2) a homogeneous table and a single rule of classification. It does so by subversively creating a myriad of private archives that disturb the panoptism of the point of view and the homogeneity of the space of classification. The multiple points of view and various angles of photography enable a better exploitation of qualities inherent in photography, such as manipulations of exposure and enlargement. An example of this, also from the domain of Israeli press photographs, is provided by Alex Levac's *Bus Line 300*, a black and white photograph. After a Palestinian terrorist squad hijacked a bus and was overpowered by Israeli soldiers, an army spokesman announced that all the terrorists who participated in the operation had been shot dead during the encounter. Alex Levac[12] was one of many press photographers on the scene and exposed a picture in his lab that showed one of the terrorists being led away alive by two Israelis.[13] There was no doubt that this man had been murdered after the event. The exposure lead to a "political scandal," to the appointment of a commission of inquiry, and to "an upheaval" in the Israeli security service. Here photography employed a critical rhetoric of freedom of expression and the right of the public to know—photography as evidence, as a means to censure power, and as an opportunity to restrain it.[14] In producing both evidence and critique, the individual photographer can assume a critical stance as against a centralist supervising position. However, the critical stance of the photographer, like the stance of Foucault's critic (analyzed above in section 2), leans on the same logic of supervision and control that is at work in the disciplinary site as a locus in which the subject is controlled and controls his or her actions.

The relations of control and resistance presented here take place in a modern space of discourse and action—a delimited space, like the museum space assembling within its premises products that can be attributed to authors, whether defined as artists or photographers. But the photographer's camera and the objects it produces are not only subjected to the relations of power that characterize the space of governmentality (subjectivization) and critique (desubjectivization). The camera has another ethos as well—not the ethos of the subject who employs the camera to confirm himself as the author of the photographic statement but its own ethos of an instrument that also interpellates the subject. Now the camera follows the subject, and now it leads it.[15] The camera has a defined purpose that the photographer seeks to

12. See an interview with Levac in chapter 10, The Picture [of the Battlefield].

13. In an earlier article (in Hebrew) on Benjamin, I noted his use of a photographic historical perspective, describing his conception of the historian as sitting in a darkroom.

14. It is also possible to develop and pinpoint the photographer's critical stance by analyzing how he or she accounts for that stance and how it serves as the object of posing a problem.

15. In Foucault, the dialectic of the visible and the invisible and of the viewer and nonviewer or potential viewer is preserved. Photography, however, invites contemplation of total transparency, with everything present and nothing concealed as a matter of principle. The same is true of death, which results from the biopower manifested in the right to take and give life. Death itself undergoes "spatialization" and network-

realize. But the photographer may turn into its victim because the camera also has a destiny—a dimension that cannot be predicted and controlled, a dimension of contingency and indeterminacy that cannot converge with the author's purposes.[16]

In intersubjective space, the camera is activated through the subject's stance in the wake of an event. At the end of the process, when the picture is printed in a newspaper or put into an album, two points of reference in time are created—first the event and then the documenting photograph. But both function also in the space composed of networks of presences[17] in which the subject doesn't really control the camera. The camera is always already there, part of the network in which the event occurs, and it can invert the point of reference in time: first the documentation and then the event (or the sense) that destiny provided for the camera that was present on the spot. These relations—between thought and reality, between purpose and destiny, between event and photo—aren't conducted only in intersubjective space, where (from the points of view that organized it) everything appears as if under control. When the person assumes the position of a viewer who commands the field of vision and suddenly is viewed by others and also is activated like an object—like a camera or a pistol, something else that attracts, tempts, or repulses—the power relations between subject and object are reversed.

The object is a presence that does not have a point of view and cannot be subjected to a course leading to an objective. For that end, a subject is needed, but the subject now proceeds according to the logic of the "order of things." The reversed relations between subject and object don't allow for a homogenous space-time in which things flow in the incline of time and prepare themselves for the historical viewpoint that weaves a continuous narrative. But the historian, the news reporter, the politician, and the critic tend to freeze on the photographic screen as if it were an intersubjective space—a space in which one doesn't see the active presence of the objects, their temptation and revulsion, or the presence of the camera itself. The organization of the discourse thus constitutes the historian, the critic, or the commentator as someone sitting down in photography's "darkroom," running the films of reality forward and backward, interpreting them, and seeking to give them a

---

ing, and terror can catch up with it at any point in the network without boundaries and without concern for the visible and the invisible. In this sense terror is transparent. When terror appears, it doesn't operate in the dialectic of being or potential being. It doesn't need to penetrate demarcated boundaries sites such as the disciplinary sites. It is like a virus spreading throughout the system.

16. For a discussion of destiny, see Latour (1994) and Baudrillard, (1981, 1990).

17. For a detailed discussion of the term *network of presences*, see chapter 8.

form that forever conceals the jumble of forms reality has assumed, thus exposed to our view.[18]

4

The camera and the photographic and computerized technologies play a crucial role in the structural transformations of the public space and the status of the museum as an expression of the existence of more or less autonomous cultural spheres. Ever since it appeared in the early nineteenth century, the camera has entailed a threat to the spatial texture of the disciplinary society because of its ability to "reduce distances" with a single snap of the button. The age of mechanical reproduction made it possible to bring near the spatially and temporally distant. The past was no longer relegated to defined loci, shut up in museums, archives, and libraries, historic city quarters, and monuments from distant periods surviving here and there in fast-growing cities. The most prevalent sociopolitical use of photography in its earliest years exploited the camera's need to be present at the same site as the photographed subject. Thus, for example, the camera always takes a sample of the place where it is active and of the event it captures, which helped photographers develop a rhetoric of authenticity and specific rules of discourse regarding the act of representing the "original." From this rhetoric and discourse evolved a new concept of truth—in art, in law, in political life, and in the press. This truth derives from the power of photography to provide evidence by the allegedly faithful, indexical relationship between the photographed and the photograph. The photograph proclaims its faithfulness. It evidences not only the photographed but also the conditions of the evidence, since its very existence makes it possible to infer the physical closeness between the photographer and the photographed—their presence in the same spatial-temporal unit.

Arguably, it is precisely this indexical relationship between the photographed and the photograph that the West parted with in the last decades of the twentieth century—and with that relationship, the rhetoric of authenticity, the rules of presenting the truth and the original, and the patterns of gaze and discourse that they

---

18. The discourse is organized around the assumption that (1) the work of art "was there" before the museum and the museum only assimilates it or (2) the event "was there" before the arrival of the camera and the camera only quoted it, froze it, and offered it a place to appear in. The discourse is organized so that its participants disregard the destiny of the things that cannot be explained by the designs of a prime mover or author. At most it can be viewed after the event, when the eye attempts to focus on the space composed of grids of presences and disregards the designs—if such they are—that these presences seek to impose on the world.

entail. A disciplinary society (so masterfully described by Foucault), relies on a succession of close, delimited, and regimented physical sites that individuals traverse in the course of their lives. It is being replaced by what Gilles Deleuze (1990) has defined as the "society of control," whose patterns of governmentality exist in networks and at junctions through which the individual must pass. These changes in forms of organizing space and the individual have immediate effects on the patterns of production and distribution of images. The developing technology of reproduction and image distribution, the implosion of place as a demarcated social and geographical unit, and the disintegration of disciplinary institutions make it possible to consume images faster, more easily, and at lower cost. Images are consumed and distributed through networks of communication and computer channels connecting to and disconnecting from countless outlets dispersed throughout public space. In fact, contemporary public space is destined for photography and is compartmentalized into an aggregation of private spatial units affiliated by network connections to television screens and computer monitors. In an age when things find their place in a specific slot or in a recognized address on the Internet and are connected by networks traversing all spheres of activity (the arts, politics, communications, and law), art cannot be restricted to defined sites of knowledge and display (museum, gallery, and studio) and to an autonomous cultural sphere.

Contemporary public space is dissolved, the various boundaries between spheres have blurred, and the question of critique is being turned upside down: Who or what critiques whom or what? Who or what has a point of view on whom or what? Who or what is changing positions in the critical statement—the public space or the critic? These questions are connected with a form of spatial organization that differs from the museal space (an intersubjective space of discourse always functioning also as a disciplinary site), refutes the logic of this space, and challenges the priority that it seeks to safeguard for itself.

5

This description of public space, the camera, critique, and subjectivity serves as a basis for a historicization of the conditions of the production of the contemporary photographic image. I broaden it to give an account of the conditions underlying the appearance of the photograph in the space of images.

Israel, the 1990s, the prolonged occupation of Palestinian territory, oppression, violence, Intifada, aggressive colonization, continuing annexation of Jerusalem in violation of international conventions and dispossessing the native Palestinian inhabitants of their right to live in the city, various forms of closure of the occupied territories, the Oslo Accords, the murder of Prime Minister Yitzhak Rabin in the wake of the signing of the agreements, Binyamin Netanyahu's rise to power, the strengthening of the religious and nationalist character of Israel as a Jewish state and the growing gaps between its Jewish and non-Jewish citizens, processes of cultural and economic globalization that aggravate the Palestinians' status as a third-world enclave within Israel, a simulation of peace agreements, spectacle politics.

The works of Barry Frydlender, Michal Heiman, Dana and Boaz Zonshine, and Efrat Shvily reflect this space of images in one way or other. None of them turns this situation into a project presented as the object of his or her work, but none can avoid being entangled in this intricate web of images.

Before addressing the images I would like to dwell on another, paradigmatic image in the context of the present discussion of the status of the image in the 1990s[19]— the murder of the prime minister of Israel on November 4, 1995. A few weeks after the murder, an amateur photographer, Ronny Kempler, announced that he had possession of a videocassette documenting the murder. Kempler was a bystander at the murder site who claimed to have had a prescience that something bad was going to happen. He rambled around the square with his camera and watched what was going on through the camera lens. Every moment seemed fraught with disaster. After roaming the square for a while, he reached the terrace overlooking the stairs from which the prime minister and his entourage were to exit the square after the demonstration. For more than twenty minutes he framed the scene of the murder, and then he captured the prime minister's back as he was walking down the stairs. A shot was heard. Suddenly Kempler appeared as someone whose prophecy had fulfilled itself. "Why did it happen to me? Why, of all people, was I chosen?" he asked after the event. Immediately after the first shot, he disassociated himself from the camera. During the next two shots he acted as if he hadn't expected disaster to strike, especially before his own camera.[20]

Kempler, by the way, was not the only person—in Israel or in the world at large—to be caught with a camera while witnessing an act (by another) or to prepare a camera for an(other's) act. The camera is a quintessential means of producing images. It is apparently an instrument in the hands of the subject, subordinate to the subject's wishes, maneuvers, and points of view, a mark of his autonomous status. The camera is a protective accessory that a person carries, a sign of autonomy, free-

---

19. On the video of Rabin's assassination, see chapter 8.

20. Was this what Zizek referred to when—in his interpretation of Lacan—he described the moment in which the Great Other returns to the subject his message in its true form (see Zizek, 1992)?

dom of movement, and gaze. It grants the subject an exterior position as observer, tourist, somebody who *came, saw, and left.* It backs up memory, becomes evidence (should he be asked to present it), provides continuity, identifies a time and place, and preserves the traces. The camera certifies that the individual has *been there.* This is the modern ethos of the camera, of art, of history that underpins the critical concept described by Foucault and developed or criticized by Edward Said, Homi K. Bhabah, Couze Venn, and others.[21] The main part of the critique of Foucault in this context (allowing for all the differences between the various critiques) comes from feminism and postcolonial studies and focuses on Foucault's failure to distinguish between different forms of power and control—specifically, among the relations of power in capitalism, colonialism, and postcolonialism. The critique of Foucault also deals with the establishing of a different subjectivity. This critique, for the most part, continues to posit space as an intersubjective space of communication, and it focuses on othernesses (which, under this or that rule of representation and control, are deprived of the position of subject). This critique poses the other as a trace, an erasure, a supplement, a phantom, a repressed element of the autonomous subject. In so doing, it continues to belittle the importance of the space composed of networks of communication and contact, a space in which the subject is always a blind spot, an object.

Regarding photography, the writings of both Foucault and his critics miss a fundamental issue. The individual wields the camera as evidence of the camera's autonomy, but the camera also and primarily offers evidence that the photographer (the "subject of the [photographic] image") is not the one who "came, saw, and left." The photographer's arrival—which is accompanied by the camera's arrival—creates an appearance that was not there prior to his or her arrival and that does not always allow the photographer to leave at will. In any case, the image that the photographer will take from "there" can be interpreted in different ways in accordance with how the "subject" of the image (the photographer) perceives both the situation to which the image relates and the image itself. The camera, then, always evidences the photographer's being enclosed within a space that is not his and that he (or anyone else, for that matter) is unable to control, a space within which the photographer is always "singular plural" (Nancy, 1996). The camera witnesses the individual as always being with others (whether instruments or other human beings)—maneuvering and

---

21. See, for example, Venn (1997). In this article Venn outlines the history of the critique of the subject through a presentation of the arguments of Edward Said, Paul Gilory, Toni Morrison, and others.

maneuvered, seeing and seen, viewing and viewed—and always also as a blind spot within a web, part of which he discerns and in relation to which he acts.

6

In the following critique of critique, I examine the limitations of critique and the conditions that make critique possible. I propose—as a critical position—to renounce the claim of the autonomous, sovereign subject to secure the critical position. I open this discussion with a description of the works of Barry Frydlender, Michal Heiman, Efrat Shvily, and Dana and Boaz Zonshine. I relate to their work only through this axis—which, as I see it, is also the common denominator that brings them together—and disregard other, no less important dimensions of their work.

Four artists, four images: a transparency produced by computer manipulation of different negatives (Barry Frydlender); a photograph from a family album that is put into a test kit to be operated in a museum setting (Michal Heiman); a passage excerpted from a staged video filmed with a static camera (Dana and Boaz Zonshine); and a traditional documentary photograph taken in an open landscape (Efrat Shvily).

Barry Frydlender
Flash. The eyes of the young man in the forefront of the photograph are popping out of his head. They become vacant and take on the blinding whiteness of the flash. A white flag. Cease-fire. He realizes that his fate is sealed. He surrenders. Surrenders to strange hands. And walks away.

Barry Frydlender, *Baptism by Fire, Dor Beach*, detail,
1993–1998

Michal Heiman, *Michal Heiman Test (M.H.T. no. 2)*, plate 57, 1998

Michal Heiman
Flash(-back)
Don't move. The photographer's at work.
But he has no camera.
Why? Do you have one?
No, my hands are empty. There's only a flash(-back) between my legs.
That doesn't count! (Smiles)

Efrat Shvily
The earth is boiling. It seethes, surges, and produces monsters. Sealed windows, sightless, eye-less, lensless. One of them has grown to the dimensions of a black screen that engulfs any

Efrat Shvily, *Malha*, black and white photograph, 1995

image. At sunset, the earth dwellers assemble around it and wait for the light to appear. The blackness continues to engulf everything.

Dana and Boaz Zonshine

The gaze scans all the stories of the building. The figure is in acceleration. The gaze chases it, but the swiftness prevents a clear distinction of the figure and the nature of the building. It is only when the figure strikes the ground that the gaze recovers and reconstructs the picture. A suicide, a fall, annihilation. The figure, too, recovers together with the gaze. It rises to its feet and walks away.

Dana and Boaz Zonshine, *Untitled* (The Wailing Wall),
video, 20-second loop, 1996

The common denominator I use—the limitations of critique and the conditions that make critique possible—leaves traces on the works' surface or in the media and practices the artists chose for their work, even though, at times, strong lighting is needed to expose it. This common denominator also found expression in the conversations I held with the five artists. These artists create for themselves (or enable themselves) to act within conditions of production, of work, or of display in which the firm position of the subject, which allows control of the (visible) space, is denied to them on different levels and for different lengths of time. Subjectivity presents itself to them as a moment inside the system of power relations within the framework of which they are both subjects and objects.

Barry Frydlender chooses the position of a viewer of a computer screen. By viewing his own photos, editing them, and making the requisite decisions before printing them, he takes a position in the middle—between the image appearing on the screen and the final result that is printed later in the lab. The image offers itself up on the screen, invites him to effect changes in it, and suggests other images. Some of the suggestions are inherent in the image, others derive from the technological equipment, and yet others derive from the singular encounter between Barry Frydlender and the computer. In his studio, Frydlender makes negatives of several pictures he took back in 1992 appear on his computer screen. What he saw in these negatives in 1992 is not what he now sees. Frydlender tries to reflect this time interval—the interval that's created in the image, in perception, in technology, in the political reality—in the final product. Time—which is not controlled even when it is managed—preoccupies him, and this is especially conspicuous in a photograph of the Israeli memorial siren,[22] the siren as the freezing of a moment, as an act of photography, as a group portrait of a nation.

Frydlender chooses as subjects for his work highly specific moments in which the figures are anonymous but generally identifiable in terms of their group affiliation and their participation in part of the photographed event, which is simply a point in the lived time of a group or a people. This is true of the Intifada photograph, *The Siren, The Drafting Party*, and *Air Force Display*. These photographs do not correspond to the simplistic and structured power relations that exist between rulers and ruled. The photograph itself always appears as an arena of power struggles that cannot be fully controlled or be assumed a priori to be stable. It is the nature of the photograph to be this arena, but the kind of treatment that Frydlender gives it

---

22. On two appointed dates in Israel—the Day of Remembrance (for fallen soldiers) and Holocaust Day—a siren is sounded for 60 seconds during which (Jewish) citizens are requested to halt all activity.

Barry Frydlender, *Birth of a Nation: Palestinians Make a
Movie*, 50 × 200 cm, 1989–1998

highlights this nature and does not resist it or attempt to control it. Thus, in the photograph *The Birth of a Nation: Palestinians Make a Movie*, Frydlender the photographer participates in power relations by operating his camera and computer and by
being operated on by them. Frydlender places himself before the computer screen
(after having placed himself in the photographed event) and directs the computer
image—in effect, producing the Intifada film, the movie made by the Palestinian directors. Of course, he does not remain in the role of the director: he is also the actor
of the event. The Palestinians in the photograph control the media (and are controlled and maneuvered by it), even if their hands are devoid of cameras. They control the representation of the Westerners (Europeans and Americans because the
Israelis are outside the picture) when presenting them as captives of their editors and
of the media ratings. The Palestinians also have for years observed the Israelis and
accumulated incriminating evidence against them—through the kaffiyehs that cover
their heads, obstruct their view, and are a symbol of their subjection to Israeli occupation. The photograph titled *The Drafting Party* is also composed of several negatives, and reveals complex and ambiguous relations of power that present the event
(a farewell party before the mandatory army enlistment of a group of young people)
in a leveling light. A common interpretation of this photograph sees it as an expression of youthful abandon, lack of responsibility, or narcissism (Shapira, 1994). This
interpretation creates an opposition between society and the young people who are
subverting it and so misses the context of the photograph (a drafting party) and the
complexity of the relationship between citizens-subjects and the state. The photo is
a kind of allegory of a crucial moment in the lives of these boys and girls, a moment
when the state is about to revoke their newly granted status as adult citizens—citizens who have rights and duties in a public space and are entitled to struggle for their
representation, their property, their bodies and their freedom of movement. Their

impending recruitment is the moment in which they will relinquish their civil rights and turn into soldiers in the state's army. Their bodies will be deprived of rights and may be stationed in occupied Lebanon, in the occupied territories of the West Bank, or in any other place. The skinny-dipping boys and girls know this and savor for a moment the illusion of freedom of the nude body, free of representative insignia and divested of duties. Only their gaze bears witness to their situation, turning blank in the face of the flash, aware of its powerlessness, waving a white flag, surrendering. Their bodily surrender to their fate may appear to show devotion to the state, but in effect the surrender disrupts the plans of the state, which needs soldiers to devote rather than abandon themselves—soldiers who fight for it rather than surrender to it in advance.

At the entrance to the exhibition space hangs a sign welcoming spectators to *Michal Heiman Test No. 2: A Test for Women Only*. If the spectator is a man, the sign directs him to have a seat and rest or leave the hall. If the spectator is a woman, she is invited to lie down on the sofa. She is offered a choice between "the public sofa," where she would take the test in the presence of an audience, or the "private sofa," where she would be isolated from her surroundings with the help of a pair of earphones. Sitting close to her there is a person—a guardian, an examiner, an analyst, an authoritative figure—ready to guide her in what is to come. In both cases, whether she has chosen to take the test in privacy or in public, she is invited to look at a series of photographs and talk about them. Yes, just like that, lying on the sofa, she would let the words flow through her, let the noises come out of her body and be articulated in recognizable syllables gathered into a sense, be thrown out of her throat; she would tell something about the world seen in the pictures, the world as it is reflected in the picture she is seeing now for the first time. Well, this is the way it goes in a room with a sofa and an authoritative figure ready to listen. But here, in the somewhat threatening and uncanny situation Heiman created for women spectators, rules are slightly different. Here the effect of these rules of a room with a sofa is conditional: they are not simply put to work but put on display, and they would work as long as someone is willing to take part in their public display. It is you, dear spectator, who is now taking part in the display of these rules on the museum's stage. And thus, when you look at these pictures and let yourself be taken by them, new pictures are emerging—pictures that have never before been inscribed in a photographic surface and are entirely yours, pictures which, perhaps, you should not present in public, to the public, but now it is too late, for these pictures are already pushing themselves forward, insisting to be shown; for a room with a sofa, Freud told us all, is the place where one is supposed to be left alone with those pictures that push

Michal Heiman, *Michal Heiman Test (M.H.T. No. 2), My Mother-in-Law, Test for Women,* Le Quartier, Quimper, 1998

themselves forward, to turn them into words, and share them with that authoritative figure sitting nearby.

Michal Heiman has collected seventy-two images in a box that imitates the "Thematic Apperception Test" (TAT), a well-known personality test used by psychologists as an authorized diagnostic tool. In this test an examiner presents a subject sitting by a table with a series of ambiguous images and invites him or her to tell a story about each image. *Michal Heiman Test No. 2 (M.H.T. No. 2)* juxtaposes three situations, the psychoanalytic, the diagnostic, and the museal and uses this juxtaposition in order to examine critically the three of them.

Michal Heiman chooses the position of the spectator looking at someone else's photographs—photographs that are taken by someone else, that have been photographed by someone else, that someone else collected. Heiman turns this quintessential position of spectator into her own, elaborating it and giving it back to the spectator, whom she transforms into the subject of the artistic image and also into the subject of the psychological image. This spectator is asked, on several levels, to assume Heiman's position and to reproduce it.

When Heiman looks at these photographs (most of them are of her mother-in-law), she is classifying according to the restrictions and advantages of her family relations with the photographed (her mother-in-law), attuned to the route her

Michal Heiman, *Michal Heiman Test (M.H.T. No. 2), My Mother-in-Law, Test for Women,* Le Quartier, Quimper, 1998

mother-in-law traced on her meticulously planned journeys as well as in random rambles. Heiman does this without relinquishing essential activities of the subject's position, such as sorting, selecting, and classifying. She performs these activities as an accumulative sum of activities familiar from two institutions and their practices—the museum and psychology. The images she presents to the spectator, the "subject" of her "test," are mediated through these two institutions and their practices. They are presented in a "test" box by an "examiner," who duplicates Heiman's positioning—but without the possibility of identity between the two of them, between them and the photographed, or between them and the subject of the test.

These relations of similarity and difference between the personae and positions of Heiman and the examiners dissolve the established hierarchical relations that institutions and their practices (such as the museum and the psychology apparatus) seek to preserve and point to their fluidity. Heiman is attracted to these two systems, seduced by one and functioning within the other, but at the same time she criticizes them, especially by turning one against the other. She bypasses the museum apparatus by way of the psychological apparatus. Within the framework of the museum institution she develops exchange relations borrowed from the psychological apparatus rather than those practiced in the museum, in which the boundaries of the subject are predetermined by the way he or she is placed in front of the artistic object.[23] The exchange relations that Heiman's installation in the museum enables reflect the psychoanalytical situation, with one crucial difference: they are not continuous in time, and the examiner/analyst cannot gain knowledge relating to the spectator/analysand and take an active part in subjectivizing him or her. Thus the therapeutic situation is divested of its characteristic power relations. By activating the general patterns of the structure of the therapeutic situation in a museum setting through the mode of the *Michal Heiman Test*, viewers have an opportunity to disrupt the museum order. This order is based on complex relations of silence, both on the part of the museum object and on the part of the museum subject, and on the distinction between the different subjects of art—the artist and the spectator. The museum spectator is invited to induce the mute object to speak—but only later and outside the boundaries of the site. Heiman's spectator is invited to induce the seen to speak at the site itself. The images Heiman offers for viewing and voicing violate the standard norms of presentation and serve as a point of departure for unexpected encounters with conveyors of parallel, contradictory, other images, encounters in which she finds herself being led no less than leading.

Michal Heiman's "test" is intended for women. It suggests that they look at a number of pictures of a woman—a mother figure and Heiman's mother-in-law—and a few pictures of women who were inscribed in a history that is shared with others. The first photographed figure is a magnified stereotype of the (Jewish) mother figure. She is more (and less) than a mother, more (and less) than a citizen of the (Jewish) state.[24] She doesn't tour the state like a tourist but looks instead rather like the proprietress who comes to collect the rent or to improve her tenants' living conditions. She embodies much of what is repressed in that state, and its close relationship to her presents an opportunity to take a straight look and see how the state "really" looks—how the overbearingness, excessiveness, and unusefulness of this figure look. This mother figure has herself photographed incessantly, in any place, on any occasion. She is always ready with the camera "just in case": this may be the decisive moment, so she had better have proofs, evidence, in her hands. For one mustn't let destiny rule the world alone.

Together with her, in the same box, are seven other women whose "decisive moment" indeed caught up with them. Each of them experienced a crucial moment or performed an act that justified a portrait, an image, an immortalization, but no cam-

---

23. For a more detailed discussion of this dimension in her work, see my Manual to the *M.H.T. No. 2* box (Azoulay, 1999b).

24. A state whose law of return grants Jews throughout the world automatic Israeli citizenship.

era was present to immortalize the moment. Their portrait is thus a portrait that does not bear witness to the decisive moment but manifests the decisive relation between them and the social order they disturbed and whose rules they sought to suspend. It thus constitutes a double portrait—a portrait of them and of the social order they challenged.[25] The first one is of the three surviving Dionne quintuplets, who, having been put on public display as children together with their two other sisters, eventually broke the silence to bring this glaring abuse of a child's body to light (and to claim damages for themselves). The second is of Ulrike Meinhof, leader of the Baader Meinhof group (a radical anarchist group active in Germany in the late sixties and early seventies), whose portrait evokes the game of the democratic state—a game in which everything is negotiable except the rules of the game and from which any player attempting to put those rules in question must be excluded. The third photograph is of Leila Khaled—the Palestinian freedom fighter who became famous for the skyjacking in which she was involved. Khaled expropriated the time of the flight passengers to point to the time and the place of which her people, the Palestinian people, had been robbed. The fourth portrait is of Eva Hesse, an artist who put her body in the center of her art long before the artistic discourse could have contained such a manifestation. In it an apparatus is saturated with violence and the tensions between an individual, a body, and a position from which to see, speak out, and act. And the last portrait is of Kochava Levy, who found herself in a hotel that was occupied by terrorists and masterfully played—with her unprecedented feat of conducting negotiations with the terrorists—the role assigned to her by history.

Dana and Boaz Zonshine pose the camera and create situations opposite it in which they share the control of the image with their various protagonists. This is true of a video like *Vertical Jump*, in which a (doll) figure is falling from a high floor into an inner courtyard. The figure lands on the ground with a bang, stands up as if nothing had happened, and walks away. In the video *Clark*, as well, a monocycle rider performs acrobatic feats by the parapet of one of the bridges across the Seine: a careless movement will topple him into the river. The video may end this way or another. They stage the scene in such a way that each time a different event occurs in it. No matter how many rehearsals are made to stage the scene, each time it will be something different and unexpected. The artists set up the situation, choose the shooting angle, edit the video works, and decide on the mode of display, but to a no lesser extent they respond to random images glimpsed from the visual flux in which they live.

---

25. For additional details about these women, see my Manual to the *M.H.T. No. 2* box (Azoulay, 1999b).

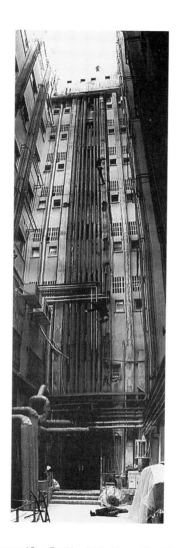

Dana and Boaz Zonshine, *Vertical Jump,* video, 1996

CHAPTER 6

In their words, they receive the works "ready-made." All that remains for them to do—from the moment they see the work—is to realize it.

This is the case, for example, in the video in which scores of planes seem to be colliding with an apartment block. Every day, in their former apartment in Tel Aviv—which is situated along the in-flying route to the nearby airport—they saw planes fly into but never out of the building, as it were. The field of vision prevented them from seeing the plane "exit" from the other side of the building, but this was enough for the plane's "entrance" into the building to be literalized—the planes entering the building. The video was shot by a static camera that the artists placed on the roof of their house. The camera documented hours of such (potential) encounters between the plane and the building. They were fascinated by the planes' daily passage over their building and obsessed by the tragic end of their flight that seemed to be destined by the flying route.

In another video, they combine linguistic and visual elements in a similar manner. The Western Wall looks as if it is inundated with the sea. In the center, between the wall and the sea, men dressed in black stand in a praying posture, swaying backward and forward in measured movements. It is sufficient to be only minimally familiar with the geography of the state of Israel to know that Jerusalem is situated on the mountain in the east and that the sea is in the west, some 50 kilometers away. Familiarity with the political climate of Israel makes it possible to see in this video a literal realization of the often-heard, frantic claim: "The Arabs want to throw us into the sea." This cliché, which for years served in answer to or argument against any negotiations with the Palestinians about the borders of the state, suddenly took on a physical form as an image of a pastoral landscape animated by the soft movements of the people populating it.

Efrat Shvily deals with direct photography—neither snapshot nor staged image. This is a standard, frontal, stylized mode of photography that draws on the distinct tradition of photographers with a personal imprint.[26] To produce these images, Shvily chose a certain disguise or mask—that of a tourist: "when I returned to Israel after spending ten years in England, Italy, and the States . . . I wanted to remain a tourist, and the camera helped very much in that respect." It is a mask that helps her to continue to see through the scorching and blinding light. Over the years, she lost control over the mask and, as evidenced by the photographs themselves, became unable to remove it at will. The mask has turned into an integral part of herself.

26. Photographers such as Walker Evans and Dan Graham (see Chevrier, 1992).

Efrat Shvily, *Ma'ale Edomim,* black and white
photograph, 1993

Through it, she sees sights that mark the boundaries of a country located in another place. This country is not hers. It is a strange country with its own laws—monstrous, untenable, abstract, utopian, apocalyptic. This country looks like a figment of the imagination but is, in fact, simply documented—the country where she lives, that she roams with her camera looking for pictures to be taken, pictures soliciting her to immortalize them, and all this within the framework of the documentary genre.

But Shvily's photographs have an air of fiction. They respect the genre, but to an equal degree they respect reality, and reality (at least in Jerusalem) looks rather like fiction. However, to recognize the fiction one has to recognize the historical facts. East Jerusalem was occupied by Israelis in 1967, together with the West Bank. The previous border between the two sides—known as the Green Line—became the protagonist of a strange reality. The people (the Israelis) who wish to efface it, to behave as if it doesn't exist, in fact behave as if it does indeed still exist and as if, on one side, live superior citizens (they themselves) and, on the other, a populace deprived of rights. Among the former were those who wanted to efface or retrace this line with their own bodies, as it were. They went to live beyond the line, aspiring to sustain the territorial continuity between its two sides, and are known as "settlers." These people are seen but do not see. Having passed from one place to another, from one area of jurisdiction to another, they nonetheless imagine themselves to be living in the same country. To them, historical reality, boundaries, and people are all negligible and invisible elements. They imagine the land of their forefathers and build it. It hovers above the ground like the phantom of an ideal country built to perfect proportions. Shvily documents them. More precisely, she documents their buildings, looking like landing strips for spaceships, like a passage in the (apocalyptic) vision of the messianic age or like the archaeological remains of a past calamity. Shvily's photographs contrive to manifest the other side of the overt power relations (those where the Israelis rule and the Palestinians are ruled) and to portray the Israeli settlers as being ruled by fantasies, false visions, and apocalyptic dreams spelling their own end, and other Israelis, in turn, as being ruled by the settlers.

Could it all have been different? Could Barry Frydlender have chosen to ignore the influence of technology? Could Michal Heiman have conceived the image outside the practice of the (psychoanalytical) couch, on which she saw more images than in the museum? Could Dana and Boaz Zonshine have directed their protagonists in a total manner? Could Efrat Shvily have seen the sites and sights she photographs without the mediation of her (or some other) mask? The answer is obvious: no. Even if they had sought to do so, none of them would have been able to control the situation and turn it into a reflection of their artistic design. At most, they could have denied these conditions, presenting themselves as autonomous subjects and signing the image with their signature, as if they were its masters. Their search for these intermediate states (in which the image lives its life and in effect proposes to them to maintain a new type of reciprocity) makes their work critical—a critique of the boundaries of the image and a critique of critique as an act of an autonomous subject.

It is possible to go even further and claim that we're talking about a form of critique without critics, without subjects. This form of critique exists within the intensified presence of new conditions for the gaze, the discourse, and the act at the close of the twentieth century, and the conditions that this critique presents with such acuity call in question the spatial organization and the forms of subjectivity from which modernity derived.

CHAPTER 7   THE [SIMULATED] CITY:

JERUSALEM

A few days after the signing of the Oslo Accords in Washington, D.C., the Israelis and the Palestinians began secret talks on the future of Jerusalem. Israeli Deputy Foreign Minister Yossi Beilin and Palestinian Abu-Masen deliberated for a year and a half, until November 1, 1995. These talks took place without the knowledge of either Prime Minister Yitzhak Rabin or Foreign Minister Shimon Peres. On November 4, 1995, three days after the talks concluded, Rabin was assassinated by an Israeli gunman in Tel Aviv's municipal square. A few days after the assassination, a draft of the agreement—known as the Beilin-Abu Masen Accord—was presented to Peres. Peres, who had stepped into the post of the murdered prime minister, rejected the agreement, contending that it wasn't the right time to deal with it. Some would have it that Peres was afraid of losing the forthcoming elections if the agreement were to become public. Instead, he preferred to suppress discussion of the future of Jerusalem and of Rabin's assassination and leave it out of his party's election campaign. Likud leader Binyamin Netanyahu, however, wanted to bring the repressed materials to the surface. He conducted an aggressive campaign under the slogan "Peres will divide Jerusalem." Underlying this slogan is the assumption that Jerusalem is united and that any division of the city will occur due to the deliberate action of a leader such as Peres, who will willfully disrupt the city's unity and the solidarity of people who have united around the idea of the city's unity. On election day in May 1996, Netanyahu's proved to be the winning campaign. Netanyahu was voted into power, while Peres and his party lost the election and joined the parliamentary opposition.

Peres suppressed discussion of the future of Jerusalem. He acknowledged the excessiveness of the city over the unifying signifier "Jerusalem" and was afraid that in any discussion of the topic of Jerusalem Peres himself would be exposed as realizing that this excessiveness (namely, the conflicts that pervade the city) constitutes a point of departure for negotiations and is not to be seen as the basis for a unifying image of the city.[1] Peres knew what everyone knows: Jerusalem is not one, is not homogeneous, and exists in the conflict-ridden present rather than the eternal history of the

---

1. Jerusalem the sacred and Jerusalem the profane, heavenly Jerusalem and worldly Jerusalem, the Jerusalem of maps and the Jerusalem of neighborhoods, the Old City of Jerusalem and the Jerusalem that has burst its own boundaries in a construction boom, Jerusalem without running water or sanitation and Jerusalem of exclusive housing compounds, Jerusalem of refugee camps and Jerusalem of expropriated lands, Jerusalem of fantasy and Jerusalem of harsh and sometimes bloody reality, Jerusalem of the secular and Jerusalem of the Ultra-Orthodox, Jerusalem of the Jewish settlers and Jerusalem of the Palestinians, Jerusalem of history and Jerusalem of the future, Jerusalem of the 1948 settlers and Jerusalem of the 1967 settlers, Jerusalem of its citizens and Jerusalem of its inhabitants, whose right to live in the city is being denied them.

Jewish nation. Netanyahu, on the other hand, who conducted a campaign that was all "virtual reality," was unafraid of this excessiveness or its ability to influence the signifier "Jerusalem," so he chose to invoke the signifier alone during the course of the campaign.

Both Peres and Netanyahu understood the power of the signifier "Jerusalem." The former wanted to get rid of it and deny its existence. The latter, perhaps to some extent because of the other's behavior, divined the issue in his crystal ball and let it work its magic.

Following the 1996 elections and Netanyahu's ascent to power, the existence of the Beilin-Abu Masen Accord became public knowledge. It was written about in the press, and its principles were presented in various forums, although the actual document was never made public. The agreement remained an unknown—a secret that people talk about but cannot see. The document contains a terrible secret: it doesn't divide Jerusalem but merely accords symbolic status to the administrators of the various parts of the city. In other words, the Beilin-Abu Masen Accord exposes the most terrible secret of all—that Jerusalem can't be divided because it isn't united in the first place. I return to the contents of the agreement later in this chapter. In May 1999, Netanyahu once again focused his election campaign on Jerusalem. This time the signifier "Jerusalem" found no echo. Ehud Barak won these elections.

During the course of the 1999 election campaign, Barak made use of televised footage in which Ehud Ulmart—rightist, Likud member, and mayor of Jerusalem—declared before an audience that neither Barak nor any other leader would divide Jerusalem. On a different occasion Ulmart even apologized to Shimon Peres and retracted his statement that Peres would divide Jerusalem, which he had voiced in the previous elections. Should we conclude that Ulmart handed power to Barak on a silver platter? Did the promise not to divide Jerusalem decide the elections? Did Ulmart's remarks carry more weight than those of Netanyahu, who declared that Jerusalem would be divided under Barak's rule? Could it be that Barak won the elections but that the voice was Ulmart's? All these questions are subsumed under a single larger question: can we ignore the connection between the city of Jerusalem, which adorns the State of Israel like a crown, and the leader who serves as the country's head of government?

On the evening that Yigal Amir assassinated the prime minister, this connection was impalpable or at least didn't appear significant. The struggle between the right and the left and between the religious and secular segments of the population, which was portrayed as a struggle between the forces of light and the forces of darkness, was seen as the background against which the assassination should be understood.[2] Here I would like to emphasize the connection between the assassination and the city of Jerusalem.

On the evening of November 4, 1995, a young man arrived in Tel Aviv's municipal square with a gun in his pocket. He took off his skullcap, concealed his religious identity, and awaited Yitzhak Rabin's departure at the conclusion of the peace rally that was taking place in the square at the time. In a confession delivered the day after the assassination, Amir portrayed Peres as the man who had led Rabin astray or, in other words, as the one responsible for the deteriorating situation in Israel due to the Oslo Accords. All the same, he emphasized, he had preferred to wait for Rabin. Peres had lent Rabin his peace-making speech. Amir preferred to ignore the author of the speech and wait for the voice, the signature, the authority, the one whose speech assumes symbolic status when it leaves his throat. He waited for Yitzhak Rabin himself. Amir's choice of Rabin rather than Peres rejected the verbal and the allegorical (the contents of speech) and chose instead the symbolic—the authentic voice, though he may choose other, loathsome voices. Expressly because Rabin had undergone a transformation—from the deliverer of Jerusalem in 1967 to the person chosen by Peres to give up Jerusalem in 1992—Amir saw him as the more dangerous, the one who could persuade people to unite behind him. From Amir's viewpoint, to put it crudely, Peres wasn't worth the bullet. Amir ascribed symbolic value to his own action by playing the scene beneath the gaze of divine providence and in a framework that allowed him to rescue the people of Israel, who had lost sight of where their leader was taking them.

Amir planted himself opposite Yitzhak Rabin on the stage of history, like a true prophet versus a false prophet. After the Oslo Accords there was a change in Israeli politics and a struggle began between the old regime of representation and the new. In the framework of the old regime, exchange relations are regularized according to transcendent and religious values that themselves are exempt from exchange. In the framework of the new, each value can in principle be exchanged or substituted. These two regimes also express themselves in two regimes of subjectivity. In the first, the subject holds an inner secret—a nucleus of truth that shapes all his or her actions and words and that is expressed by all his or her actions and words. In the second, subjects participate in mimetic relations between themselves and their surroundings. Both these contradictory elements of subjectivity were contained in the single figure of Rabin. His figure manifested both deviation from them and their sublation

---

2. In the film *A Sign from Heaven*, which I directed in 1999, I attempted to trace the pattern for a rather different interpretation of the assassination.

(termination but simultaneous preservation). Rabin in the flesh symbolized the possibility of reconciliation between these two elements. Rabin—whose voice in the past had been the voice of transcendent truth, the historic truth of the Jewish people—had become in the present someone who borrows a voice from other mortals. Amir wanted to save the people of Israel from Rabin, save Rabin from Peres, and save Rabin from himself—and all this on behalf of the people of Israel.

Amir was concerned for the fate of the land of Israel, but he was no less concerned about the danger posed by the mimetic subject. The mimetic subject imitates others, has no inner truth, does not truly belong to history, the community, the nation, tradition, or religion. The subject imitates another, follows it, is seduced by its suggestions. The subject has no boundaries and reflects everything it encounters in its path. Amir, who wanted to extirpate this subject, did so, paradoxically, while manifesting that he was just the same. An hour before assassinating Rabin, Amir took the skullcap off his head. He got rid of the symbol differentiating him from the secular population and identifying him as the other. The removal of the skullcap can be interpreted as simply a camouflage action, but it is difficult not to regard it as expressing a desire to assimilate, to enter into mimetic relations with the other. After Amir removed his skullcap, he gripped the gun in his pocket and waited in a military-style ambush for his target. Like a devoted soldier, he stood on guard and rose to defend his nation. He had done so as a soldier fighting against the Muslim enemy, and now he did so as a soldier fighting against the Jewish enemy.

When the secret of the Oslo talks was disclosed, a political and psychological barrier that had constrained Israeli politics since the 1967 war was broken, and a radical change ensued in the structure of the political discourse. Since the mid-1970s, the Israeli left had developed the practice of simulating peace talks (talking about what could be or should be but without the power or will to negotiate real agreements) with the Palestinian leadership.[3] Beside talks of this nature conducted by the left (which was then in the opposition in Parliament), secret talks apparently were also conducted by Mosṡad agents (the Israeli Intelligence Service acting outside Israel) and other official representatives, there were certainly rumors to that effect. In other words, the opposition openly simulated negotiations, while there were indications that the authorities were secretly simulating negotiations. In the beginning, in their secrecy, the Oslo talks were a combination of these two practices: the group dynamics of the left's open simulation, and the secrecy of the government's simulation

---

3. For discussions of the simulation of the peace talks, see Azoulay and Ophir (1998).

prior to Oslo. Before Oslo, the talks were never the real thing, nor were they a substitute for it. They were just a presentation of what could or should be. In Oslo the simulation became the substitute, and then it became the real thing. Only when the Israeli government publicly acknowledged the talks did the change occur: the talks, which had been a simulation of negotiations, turned into real negotiations.

What is the mark of real negotiations? Like anything real, they have a visible and an invisible part and neither can be entirely canceled out, whereas a simulation, being two-dimensional and lacking depth, is either entirely open or entirely secret, and it dissipates when the other side of the show—open or secret, it makes no difference—is exposed. The secret talks conducted by the government, if such there were, had to dissipate the moment that rumor of them leaked out, for the state was strictly prohibited from talking with the Palestinian Liberation Organization. The open talks conducted by the left also had to dissipate the moment it appeared that an official element was involved in them behind the scenes, for the left couldn't possibly represent the state.

The greatest transformation wrought by the Oslo Accords since they became public has been primarily (both in principle and in actions taken in response to Oslo) a change in the regime of representation that once dominated political discourse in Israel, especially with respect to the ideal that has informed Israeli political rhetoric—namely, "peace." For decades peace had been whispered and shouted by people as a signifier to which the proper referent would be supplied by everyone when the conditions for peace arrived. Everyone had known that simply saying "peace" didn't make peace happen. But now that the infinite distance was suddenly slashed, peace seemed within reach, just behind the door: palpable and threatening to those who had always felt that peace could be real only if it was false, palpable and inviting to those who had always believed in the possibility of its realization or had come to believe in it now. The relation between signifier and referent became mysterious, and both sides expressed an urgent need to ascertain its character. Everyone belabored the signifier to disclose its true hidden referent. The signifier turned into a punching bag that everyone struck in vain, for it remained a ball of rags, hot air, a piece of paper that could not divulge the true referent. This all happened, so it seems, because of the nature of the interim agreement.

Oslo proclaimed a transition from occupation as a de facto permanent situation to occupation as a de facto temporary situation and an intent for a transition from de jure occupation to de facto independence and even de jure independence. It was a transition to transitional conditions. From the moment the Oslo talks came out of

the closet, "the peace process" became an opportunity to simulate the end of the present and future occupation. You'll never be able to know that the occupation has ended. The state of transition is a state of occupation, as much as it's a state of an occupation coming to its end. Israel has to look like a conqueror (although it is no longer a conqueror) because a peace agreement has yet to be negotiated. The Palestinians have to look like freedom fighters (in the areas and with respect to the issues that have yet to be agreed on) because the state of occupation continues. The Orient House is a symbol of the Palestinians' continuing struggle over Jerusalem, and for a long time the Palestinians abandoned the entire eastern part of the city to Israeli encroachment at the price of simulating sovereignty over a single building. Har Homah[4] is a symbol of the Israeli government's determination to retain control of greater Jerusalem and prevent its division, but for a long time now all construction activity at the site has been frozen.

The external signs of the end of the occupation—the tokens of Palestinian sovereignty—are the only evidence that the occupation is about to end or that peace is about to arrive. The simulation of the peace process and of the end of the occupation continues under the new regime, and it will continue even if Palestinian independence is eventually declared. The declaration (of a Palestinian State, for example) itself has a clear simulative character because it explicitly recognizes any declaration of independence as a simulation of independence and any talk about the anticipated declaration as a simulation of the declaration. It constitutes Israeli and Palestinian recognition of the independence of the simulation. The Israelis have extended such recognition for some time, after summarily dismissing the Palestinian people for years and raising them from the dust by virtue of this dismissal. Now they are summarily uniting Jerusalem and actually dividing it by virtue of these declarations, which testify time and again that they're the main adhesive holding the "reunited" city together.

Israeli recognition of the simulation and its independence begins in Jerusalem, which has become the distinct site of the simulation, its locus. Since the Israeli conquest in 1967, Israel's takeover of Jerusalem has come to resemble the stance of a narcissus at the edge of a swamp, generating itself with an excessive regard for its own reflection in the water. Every time this Narcissus sees a reflection other than what he wants to see, he employs one of the three mechanisms at his disposal for turning

---

4. Har Homah is a new Jewish settlement within East Jerusalem that was built with the approval of the government.

it into the desired reflection—cartography, the legal apparatus, and planning and housing.[5]

It is a duplicitous practice. On one hand, Jerusalem can be acted on: it can be fortified, built, expanded, or contracted, all in the framework of an economy of demographic and political interests. On the other hand, Jerusalem can be preserved outside any economy, and its transcendental standing can be preserved. But due to the need to manufacture more and more Jerusalem to maintain the demographic balance, the city's transcendent status has been pressed into service as a resource that can be used to baptize more areas in the name of Jerusalem. Immediately after the conquest of Jerusalem in 1967, Israel turned the city's transcendent status into a resource and the city itself into the land that supplies this resource and testifies to its existence. As I've said before, Israel alone controlled the allocation of this resource and its distribution over adjacent areas, the determination of the city's actual boundaries, and, in consequence, the right of its inhabitants to become residents.

Over several decades Israel portrayed the Palestinians as an entity that could not be negotiated with and Jerusalem as a city that could not be negotiated over. Once the psychological barrier concerning the Palestinians broke down and direct negotiations with them began, it was clear that in one way or another Jerusalem, too, would become part of the negotiations. In the Oslo Accords it was agreed that the administration of Jerusalem would come up for discussion in the framework of the permanent status talks. Thus both the Israelis and the Palestinians could be proud of their achievement—the Israelis for signing an agreement without agreeing to the division of Jerusalem and the Palestinians for having established Jerusalem as a negotiable subject. Actually, to sign the Oslo Accords the Israelis had to share the secrets of the simulated talks (in other words, the control of the simulated talks) with the Palestinians. As long as the simulation was managed by Israel alone, Jerusalem's transcendent status was ensured. When the barriers came down and the Palestinians became partners to negotiations, Jerusalem lost its unequivocal status and became a polysemic sign at the center of a plethora of conflicting interpretations.

Since the Oslo Accords, simulated talks have become political reality. The simulation hasn't canceled out the meanings but multiplied them in conflicting directions. The double meanings multiply and propagate at an amazing rate, and no suspicion of pretense can be proved. The "real intentions" cannot be exposed—not just because intentions are revealed through additional signs such as gestures, sayings, and actions

---

5. See chapter 9.

but because the "state of transition" itself endows a double meaning to any such sign. The more simulations accumulate and the more possibilities of interpretation multiply, the greater becomes the need for clarity. Highly motivated individuals with a strong messianic bent couldn't tolerate the simulative character of the historic situation. Yigal Amir expressed the reaction of one who pines for an unequivocal and final interpretation of political reality. He assumed that he was in possession of such an interpretation, and he was convinced that his interpretation was exactly opposed to the illusion in which everyone else was caught up. His assassination of Rabin in Tel Aviv's municipal square on the evening of November 4, 1995, took place in the glare of the spotlights. It expressed the arrogance of bringing into the light this inflexible interpretation and imposing it on an immeasurably more ambivalent reality Yitzhak Rabin's assassination was an ultimate attempt to burst through the tissue of simulations to allow reality, the "naked truth," to appear as it really is.

On November 4, 1995, with three shots of his gun, Yigal Amir demanded that the simulations be abandoned once and for all, he demanded a release from the immanent simulative quality imposed by the conditions of historical reality and a return to comforting and unequivocal distinctions—between war and peace, liberation and subjugation, the real and the virtual, the true and the false. Amir's action in the municipal square expressed a desire for a return to the real, to familiar absolutes. His action, like other violent actions which demand the appearance of the real, ignores the power of the dialectical relations between police and terrorism, unemployment and production, an event and its media images. He and others like him also find it difficult to see the global, viral networks of government, production, and media that repeatedly eradicate any boundaries that local elements erect between nations, national territories, or social spheres and that impose simulation as the only regime of representation. When simulation is the regime of representation, one can act on reality only by means of simulation. Any attempt to impose upon reality a violent event—which will tear away once and for all the contradictory layers of images piled on top of each other—is met immediately by a response from the various global networks. These networks try to restore the simulative dimension of the event and endow it with meanings that are consistent with the existing order and that are incapable of undermining prevalent conditions: hybrid areas, transitional period, a blurring of unequivocal distinctions. Any attempt to symbolically represent reality with an unequivocal interpretation that separates the real from the virtual encounters resistance. Instead of revealing the truth about the reality subject to interpretation, it conceals both reality and the simulative conditions of the interpretative activity itself.

THE [SIMULATED] CITY

Yitzhak Rabin was assassinated, but the truth wasn't revealed. He was mourned by all, and the grief expressed knew no boundaries between right and left. Those few who dared to say something concerning the assassination that didn't confirm the consensus that had been arrived at only hours after the crime or who didn't open their remarks with "I condemn" became immediately suspect as possible collaborators and in some cases were taken in for questioning by the police. Those in Rabin's party, under the direction of Shimon Peres, embraced the atmosphere of mourning that descended on the country and joined in depoliticizing the assassination, which meant removing it from the exchange economy of the elections. Binyamin Netanyahu, by contrast, didn't pass up the opportunity to divulge the truth that Yigal Amir had failed to expose in the municipal square and proclaimed the "truth" that had been denied: "Peres will divide Jerusalem." Unlike the Labor Party, which attempted, after the signing of the Oslo Accords, to play the simulation game with the Palestinians, Netanyahu stated an unequivocal formula from which any obscurity was removed: Peres would divide Jerusalem. Netanyahu played the simulation game masterfully. Having expropriated "peace" from the Labor movement under the slogan "Peace with security," he understood that to win in a regime of simulations he must create the simulation of an unequivocal truth, as well as a simulation of sole possession of the simulation.

During the three years he was in power, Netanyahu simulated a continuation of the peace process. He failed to understand, however, that simulation isn't a one-man show but a new regime of representation that contains everyone. In the elections of May 1999, when Netanyahu once again tried to play the Jerusalem card, he was roundly defeated. It turned out that the division of Jerusalem, in itself, wasn't such a threatening issue. In 1996, the signifier "Jerusalem" had functioned as a rallying point for various political and religious factions. In 1999, the same signifier appeared illusionary and irrelevant, a ghost that Netanyahu had raised from the grave. He turned the Orient House into a symbol of the all-out war over Jerusalem, but the Orient House didn't appear to be more than it is—a symbol. The voters for Barak apparently preferred to support a policy of dividing the city's symbols without dividing the city itself, leaving the city "in our hands" and giving it to the Palestinians at the same time.

The most important point in the Beilin-Abu Masen Accord is an agreement on the flexibility of Jerusalem's boundaries. This means that Palestinians won't condemn Israel for having expanded Jerusalem's boundaries for years, while Israelis will give up their sole proprietorship of the flexing process. Instead of one side denying its actions while the other side condemns them and demands the return of what has

been stolen, both sides in effect agree to place Jerusalem on the operating table, re-nounce its status as a missing object in the discourse, and turn it into an object that is present to the view and to intervention and into speech that is guided by an ob-servant view and regularized, systematic intervention. In effect, the two sides have agreed to be partners in creating the simulation of the city. As evidence of this agree-ment, Abu-Dis, the seat of the new Palestinian national institutions, is due to rise at a distance of 2.3 kilometers east of the El-Aqsa Mosque, exactly the same distance at which Israel's Knesset is located west of the El-Aqsa Mosque.

By assassinating Rabin in Jerusalem's municipal square, Yigal Amir sought to di-vulge the truth about Rabin's plans for the city, which had been suppressed during negotiations with the Palestinians. Immediately after the assassination, Binyamin Netanyahu gave this truth a voice when he warned that Peres would divide Jeru-salem. Peres thought that if he underplayed Rabin's assassination and any plans for sharing the administration of Jerusalem, he would win the people's trust. Today, af-ter Netanyahu's removal from office and the election of Ehud Barak, it seems that Amir's pretension to divulge the truth about Jerusalem is about to be expressed in the most literal way. The Beilin-Abu Masen Accord puts Jerusalem on display and shows that many of the city's characteristics aren't latent in the object "Jerusalem" itself but stem from its place in the symbolic order. Abu-Dis, located at a distance of 2.3 kilo-meters from the El-Aqsa Mosque, can turn into Jerusalem just as new neighbor-hoods outside Jerusalem built after 1967 were declared part of Jerusalem in the past. So, too, sovereignty will no longer derive from showing the flag: according to the Beilin-Abu Masen Accord, the Palestinians will raise one over the El-Aqsa Mosque.

CHAPTER 8   THE FLOODLIT ARENA [OF MURDER]:

YITZHAK RABIN

The fundamental event of the modern age is the conquest of the world as picture.
—HEIDEGGER (1996, 59)

BEFORE THE LAW

Saturday, November 4, 1995. An illuminated plaza. Yigal Amir is sitting on a big planter at the back of the municipal building by the plaza. He is waiting for Prime Minister Yitzhak Rabin's departure from a rally in support of the government's peace policy, which took place that evening at the plaza. Ronny Kempler, an amateur photographer, is ejected from the security zone by a policeman and moves away to the roof of a nearby building to get a wider view of the area. Rabin descends the staircase and approaches his car. Amir draws a 9 millimeter Beretta pistol and fires three shots at the prime minister's back. A few weeks after the assassination, Ronny Kempler reveals to the Commission of Inquiry that he possesses a video testimony of the assassination.

Four months after the assassination, Amir's trial came to an end. He was found guilty and sentenced to life imprisonment. On the day sentence was pronounced, the Minister of Justice summarized the trial as another chapter in the evenhandedness of Israel's democracy: "I asked the critics at the time not to interfere in the course of the trial because in a lawful and democratic state the accused are not tried in the media, even when somebody commits the most horrendous crime before a television camera" (David Libai, quoted in Alon, 1996, p. 39).

The camera, said the Minister of Justice, was simply one of the eyewitnesses, and its testimony had still to withstand the test of legal discourse in court. Democracy, he said, as if it was a matter of fact, sets the stage for the struggle between Amir and his assassinated prime minister. However, is the camera really just one of the witnesses? Did not it take part in the event itself? Is democracy such a self-evident framework for the struggle? Isn't it one of the major things at stake?

THE ARENA

On Saturday, November 4, 1995, tens of thousands of people were crowded in the Malchei-Israel Plaza to demonstrate their support of the government's peace policy. These tens of thousands of demonstrators wished to express, by their very presence in the plaza, a common view and to preform a political act for the benefit of the peace process. They made tens of thousands of demopresentations.

Had a photographer been in a helicopter hovering above the plaza, he or she would have captured a regular movement of thousands of human ornaments, each knowing its place and its way and calculating its trajectory so as not to bump into others. Coming closer to the crowd the photographer would have framed people who are masters of civic manners—conducting their bodies in civic space, keeping a bodily distance and bridging it, maintaining a proper walking pace, properly gathering in a crowd, and keeping eye and ear contact with the central stage without being dominated by it. Those individuals, whose movement and behavior seemed to be self-orchestrated, knew how to take part in the crowd and how to conduct their civilized bodies to create the mosaic of the crowd in the city's public space.

That evening the plaza was lit by spotlights that delineated its architecture, revealing an architectural design that adopts the crowd as a constitutive element. The demonstration exposed how eloquently the design of the plaza articulated an awareness of questions of power and representation in a democracy. The plaza is organized along two well-balanced axes, horizontal and vertical. The large square is laid down as a two-dimensional substratum implanted in stone, like a standing screen that was laid horizontally. The temporary stage is a slightly elevated three-dimensional structure that is placed along one axis, the already elevated balcony of the city hall. The stage elevates the leaders who have called for the gathering and who claim to represent the crowd, but the elevation remains temporary, and its ephemeral nature is never erased.

Demonstrations for or against the peace process frequently take place at the plaza. As a ritual of a sort, the act of demonstration has become a cliché, a commonplace in the place of the common. Once a year, the army takes its turn in the sequence of demonstrations, and the people are invited to adore the spectacle of state power—including tanks in the plaza. Once a year there is a book sale, too, which meets the needs of the spirit and creates them at the same time, and everyone is invited to take part. The crowd at the plaza changes its appearance, manners, and patterns of movement according to the occasion of the gathering, whether demonstration or fair. Yet the same eloquent harmony always remains between the movement of the crowd and the spatial proportions that the plaza offers its gathering—the same proportion between square and stage and between the flattened horizontal "screen" that carries the crowd and the vertical balcony of the city hall that overlooks it. This harmony and these proportions, so it seems, demarcate in advance, in a civic manner, the democratic, civic struggles over the nation's common good.

When Yigal Amir came to the plaza on that Saturday evening, he felt estranged from the spectacle of democracy and excluded from the people who (to him) happily agreed to sell their land and their past. He was not one of them and did not have any official position from which to speak to them. This sense of alienation was vividly expressed in different confessions that Amir made to the police and through it to media in the days following the assassination. Because he felt himself to be a stranger to democratic discourse, Amir could look at this discourse from a distance and with the gaze of an outsider. From his external position Amir created a coherent picture of a certain state of affairs that he had long dreamed of influencing.

Feeling himself lonely in that position, Amir looked on those around him with condescension (because he felt that he knew best) and sadness (because he felt that many were being led astray by a weak, blind leadership). He took the position of one who sees clearly what others fail to grasp and therefore must take responsibility for action. But although lonely, he was not alone, and his responsibility for the people was (in his eyes) assumed under the eye of a spectator who oversaw the entire scene—a provident God. Amir was a self-appointed prophet of that God and felt that he was watched by an all-seeing eye that shared with him the view of the crowd, its leaders, their blindness, and the coming disaster. But that eye from above also saw him seeing all this and therefore expected him to intervene in the scene. To act, Amir had to maintain or at least imagine God's point of view to maintain the distance between his external position and the scene in which he was about to enter (both the democratic event and the history of which it was an event). "I am not sorry for Rabin," he said later. "I wanted that in heaven they will see that someone from the people did it."

A short time before the end of the demonstration, Amir moved closer to the back wall of the city hall and sat down on one of the large, white, round planters placed near the edge of the pavement. He turned the planter into a chair in history's waiting room, as he was soon to turn the area behind the city hall into the heart of an historic event. He was waiting for Yitzhak Rabin, who was about to leave the demonstration and enter his car, which was parked a few steps away. Amir, who felt estranged and excluded in the main square and did not know how to behave there, was easily integrated among the guardians, policemen, and secret agents who populated the area, presumably more attentive than ever. He mingled easily with all those cogs of the more or less clandestine state apparatuses from which the overt, democratic happening could never be really separated. He looked like one of them; in slightly different circumstances, he could have been one of them (and some of them, perhaps, could have taken his place). As he was sitting there on the large planter, chatting coolly with a policeman who stood nearby, his presence behind the city hall seemed entirely natural to all those who should have questioned it.

Another man passed that evening through this same area of shadows and suspended suspicions. This was Ronny Kempler, an amateur photographer (or at least this was how the press presented him). Kempler was seduced by the shadows of the backstage area and tried to place himself there to wait for Rabin's arrival. But he was chased away from the secured zone by a policeman. He looked for another point of view that would allow him to take shots of the scene and finally climbed the roof of a nearby building, securing a clear view of the area Rabin had to cross to reach his car. The backstage area now was watched from three points of view—that of an ancient God, that of a future assassin, and that of an obscure photographer. These three gazes were doomed to intersect.

TELOS

Amir's purpose—Rabin's assassination—was the pinnacle of a critical practice with regard to history. For Amir, history is a clear visual field that provides select individuals with the opportunity to realize their vision in a single act. At the same time, history (or God as its metasubject) uses individuals as instruments for the realization of its telos. Being the instrument of history, Amir can nevertheless be conceived of as a critical subject because he sees what others cannot see. By the assassin's own admission, since the signing of the Oslo agreements he had several times intended to murder the prime minister. On the evening of the assassination, he'd picked up certain signs and interpreted them as signs from heaven, indicating that the way he'd chosen to deal with Yitzhak Rabin was the correct way. Amir had a clearcut purpose—assassination of the prime minister. This purpose was translated into a few plans of action, which, until that evening of November 4, 1995, had failed in the absence of signs from heaven and suitable circumstances. The assassinated prime minister also had a plan of action—completion of the peace process he had begun two years earlier.

The plaza, as I try to show later, became for a while the space where Israel's history was unfolding. From Amir's point of view only he and Rabin stood in that space. Rabin was standing on the stage seeking to govern the people by giving them an understanding of the boundaries of governance. Amir was roaming in the square among the crowd wishing to redeem the people from this governance by imposing an act of violence on their governor. Amir imposed on both of them a fateful encounter that took place under the glaring light and watchful eye of a divine supervision (the camera?) suspended above them as in the day of judgment.

DIFFÉREND[1]

I here discuss the question of critique in terms of point of view and spatial relations. My assumption is that a critical attitude is always a simulation of an exterior point of

---

1. The term *différend* comes from Jean-François Lyotard. It refers to the impossibility of expressing the contentions of one side to a dispute by using the language of the other side.

view in relation to the discourse or object to be criticized. Amir's critique lay outside the language of hegemonic discourse. In Lyotard's terms, between his religious discourse and the hegemonic one there was a *différend*. To adopt a critical stance he did not have to simulate an external position, he was pushed into one. He actually saw and spoke from outside the hegemonic discourse, and finally he also acted from outside.

Standing outside the hegemonic discourse, Amir does not recognize its authority and rules, as much as the latter does not recognize the authority of the rabbinical discourse, one of whose versions Amir practices. The two discourses are mutually exclusive. The gap between the state's hegemonic discourse and Amir's seems unbridgeable, at least from Amir's position in his own discourse. His statements (or interpretations) can hardly be formulated, let alone be legitimized, in the other discourse. Long before the murderous act, Amir's discursive practices expose the limits of hegemonic democratic discourse and challenge the very basis of its legitimacy. The sacred freedom of expression evidently applies only to what can be formulated and heard according to the rules of democratic discourse. In other words, Amir highlights the limits of democracy by showing what cannot be *heard*. In Lyotard's terms, he is a witness of *différend*.

TWO SPACES OF SIGNIFICATION

I present below the political plans of both Yigal Amir and Yitzhak Rabin as critical activities with regard to two spaces of meaning.[2] I intend to conduct this discussion of the assassination (as a critical act) and of criticism (as a violent activity) on the borderline between two spaces—the intersubjective space imposed by subjects and the space composed of networks in which each subject is also a presence existing beside other objects. A critical act imposes an intersubjective space of discourse and action, fixing the distinction between subject (as a pole of action, speech, and gaze) and object (as a pole wherein action, speech, and gaze converge). This distinction between subject and object is anchored and established in specific forms of spatial organization, particularly in disciplinary sites (as these sites were understood and analyzed by Foucault). Disciplinary sites are organized as homogeneous visual fields that unfold through homogeneous temporality and enable relatively fixed and manageable rela-

---

2. While acting from a defined position as subject, both Yitzhak Rabin and Yigal Amir failed to achieve the purposes they'd set for themselves. Realization of their plan led to a result contrary to the desired one: In the one case, Rabin turned from the architect of the process into its victim; in the other, the assassination led to an acceleration of the peace process and to an intensification of public support for it.

tions between a point of view and its objects. The critical position is one such point of view, from which one gazes at a homogeneous visual field. The critical point of view, however, takes place in another space, which it cannot see—the space composed of networks of "blind presences" that cannot be managed or disciplined.

THE THEORETICAL MOVE

Spatial analysis is crucial for understanding the assassination as the violent culmination of a particular genre of critical practice. Amir's claim—that his act expressed and was justified by his critique of Zionist democracy—is taken seriously here. A critical stance or position, it is argued below, should be analyzed in terms of the things that could (or could not) be said about it, the things that could (or could not) be seen from it, and the spatial conditions that enable and constrain the critical gaze. Amir's critical stance is thus reconstructed and represented in relation to its spatial and visual characteristics—the spatial relations in the scene of the assassination and the three distinct points of view of the murderer, of his victim, and of the photographer who documented the event.

Through a discussion of Michel Foucault and criticism of the disciplinary site, I analyze the relation between these two spaces (the intersubjective space and the space composed of networks) and present them as heteronomous spaces, neither of which can be reduced to the other. By analyzing Amir's position as a critical position, I compare his position to a sequence of other critical positions (institutionalized positions, such as that of the curatorial agent in a museum or the photographer) within Western contemporary culture and try to point out its limitations, its violence, and its destiny. Such critical positions exist in the intersubjective space of discourse and are closely linked to disciplinary and supervisory practices, as I argue later by using Foucault, against himself. The long discussion of disciplinary site leads finally to the scene of the crime to look at it once again, this time through the lens of the camera that documented the assassination. I return to the scene of the assassination and attempt to read it as a place of eventuation and a place of interruption—a break in the continuous flow in the channels of interaction and communication in the various networks. I discuss the assassination not only as an ethical model but as an aesthetic one, not only as a planned and purposeful event but as a purposeless activity, as a movement in various networks that cannot be reduced to intentions and plans.

INTERSUBJECTIVE SPACE AND NETWORKS OF BLIND PRESENCES

In schematic fashion, modernity is generally identified with the appearance and establishment of an intersubjective space of discourse and action—the "public sphere" (see Habermas, 1989)—whereas postmodernity is identified with a space of relay networks that make up the global village (see De Duve, 1989; Lyotard, 1986). These two spaces are generally depicted as successive in time. I contend that public space, as a common space,[3] is concurrently experiencing its own dissolution and the emergence of reformed private spaces interlinked among themselves (by means of television, telephone, and Internet). A virtual public space now functions in parallel to the public sphere. The logic that enables public space to be organized as an intersubjective space also guides its dissolution into relay networks between private spaces.

Intersubjective spaces of action and discourse are imposed all the time, continuously, by everyone. In intersubjective space, observation and control of the world are performed from a relatively fixed point of view. Each such fixed point of view momentarily considers itself external to the world but is also intertwined in a network of points of view that cancel each other out by functioning as points of presence and relay stations. Thus, for example, the point of view of each of the policemen at the rally has, in principle, another dimension—being a point of blind presence, that cannot fully observe itself from outside as a presence within the network (on which he doesn't have a point of view). His point of view is operated by the network in which it is intertwined—to be shocked, to be transferred from place to place, to serve as an instrument for relaying messages, goods or viruses, to infect or to be infected. An intersubjective space cannot be reduced to a space that consists of networks of objective presences (and vice versa); the two cannot be united within the same visual field. But the two spaces exist concurrently in unsynchronized fashion, without a point of view to observe them. Synchronization and homogenization are a precondition for a point of view.

Beside the intersubjective space of action and discourse, I attempt to reconstruct, as an additional space—the space of relay networks in which each subject is also an objective presence existing beside other objects. A basic characteristic of this space is that it is composed of networks of presences that lack points of view to the network. A presence—as apart from and together with other presences—is the basic unit of the various networks. Perceived from an intersubjective space, these presences may take the form of signs; otherwise, their entire existence is predicated on their position within the network, which is nothing other than the network of relations among various presences.

---

3. Public space is common in at least two senses of the word. It is a space in which every citizen has an equal right to accessibility and movement. It is a space in which the social contract is formulated: its expressions and institutions are accorded "visibility" and help shape the individual's identity and modes of behavior.

I intend to conduct this discussion of the assassination (as a critical act) and discussion of criticism (as a violent activity) on the borderline of tension between these two spaces. My thesis is that the two cannot be compounded into one and therefore cannot be compounded into a unity of time—except for the time and space of a text, like the present one, which views them after the event.

REREADING FOUCAULT'S DISCIPLINARY SITES

Foucault (1986) opens his essay "Of Other Spaces" by asserting that the greatest obsession that haunted the nineteenth century was history. The twentieth century, adds Foucault, would perhaps be the epoch of space: "We are in the epoch of simultaneity, we are in the epoch of juxtaposition, the epoch of the near and far, of the side by side, of the dispersed" (Foucault, 1986, 22). In his various studies Foucault develops the concept of discourse as a criticism of conceptions of subjectivity and history and endows it with materiality, space, and the structure of a network. In the above quote from his essay "Of Other Spaces," as well as in his various studies of prisons and other spaces (such as factories, schools, barracks, and hospitals) that resemble prisons, Foucault describes a paradigm shift from space to time.[4] But this shift, I contend, takes place within the framework of the first paradigm—historical time—which makes it possible to present these two paradigms as successive. Despite everything Foucault said about history and historicity, history here serves as a homogeneous container, and the critic, archaeologist, and later genealogist are depicted as having a point of view external to it.

In 1978, in his first lecture dealing with Kant's essay on the Enlightenment, Foucault proposed a "historico-philosophical" perspective for analyzing criticism as practice. Critique is the other side of control, and governmentality (*gouvernementalité*) is a new form of power relation which became established in the eighteenth century as feudalism and absolute monarchy faded. Wherever this form of government predominates, claims Foucault, criticism can, in principle, be identified as "the art of not being governed." Foucault locates the first appearance of governmentality in sixteenth-century Christianity. He refers to mechanisms and practices of intervention in the lives of individuals that were developed by the Catholic clergy and were without precedent in ancient times. The idea that the individual, regardless of gender, age, or status, must be managed to arrive at redemption—an idea that found expression in a variety of mechanisms of control and management—Foucault

---

4. In his various books, Foucault deals with several disciplinary spaces including the prison (Foucault, 1975) and the clinic (Foucault, 1963).

contends penetrated into the public sphere. Critique appeared in parallel to these mechanisms and at a later stage became institutionalized in several directions such as Kant's critical project, and even before that among professional critics. Governmentality developed as an art, contends Foucault, as did critique, the art of not being governed (*l'art de ne pas être gouverné*). This continuing and permanent gyration between the two results in an accelerated development of the practices of governmentality accompanied by a constant questioning "how not to be so controlled, by these or other factors, in the name of certain principles, in behalf of such aims or by means of such or other procedures" (Foucault, 1978, 37). As opposed to governmentality (those mechanisms of power that use the truth to subjugate individuals), critique is "the movement by means of which the subject claims the right to question the truth regarding the results of its power, and to question power regarding its discourses of truth" (Foucault, 1978, 39). If so, critique, according to Foucault, is the art of voluntary nonsubjugation (*desassujetisement*)—resistance.

Foucault draws a parallel between his proposed definition of critique and Kant's definition of the Enlightenment.[5] Kant describes humanity as being in a state of minority. The way to escape this condition and achieve maturity, according to Foucault's reading of Kant, is by means of critique of religion, of justice (natural law constraining the authority of government), and of (scientific) knowledge. By means of the same three axes, Foucault describes both the development of the art of governmentality and the institutionalization of critique. Critique, according to Kant, shows reason its limits and tells knowledge how far it may go without losing its validity. Critique, according to Kant, is not only what we do with such or another measure of courage but also the idea we have of our knowledge and of its limitations.[6] Thus, the individual will be able to discover the principle of autonomy, to posit the boundaries within which he will no longer have to hear the injunction: "Obey!" Kant's negative conception of critique (the imposition of limits) is turned by Foucault into a "positive" action (the transgression of limits): "In what is presented as universal, necessary, obligatory, [one has to identify] whatever part of the thing is particular, circumstantial, and an effect of arbitrary constraints. In summary, we are speaking of changing the critique that operates within a form of necessary restriction into a practical critique within the form of a possible border crossing" (Foucault, 1994, 4:574). On the few other occasions that Foucault discusses critique, the

---

5. See the two versions of Foucault's "What Is Enlightenment?" (Foucault, 1994, vol. 4).

6. In the version of "What Is Enlightenment?" published in on 1984, Foucault discusses the two conceptions of critique in Kant (Foucault, 1994, vol. 4).

discussion is always conducted in connection with Kant's critique. With both Kant and Foucault, critique demands a point of view and a subject to comprehend it. Critique is a reflexive position, a reflexive relation to the present.[7] Foucault's historicocritical or historicophilosophical practice does not deal with the legitimacy of knowledge but studies its production and institutionalization (knowledge undetached from power and power undetached from knowledge) and reexamines its scope.

In a book provocatively entitled *Forget Foucault*, Baudrillard (1987) assails Foucault, contending that his discourse is in the nature of a mirror posed opposite the power he describes, reflecting the power relations and reproducing them (Baudrillard, 1987, 10; see also Baudrillard, 1979, ch. 1). Baudrillard focuses his criticism on Foucault's (1976) *History of Sexuality*. In that book, Foucault criticizes the *repressive hypothesis*—that understands systems of rules, obligations, prohibitions, and restrictions as mechanisms of mere repression, and assumes sexuality to be an authentic truth of the individual, and that sexuality must be liberated from repression so that truth can appear. Foucault emphasizes the productivity of these "repressive" systems and contends that the mechanisms and practices that repress sexual activity are exactly those that give rise to the production and endless reproduction of sexuality in its various modes and types. Baudrillard argues that Foucault—and his critique of the repressive hypothesis—remained trapped within the conceptual framework of the political economy. According to Baudrillard, production, one of the central concepts of political economy, stands at the center of Foucault's critical discussion of repression. Baudrillard identifies Foucault's paradigm of production—which is not specific to the analysis of sexuality but anchors his conception of power as well—with his paradigm of liberation, viewing both of them as the shackles binding Foucault to the discourse he is studying.[8]

Foucault abandons the traditional conception of power as linear and finite and replaces it with fields of power relations. In both cases: "We have made, and have wanted to make, an irreversible agency (instance) out of both sex and power; and out of desire we have made a force or irreversible energy (a stock of energy, needless to say, since desire is never far from capital). For we give meaning, following our use of

---

7. This relation, Foucault claims, exists through three axes—power, truth, and subject.

8. In later texts to which Baudrillard doesn't refer, Foucault extends his discussion of production and liberty around the conception of the subject's autonomy. In his discussion of the subject in the article "What Is Enlightenment?" for example, Foucault (1994, vol. 4) claims that the practice of critique is the work of deconstructing the necessary and contending critically with what isn't, or is no longer, necessary for establishing ourselves as autonomous subjects.

the imaginary, only to what is irreversible" (Baudrillard, 1987, 47). Both sexuality and power take part in a ceaseless process of production and exchange, heeding a vital principle of capital: "The chain of investments and reinvestments must never stop" (Baudrillard, 1987, 25). Baudrillard's criticism of Foucault can be predicated on a basic claim: Foucault is a part of the object of his critique and of the power relations he describes. Foucault would not have disagreed.[9] In "What Is Critique?" Foucault (1978) depicts critique as dependent on its object: action, speech, or thought refers to what exists and constitutes a part of it (part of the criticized discourse). I assume, as well, that Foucault and Baudrillard, two French philosophers whose writings appeared at about the same time, shared in the same discourse—an assumption that is also corroborated by some of their theoretical assumptions.[10] However, each of them served as (or manufactured) an entirely different mirror for the world they describe.[11] This difference cannot be ascribed to theoretical differ-

---

9. Baudrillard (1987) deals with the question of history in Foucault and the conception of time and space it entails in only one place—the title of the book, from which a reference to the dimension of time may be derived. The title *Forget Foucault* remains enigmatic throughout the book. It can be interpreted as a provocative appeal contending that it's best to forget about Foucault: his writings are *passé*. But the proposal to forget could be an appeal to Foucault himself—to forget, to instill the dimension of forgetfulness into the discussion, to abolish memory in Foucault (that is, the modes of discourse that are responsive and subservient to historical logic).

10. Their central common assumption, which they share with other poststructuralist thinkers, is that there is nothing external to the discourse (*il n'y a pas d'hors texte*). Foucault and Baudrillard, each in his own way, claim that it is impossible to be outside the discourse that they are criticizing.

11. The point of view and the field of vision must deal with the specificity (or lack of it) of critique as a point of view. The contention that the critic cannot hold a position that is external to objects of discussion needs to be developed and elaborated into the contention that the critic's position has been conscripted by the discourse and that the occupiers of positions that critique has identified as the discourse's official agents have also been conscripted by the discourse.

I would like to describe the relation between point of view (position) and field of vision in terms of a graph. Its two axes represent, respectively, the object of description and the descriptive position. The critic's descriptive position is dependent on the object of critique; just as the critic simulates its control over the object, he is interpellated by it and looses control. An example of this relationship is the deconstruction of the subject. Changes in the objective conditions of discourse that took place throughout the twentieth century—as a result of the proliferation of technology such as photography, television, and computers—led to the spatialization of the subject or to the anchoring of the subject's deconstruction in the objective space. The critique of the conception of the subject described in the writings of several poststructuralist thinkers, whose position is a model of the critical position, is homologous with these changes. The critique of the subject (in the writings of Michel Foucault, Pierre Bourdieu, Louis Althusser, and other poststructuralists) examines an outmoded idea of subjectivity but announces a new subjectivity that is organized by the objective world of objects (with which most mundane negotiations are conducted). In other words, these thinkers' critical transition from a regime of depth metaphors to one of metaphors of flattened networks made it possible for them to speak the world (rather than about the world) better, to serve as an additional extension of it, and thus to participate in orientating the graph. In this way the computer manufacturer's interest coincides with the critical interest of the cultural critic, and both in the final analysis are conscripted in behalf of a similar goal.

ences alone but has to do with the visual field and point of view each adopted with regard to the world. Foucault's point of view, I maintain, is reflexive and seeks to impose a space of intersubjective discourse; Baudrillard's is devoid of purpose, an aesthetic point of view that examines the activity of networks of presences.[12]

CRITICAL POSITION AND CRITICAL POINT OF VIEW

To understand Foucault's discussion of critique, we must first delineate the boundaries of Foucault's visual field and the point of view that he focuses on this field. In one of the many interviews he granted, Foucault was asked to explain what makes his theory special: "The difference isn't in the theory, but in the object, in the point of view. Usually, the theory of power speaks of it in terms of law and raises the question of its legitimacy, of its boundary and of its source. My research revolves around the techniques of power, around the technology of power" (Foucault 1994, 3:532). Foucault wishes to change the point of view. He criticizes the discipline of history, which posed at its center a constituting subject (*sujet constituant*), as well as the Marxist program of research, which in the final analysis predicated everything on interests and ideology. To replace them, he stretches a comprehensive historic canvas of a different weave. Foucault positions discipline as the object of his research and writes its history: discipline as the collection of practices of subjecting to rules, supervising, monitoring, bringing to justice, applying authority, delimiting boundaries—and in general as the modern game between subject, power, and truth. Discipline—the discipline of knowledge and the discipline of the self by the self and others—became institutionalized, according to Foucault, in the form of a unity of discourse in the modern epoch. Instead of the historical discipline in the domain of knowledge, Foucault offers the history of the discipline of the individual as somebody subject to relations of knowledge and power, with the individual as the subject of knowledge and power and their object as well. In the first place, Foucault studies discipline in the institutional sites clearly devoted to it, such as the prison or clinic. The disciplinary

---

Later I examine the objective spatialization of the subject by means of communication networks (currently epitomized by the information superhighway on the Internet) to understand the social structure that narrows the distinction between communication channels and information, between medium and discourse, and in general between interior and exterior, turning the very presence of the network into the central medium of thought, speech, and action.

12. Gilles Deleuze (1990) proposes a framework for the discussion of controlled societies (*societés de côntrol*) as the social and spatial form of organization that has succeeded the disciplinary society (Deleuze, 1990). His assumptions are similar to Baudrillard's. In effect, Deleuze's article posits the possibility of organizing the relation between Foucault and Baudrillard as sequential, whereas I am trying to present them as two simultaneous readings of space.

society is organized by means of those institutions, which exercise power over bodies and collect data about individuals. These interventions are guided by prior knowledge that makes it possible to create new knowledge. The individual enters one of these units and undergoes a certain process whose termination has been predefined: something has been completed, a task has been accomplished, or a given period of time has elapsed. Within these institutions, individuals learn to position themselves as needing to be interpreted, and as beings whose actions and thoughts have meaning. Individuals enter school and complete a course of study, emerging more or less educated after a certain number of years; they enter the clinic and emerge from it after being cured; they are sent to prison and emerge from it at the conclusion of the sentence. In these confined spaces, the individual is manufactured as an object of observation, study, and manipulation.

The individual cannot fulfill the purpose to which the disciplinary site is dedicated without actually being inside it. There is no replacement for these sites; only copies scattered over the entire social space. The disciplinary site is a homogeneous and synchronized physical space, wherein sojourn individuals who are subject to a superior gaze that supervises this space and creates boundaries of standardization and normality. What lies beyond these boundaries is rejected as deviating from the norm. The disciplinary sites are structured according to the logic of places of confinement (where the deviant is imprisoned), signify the boundary of normality, but at the same time create both the normal and the deviant.

Foucault defines his critical practice as a "historicophilosophical practice."[13] The critique contained within the practice is expressed principally in the transformation of the point of view and visual field that delimit and redefine the object of study of the archaeologist or genealogist. Both are critical by definition, unlike the historian or philosopher. The visual field of the archaeologist or genealogist encompasses not only the uttered statements (*énoncés*) but the conditions for their production as well, in a way that amalgamates the knowledge, the procedures employed to produce it, the various forms of organizing the space in which it is produced, and the power relations that make it possible. In this sense, the disciplinary sites furnished Foucault with an optimal visual field for his research in which all of these were

---

13. This definition constitutes a veiled critique of two disciplines—history and philosophy—that offer themselves to Foucault's critical view as closed objects of knowledge that he can encompass and critique. Foucault assumes the object of his critique, observes it from a certain (the critical) point of view, and proposes an alternative. Foucault's critical practice identifies an institutionalized discourse (the historical discourse, for example) that has been sealed off from other fields of discourse, points to its limitations, and suggests an alternative.

captured in delimited and stabilized fields of visibility.[14] To paraphrase Foucault's remarks in his essay on critique, wherever there is governmentality, resistance or critique may develop. Only as opposed to the confined disciplinary sites (which determine the space of normalcy and deviation) could reflexive critical research establish itself.

However, if these sites furnished Foucault with a visual field and point of view, then on the basis of Foucault's own discussion, I ask whether Foucault's point of view itself is not already structured within the logic of the site. To be able to criticize discipline, Foucault is necessarily dependent on the panoptic point of view of the disciplinary site. Both Foucault as critic, as well as those occupying other positions within the disciplinary discourse and apparatus, assume a common visual field. From this field one seeks to establish a boundary of normality, while another seeks to restrict the application and validity of that boundary by revealing it as a historically determined boundary that is neither universal, necessary, nor eternal: "Critique exists only in relation to something else, it is a point of view to a domain that it wishes to police, lacking the ability to constitute its laws" (Foucault, 1978, 39). Foucault's critical position is a part of the disciplinary discourse that he is criticizing. Within the framework of certain positions in this discourse, boundaries are determined, while within the framework of other positions (such as the one that Foucault himself occupies), an attempt is made to restrict the applicability of these boundaries. This discourse, inclusive of both types of position mentioned above, takes place in a more or less homogeneous space that is amenable to control and observation (from the critic's position as well) and that makes possible the panoptic action of establishing a boundary and restricting it. This homogeneous space makes it possible for the supervisor and critic to exchange points of view because both points of view intersect each other inside the same visual field—the disciplinary site. However, there is one fundamental difference between the supervisor in his control tower and Foucault as critic: the former is situated within the physical site, but the latter isn't.

What, then, is Foucault's point of view regarding the disciplinary site? Where exactly is his visual field—in the texts, in the archive, in the architectural plans, in the photographs?

Foucault's concept of discourse enables him to transcend the demarcated, particular physical site, in which the subject is disciplined, and to speak of networks of discourse of which the subject is a function. However, these are not networks of

14. On site and heterotopia, see "Of Other Spaces" (Foucault 1986).

THE FLOODLIT ARENA [OF MURDER]

objective presences; they cannot operate without the presence of subjects in positions of observation and speech. Foucault describes these networks as flooded with light, of the kind cast by the French Revolution on the social space to banish the dark areas, hidden from view. The philosophies of the eighteenth century, according to Foucault, sought to bypass the problem of punishment and arrive at a completely illuminated visual field, a state in which "human beings won't even be able to behave badly, because they will feel so bathed and immersed in an absolute field of visibility in which the opinion of others, the gaze of others, the discourse of others will prevent them from doing what is bad or injurious" (Foucault 1994, 3:196). The discipline transcends the physical sites devoted to it and comes to rest in the networked individual—which is what Foucault attempted to study by means of the concepts of discourse, practices, strategies, and networks of power relations. Foucault uses networking of power, relations between knowledge and power, and control by means of regulating networks to criticize previous analyses of the subject and of power and presented the histories of the specific forms of relations of knowledge and power. But all these concepts and images share a common visual field with the agents of the ruling power (in the widest sense of the term), who also wish to cast more light on the arena. When "the [visual] resolution of the fields of power" (the image of resolution is Foucault's) is increased, critics are able to join other agents who wish to improve the resolution and to cast additional light on the fields of power. A critical writing of the history of discipline that aims to restrict its arbitrariness requires observing discipline and identifying its boundaries. Observing discipline means observing the site in which it is produced or observing the individuals to whom it has been relocated.

Instead of a history of subjects, with Foucault we turn to a history of relations of knowledge and power, of which the subject is an effect or function. This shift includes a spatialization of the subject and the creation of networks of relations that are given to observation, prediction, and supervision—either from "inside" (the supervisor's position) or from "outside" (the critic's position). The critic's visual field remains homogeneous; its components can be placed together or projected on a single table, and the transformations that take place in it—including the breaks—can be clearly seen. The visual field achieves its homogeneity by dint of being an intersubjective space of discourse and action; the power relations in this space are such that, at every point, any act of control may arouse resistance. It is one subject's position against that of another. The entire space is governed by subjects. For example, in the ultimate in control structures—the panopticon—even the observers are observed in turn, and the walls that are built to prevent masturbation can also provide a cover for it.[15] The network model of the discourse in Foucault is achieved as a result of the conversion of intersubjective spaces of discourse and action. It slightly resembles the vision of the French Revolution.

In this way, even when Foucault attempts to transcend the disciplinary site as a demarcated intersubjective space and develops the concept of discourse, he remains within the boundaries of discipline and of history. When discipline comes to rest in the individual, when it is networked over the entire social space and exhibits more and more phenomena that can no longer be observed at the physical site of the confined institution, Foucault turns to history to reconstruct the shattered visual field. History—the homogeneous and empty container in which the discourse is unfolded and that reveals the breaks that have occurred in it—provides Foucault with a sort of virtual disciplinary site as well as a point of view that both establishes it and is established by it. This disciplinary site is not a closed unit of space or alternately a place of confinement; it is a virtual and homogeneous unit of time and space: "When the constituting subject is got rid of, the subject itself must be got rid of—that is, arrive at an analysis that may account for the constitution of the subject in the course of history. And this is what I term genealogy—that is, a form of history that accounts for the constitution of the knowledges, fields of discourse, domains of objects, etc., without relying on the subject" (Foucault 1994, 3:147).

Foucault's subject has undergone spatialization and has been deconstructed into positions of addresser and addressee. But, in the last analysis, he is acting, speaking, seeing, and being seen in an empty and homogeneous space-time—history's disciplinary site. History can be written, within and from this site, as the history of relations of knowledge and power, of governing and of being governed, of subjects and by subjects. Foucault in effect establishes an empty and homogeneous visual field in which the history of the subject—of what this subject says, thinks, and does—accumulates. Foucault's critique of the discipline of history led him to spatialize the subject, the view, and the power and to organize them within the framework of networks of relations (relations of power and knowledge). Power that is spatialized lacks a source; the gaze that is spatialized is deprived of a focal point. The spatialization of both power and gaze—meant to uproot the notion of origin and to speak in its stead of an entanglement of branchings lacking beginning or end—creates a network lacking a center of relations between different points. However, these branchings nevertheless can observe and control, within mutable relations of power that exist in

---

15. On the panopticon, see Foucault (1975b). On sexuality and architecture, see Foucault (1976).

the tension between potential power and effective power, legitimate power and arbitrary power, the seen and the unseen.

Every point in the Foucaultian network of power relations is a position that can be grasped only by a subject and that in paradoxical fashion preserves, like a cell, the logic of force as stemming from a source and of a focal gaze. This position may enable the subject to regain autonomy, which in this context means taking a point of view on the verge of the visual field without being a presence within it. However, this point of view is a fantasy that exists only with regard to the virtual disciplinary site described above, which forcibly fuses different perspectives into a single focus and attempts to manufacture a virtual visual field by purporting to overcome the discontinuity and unruliness of both the view and the visual field in the modern epoch. This discontinuity was already characterized by Benjamin, who identified it as the central modern experience and described it as shock. In his essay "On the Work of Art in the Age of Technical Reproduction," Benjamin (1978) bases his argument on a Freudian assumption that consciousness is a protective armor against stimulation and shock, which bridges the gaps in the visual field. The virtual disciplinary site—which fuses history, subjectivity, and truth in the body of the individual—seems a way of dealing with the experience of shock, the discontinuity, the conflict, and the loss of space-time synchronization. With Foucault, by contrast, the disciplinary site (as a field of observation) and the human (albeit spatialized) point of view attempt to deal with what the eye can't see, with what the point of view makes impossible to rehabilitate, with the discrepancy between the intersubjective space of discourse and action and blind objective presence in a network.

In summary, Foucault views the critic as someone who can adopt the reflexive point of view and grasp more clearly what the various agents of power grasp. He is not concerned with the dependency between his view and the visual field of discourse, within which he speaks. Foucault thematizes the critic's participation in the discourse he is criticizing but not the "curve" on which the critic is situated—this curve being what describes the actual mutual relations between the point of view manufactured by the critic and the network in which it is intertwined. The Foucaultian critic envisions the point of view as situated in an intersubjective space of discourse and action but ignores its intertwinement in other networks, in which it is no longer a point of view but merely a presence.

Governmentality and critique structure an intersubjective space of discourse and action. Governmentality manufactures subjects. Critique, whose function is to resist, seeks to desubjectivize (*desujetissement*) them. Using the concepts of discourse and statement (*énoncé*), Foucault performed a desubjectivization that spatialized the subject, repudiated its identity as a generative source, and turned it into a function of the discourse and its phrases. However, the subject that has undergone spatialization hasn't swept along the critical position or its point of view, which remains in the nature of a position of an autonomous subject. When Foucault spatializes the gaze, pointing to the reorganization of various spaces of observation, he ultimately ascribes these observatory positions to a subject. Here, too, desubjectivization of the point of view leads to a situation where the gaze has no subjective source, although it doesn't exist outside the subject in whom it is incarnated. The subject is the point of departure and the point of convergence of the critical practice, the scheme of which Foucault draws by means of three central questions: how are we constituted as subjects of our knowledge (our mastery over things), as subjects that absorb and exercise power (our attitude toward others), and as moral subjects of our actions (our attitude to ourselves)?

THE DISSOLUTION OF MUSEUM INTERSUBJECTIVE SPACE

The museum can illustrate the tension between the intersubjective space of discourse and action and the space composed of networks of presences. The museum is a disciplinary site par excellence that functions within the intersubjective space of discourse. The individual is invited to the museum to pose before an object exhibited as worthy of interpretation. The museum conjoins observation with a more or less systematic interpretive activity. Through the act of interpretation, the individual positions the displayed object as a sign that must be interpreted and constitutes himself as an interpreting subject. This encounter is part of the "establishment procedures of reality" (Lyotard, 1983) or "the realization of the world" (Baudrillard, 1983), in which the world is organized as a collection of testimonies and signs whose immanent meaning must be deciphered.[16] From its start in the eighteenth century, the museum has functioned within the logic of the disciplinary site, both in its temporal and spatial organization and in the establishment of its authority to collect, exhibit, and interpret. The ethos of the equality among spectators regarding the object underlies the establishment of the first museums. The museum—as a place that exhibits authentic objects from art, history, or anthropology—achieves its status as the place of the unique and the authentic. The museum exposes unique objects before a universal individual. The democratic regime it maintains affords each and every individual access to the object exhibited therein. To exercise equality regarding the

---

16. Reality, contends Lyotard, isn't given to one subject or another but is the state of the referent (what someone talks about) that stems from the act of "establishing reality" (Lyotard, 1983).

object, individuals must arrive at the specific museum site, pose before the object (a system of signs to be interpreted), and constitute themselves as interpreting subjects. As interpreting subjects, they acknowledge that the sign contains a meaning that they (or people more authorized than themselves) must expose and that this meaning cannot be exposed utterly, once and for all. The museum is one of the central sites in which the individual is invited to exercise civil equality regarding the object, as well as to take part in the public manifestation of this equality.

Beside, as well as in opposition to, the process of democratization, a central authority establishes itself in a position to pull the strings of interpretation, exercise central control over an entire field of interpreters, and singlehandedly determine which objects are worthy of preservation. A culture of experts develops inside museums, which authorizes itself to represent the universal interests of the spectators as well as what spectators are supposed to learn from what they see. A field of conflict eventually arises between these two processes of democratization and the institutionalization of a culture of experts. In opposition to the museum culture of experts, particular groups seek to appropriate representation inside the museums from the universal experts and represent themselves by themselves. The rapid proliferation of museums dedicated to a particular purpose (such as the Museum of the History of the Post during the Holocaust or African women's art) is an outcome of this conflict. These specialized museums express a critical position that points to the way in which values represented as universal actually represent a particular group and thereby repress all the others. This critical position has led to an accelerated privatization of the museum site and its attendant discourse practices. Such an accelerated process took place in Israel during the 1970s, when dozens of historical museums were established, each of them dedicated to the history of one particular group that considered itself left out from the museums that serve as repositories for the metanarrative of the entire nation (Azoulay, 1999).

The reproduction of the model of museum activity and its propagation over the social space, along with the loss of "the" museum, seem to be a direct continuation of the process of democratization in culture and an expression of its intensification, while established critical positions are represented as responsible for the acceleration of this process. Every community, every group, indeed each individual can achieve perpetuation. There's a wide variety of opportunities—a photographic portrait, a monument by the side of the road, a commemorative testimonial at the local museum, a stone at Yad Vashem's Valley of the Communities, or a file at the computerized museum of family genealogy at the Museum of the Jewish Diaspora. The individual achieves in ultimate fashion equality before the object, by producing, representing, and consuming that object. In the course of this process, the object is transformed from a sign worthy of interpretation into a mirror embedded inside a network of mirrors. At the Museum of the Jewish Diaspora, for example, the individual accesses a computerized data bank of Jewish families in the Diaspora and types in a family name. The family story is printed on an elegant scroll that can be taken home. At the United States Holocaust Memorial Museum in Washington, D.C., the individual may type personal details into the computer, which adapts to the individual the personal story of a namesake, an alter ego, a Jew who lived in Europe fifty years ago and went through the Holocaust. Each person finds an exact counterpart in details of gender, status, economic condition, and so on. The modernist museum is a disciplinary site with a panoptic point of view to the past and its relics, from which it is possible to categorize, subsume, and represent. The museum has now lost its depth; beside the panoptic point of view, a network is formed of individuals lacking a point of view, each of whom has a name and an address. On the one hand, everyone has access to a practice of representation that doesn't represent anything (personal commemoration); on the other hand, a practice of representation is being conducted that lays claim to representing everything, though hardly anyone has access to it (the modernist expert).

THE DISSOLUTION OF THE CRITICAL POSITION

In the intersubjective space of discourse and action, the process of personal commemoration is described as a triumph of critical activity. Critique has laid bare the particular in universal representation and demanded the right for particular groups to preserve and represent their own particularity by themselves, enabling the inclusion of minority and specialized groups in the practice of museum representation. But concurrently with this process, other things have transpired in the second space, composed of networks of presences. The process of privatization of the public space has been accelerated, and a network has been formed of interactive sites that apparently participate in museum discourse and practices without representing anything, except their own reflection as it appears in a kind of mirror provided for them by the museum. These sites reflect the attainment of a place of representation, although no common representation has plain visibility in the public space. Negotiations toward the particularization of representation have led museum discourse and practices to a sort of "zero degree" representation, in which representation no longer represents anything or anybody except itself: it is the thing itself, a presentation without reflection. Thus, for example, are the museum data banks contrived: individuals are invited to identify themselves by name, and gigantic commemorative walls are filled with names, millions of memorial candles, millions of names in a data bank (Yad Vashem, the Museum of the Jewish Diaspora, the U.S. Holocaust Memorial Museum, the Vietnam Veterans Memorial). An exhaustive particularization of space has been achieved—to each his own cell, language, picture, representation. What is represented is only the name, the label signifying the place of the individual in the network—name, address, and picture. This is a breaking up of collective sites of confinement (which make possible a common point of view and practices of universal representation) into private places of confinement in which everyone is represented. Each and every individual becomes an enclosed unit that needs input from and output to the network only to see itself in the mirror and ascertain that the network is indeed functioning properly. Representation is no longer representation of the other but only of the self, which is nothing other than a positioning of the self as a presence in the network.[17] The network creates an opportunity for individuals to represent themselves and to acknowledge themselves as authorized to represent themselves—but only as a presence in a network.[18]

THE MASS, THE NETWORK, AND THE SITE OF THE ASSASSINATION

With the loss of a representative dimension, discipline is disseminated among its old sites at the heart of the public sphere and at the private sites that are the locations of the individual in the network. Discipline is disseminated throughout the network in a way that reduces (but doesn't eliminate) the need for a panoptic point of view to a common space in which individuals act under supervision. The individual supervises and is supervised merely by being connected to the network. Individuals feed the network, and it feeds them.

The virtual networks and the mass have now become the two forms of public space in which the individual takes part.[19] Individuals are intertwined in networks of particular presences in which they, like other objective presences in the same networks, operate and are operated on. Examples of such networks are automatic bank tellers, shopping malls, data banks, the Internet, telephones, and fax machines. Those who plug into the network enable the network to function, reproduce, and improve its internal divisions and supports its continued existence. Personal contribution to

---

17. The passage from representation to a presence in the network is an inversed symmetrical image of Benjamin's description of the passage of a work of art from its cult value to display value.

18. This process goes beyond the museum sphere. See Baudrillard's discussion on rights (Baudrillard, 1990).

19. On the network and the individual, see Deleuze (1990), Ophir (1998), Tacher (1992), and Azoulay (1992).

the maintenance of the telephone network, for example, consists of using the telephone. By means of a speech act directed toward an identified individual at the other end of the line, the telephone user is acting within the network as though it were an intersubjective space of discourse and action, although his presence in the network contributes to its density or spaciousness in a way that he does not control or monitor.[20] For example, when too many subscribers use the network at the same time, it may be disrupted or even break down. In such a case, the intersubjective space in which the user has been functioning is rudely interrupted and becomes a limbo.

Happenings of this sort inside the network create new environments of events, which cannot be managed or controlled from the individual user's space of discourse and action. At this moment the expert appears. For the expert, the network is an object that can be monitored and is ready for manipulation. The subjects who use it are nothing more than the connection points or dead nerve endings of this object. On the one hand, the expert's space of discourse and action is extended into an appointed segment of the network (never more than a section). On the other hand, the user's space of discourse and action is extended inside the network, taking no account of and in utter disregard of its materiality. Between these two spaces of discourse and action, which in principle are equivalent, extends the network as a space that is distinct from these intersubjective spaces.

A similar description could be applied to the second form of the individual's participation in the public space—being part of the mass. Gathering in at a rally, for example, creates a network of simultaneous presences. The intersubjective space of discourse that is the rally requires a privileged point of representation—the central podium, for example, or a television camera. But both the podium and the camera are at one and the same time a part of the mass, interlinked with it and subject to being swallowed up by it at any moment. The speaker at the rally, who represents the mass within the framework of a space of discourse and action, is at the same time linked to it in unmediated fashion. The mass is a link over which the speaker has no control. By rubbing against the crowd, the speaker inflames it or induces a tedium that causes a weakening of the network and a breakup of the gathering. But even in this instance, the speaker's intersubjective space is intertwined in the network independently of the intent of the agents acting within it.

At the rally in support of the government's peace process at which Yitzhak Rabin was assassinated, the mass created waves of movement in a public space, rocked

---

20. On density and spaciousness in the network, see the discussion of the community in Nancy (1990).

to the rhythm of the songs, and split up into smaller groupings. The leaders who spoke from the podium (principally at the news media) could hardly be heard in the plaza. The intersubjective space of the speakers from the podium was almost entirely detached from the mass although the speakers themselves weren't physically detached from the network of the gathering. A hundred thousand demonstrators signified with their bodies a density in the network, which ultimately attracted to itself an event—the assassination of the prime minister.

SIGNS AND SIGNS FROM HEAVEN

At the moment of the assassination, the generator of the event, Yigal Amir, acted in both spaces and created a unique convergence of the two. A privileged point appeared in the network and magnetized the entire space of presences. The assassination for a short time imposed on the plaza a single intersubjective space of discourse and action, in which every sign has meaning and all the signs combine into a single narrative, which in the context of the event serves as a metanarrative. Everything that could be slotted into the causal sequences as testimony (in the channels of prediction and explication of the main protagonists' actions) was earmarked for decipherment. Almost everything became a sign that experts of various sorts were invited to interpret. Journalists, politicians, family members, "youth," psychologists, criminologists, and pathologists all proposed an interpretive story. Experts sought signs, signs sought experts, and the entire country boiled over with signs. However, this was not the intersubjective space (which I describe below) that Amir had sought to impose on the event.

Yigal Amir was caught in the act and confessed to the assassination that very evening. He stated clearly that his mission had been to eliminate Yitzhak Rabin from the political arena. The various experts—journalists, jurists, and psychologists—interpreted his explicit remarks as a coverup for his true, concealed intent. Amir's explicit remarks, his confessions, and the open, floodlit crime scene made it difficult for the experts and interpreters of the murder to perform their jobs. Usually, experts know how to operate in a twilight zone between the hidden and the manifest, between the arcane and the explicit (like the expert interpreters at the museum). But the assassination took place between the manifest and the hypermanifest, the explicit and the hyperexplicit. To perform their jobs, these interpreters created a discrepancy between Amir's explicit remarks and actions (which could not have been more explicit) and his hidden intentions. Amir candidly admitted there had been no conspiracy, no long-term plan of action, no strategy. Amir hadn't planned to capture power or incite an uprising. Yigal Amir had been self-appointed over a small but fateful section of a plan of action that wasn't carried out—to paralyze the prime minister or, in his words, "to remove him from the course" and thus to stop the peace process. Amir imposed on reality an intersubjective space of discourse and action, and within its framework he conceived of himself as a critical subject who was accountable for his speech and actions and was seeking to change the course of history and save the Jewish people from their government. However, the assassination was comprehended by many interpreters (at least in the initial period following the assassination) as part of a conspiracy and Amir as a member of an underground. To their minds, Amir had openly committed his part of the mission—and successfully, from his point of view—but the entire plan remained hidden from view. The implicit dark side of his actions was imputed to him by others who needed this side, for their job has been to interpret it. However, there had been no prior mission, and there was no mission to follow. Amir had performed his part in a plan of action that didn't exist.

Yigal Amir sought to claim the position of an external critic of the discourse. He considered the speaking positions offered to him by the government to be insufficient and inadequate for fighting what he viewed as a course leading to bloodshed and destruction. This is a critical position with regard to the ruling power and its actions and even more radically with regard to the democratic system in general—the system of justice, the conception of truth underlying it, democratic procedures of speech and action, the secular norms for the institutionalization of political authority, and so on.[21]

NATIONAL CONFESSION

The assassination was a unique event, which by its very nature transcended any causal connection given to prediction. It immediately gave rise to new practices of confessional mourning ("Rabin and I"), which propagated in all spheres of activity—political, media, educational, and private. These practices were part of an overall effort to mend the continuities disrupted as a result of the surprise engendered by the event. Various experts—some having expertise that stemmed from past events (President Kennedy's assassination, for example) and others staking their claim on this particular event (Etan Haber, spokesperson for the prime minister's office, for example)—provided models for dealing with the assassination. Characteristic of them all was the

---

21. All through Amir's trial, the defendant and his attorneys made attempts to repudiate, directly and indirectly, the conception of testimony on which the court relies. For the purpose of illustration, I mention only the request for an autopsy and the denial of any murderous intent.

immediate rehabilitation of temporal continuities in such a way that personal and national history could absorb both Rabin and Amir. As soon as the assassination became known, the two protagonists of the event—the assassin and the assassinated—were depicted as two characters whose biographies led one to become the victim of a foul murder and the other to become author of that murder: Rabin as "author of the peace" and Amir as "author of Rabin's murder." Along with these two biographies began a creative ferment of personal confessions on a national scale. Countless opportunities were extended so that each and every one could tell a story or refashion it under the circumstances—authentic recollections of a first meeting with Rabin, admissions of a change in attitude toward him over the years, until the suppression of the Intifada, until Oslo. By means of writing, speech, and a plethora of photographers, the historical narrative began to cover the event with astonishing rapidity and to erase intensively everything that interrupted the existing social and cultural order.

The practices of confession and mourning were orchestrated within networks of discourse and social interactions and also created new visual fields begging for interference, supervision, and management of a new type. Thus, for example, the term "sterile area" appeared in the discourse, and the practice of VIP security suddenly became something concrete, for which somebody was responsible and had been appointed to produce, maintain, and manage.[22] The networks of national confession made it easy to identify those who refused "to plug into the network." In the days following the assassination, there were many instances of arrest or detention for questioning on suspicion of expressing empathy with or joy at the assassination or even of failing to condemn it. Not all of the questionings were performed by the police. People volunteered to report on fellow workers or on people they didn't know who had been seen talking about the assassination in public venues. Supervision was maintained within a framework of "self"-regulatory networks, in which people supervise each other on their own private initiative. Each supervised one portion of the network. This hubbub of supervision took the form of personal confessions of fear, feelings of guilt, confusion, and anger and of a determined resolve to put up with "No more!" But these confessions were almost always directed toward identifying creatures similar to Yigal Amir.

The assumption underlying this supervisory behavior was that it is possible to deduce from the assassination a causal sequence whose nucleus or source is Yigal

---

22. According to the testimony of several bodyguards, the concept of "sterile area" had been unfamiliar to them prior to the investigations, in which it came up for the first time. From the moment the term was coined, it retroactively became a touchstone for examining the event.

Amir as a type. Anyone with a psychological and sociological profile that resembled Amir in speech or action should be investigated. Regimes of surveillance and supervision of this type read the world as an intersubjective space of intentional actions, inclusive of which are discursive acts—a space in which every enunciation or action is attributed to a subject possessing consciousness and will and is therefore amenable to control, restriction, or counteraction. Thus, for example, instead of the ten police officers posted in an area of VIP security, twenty would be posted, and they would be better able to spot a potential infiltrator, whose criminal intent could be identified and whose planned action could be prevented. But this analysis (which sees only an intersubjective space in which there are active subjects—police officers and suspects) misses an entire visual field in which each of the subjects, including the police themselves, is also present as an object—tempting or repelling but lacking consciousness or intent, simply a relay station in a communication and relay network. Therefore, the supervision and management of their space of control are only partial and could at any moment be subverted. So it was when Yigal Amir arrived at the site of the assassination and used the police officers themselves to take action. He used their very own supervisory position—from which it had been deduced that if he were there, it was undoubtedly under supervision—to infiltrate it.

CRITICAL SUBJECT AND GUERILLA FIGHTER

The assassination of Rabin was a guerrilla action on the part of an individual who apparently operated independently and without accomplices. Amir felt he wasn't a part of the group of empowered citizens. Furthermore, he chose not to be a part of any other network of individuals. By his own admission, during the period prior to the assassination he stopped consulting with friends and relatives and had little contact with other people. The reports of psychologists who met with him, as well as biographical details gathered by several journalists, point to an almost total withdrawal from various frameworks of social interaction that might have, to a certain degree at least, made his intentions and actions visible and thus amenable to supervision and regulation. Amir was an independent guerrilla fighter, who in the period before the assassination, as well as during the act itself, managed to evade various networks of communication and avoided exposing himself in the visible positions that joining a network would have necessitated. He evaded those networks in which he had formerly been embedded and sought to reach the center of discourse, the center of the political stage, and finally of the scene of history and from there to impose his critique—to transform "the weapon of criticism" into "criticism by means of arms." He sought to withdraw from social networks that offer established channels of change or critique to be able to burst on them in a flash and appear as the generator of a redemptive change. Amir's guerrilla action was the result of a refusal to acknowledge the fundamental assumptions of "establishing reality" that are operative in a democratic system. In fact, when that guerrilla action did occur, the democratic system itself was exposed as "the other" who'd been negated. Amir, as the spokesperson and "author" of the assassination, remained outside the discourse, having been distanced from it by the various agents of democracy.

YIGAL AMIR AND YITZHAK RABIN: A MORTAL FACE-TO-FACE

In Amir's intersubjective space there were two positions of speech and action of equal status—that of himself and that of Yitzhak Rabin. In the act of assassination, Amir sought to appropriate the position of an omnipresent spokesperson. He comprehended the prime minister in the same manner, as a focal point on the boundary of an intersubjective space and in effect outside it. He conceived of Rabin as an omnipotent individual shaping reality to his will. Amir treated him as an independent sign whose meaning was immanent—a spontaneous source of freedom and action that was not dependent on the network of differences between this sign and others. The elimination of this power source from the political arena, so he thought, would make it possible to redeem the nation. For him, Yitzhak Rabin was a privileged sign, and Amir sought to position Rabin as someone operating outside the intersubjective space but independently within the networks of objective presences as well. Amir, who was opposed to the government's peace process and viewed it as a catastrophe for the Jewish people, identified the process as stemming from a specific author. Therefore, when he sought to arrest the process, he aimed at the man he considered its author. In his guerrilla action, Amir was relying on a double identification of a privileged sign. He identified himself as someone who could operate outside the space of discourse and the networks of objective presences to liquidate the man that he considered to be acting also outside this space and these networks. Amir established an arena in which he and the prime minister could contend among themselves as to who would shape the course of reality.

The crime perpetrated by Yigal Amir, being the guerrilla action of a single individual, was in the nature of an eventuation that isn't compounded within the controlled sequences of times and events and therefore cannot be predicated on causal explanations of purpose and realization. This eventuation sent shock waves through the central junctions of several fields of discourse and interrupted the sequences of time in a manner that made necessary a massive mustering of resources to immediately rehabilitate them. Within scarcely minutes, new and dense networks of new intersubjective spaces of confession and national mourning were generated, which made visible whoever refused to plug into them. The actions undertaken to renew the flow of statements in the channels earmarked for that purpose, as well as their proper linkage, were performed with surprising rapidity, also making possible the creation of new visual fields that could be managed and supervised.

PHOTOGRAPHY AND CRITICAL POSITION

To this day, photography takes part in the practices of both governmentality and critique. The camera lens—which, ever since the invention of photography, has often replaced the human eye—is generally represented as being in the hands of the subject who operates it. The camera lens, on its own, cannot assume the critical point of view formulated by Foucault, unless a subject organizes what is seen and endows it with meaning. Only when it is governed in connection with a logic typical of the disciplinary site and operated by a reflexive subject can the camera lens take part in what Foucault terms as a "critical ontology of ourselves." Only then is it possible "to treat it not in the manner of a theory, a doctrine, nor even a fixed corpus of accumulated knowledge, [it will be possible] to treat it as an approach, an ethos, a philosophical life in which the critique of what we do is, at one and the same time, a historical analysis of the boundaries imposed on us and an examination of their possible crossing" (Foucault 1994, 4:577).

Photography has made a unique and complementary contribution to the attempts to regulate the social body, as well as to attempts to criticize these attempts. At the disciplinary sites devoted to teaching (schools), to healing (clinics), and to punishment (prisons), the training and domestication of the individual have also been undertaken: deviations have been rectified and adapted to a standard model. Since its first appearance, photography has taken part in these practices.[23] The homology between photography and the disciplinary site was due to the conception of a common intersubjective space that served as a necessary premise for any encounter between the intervening agent at the disciplinary site and the "client" or between the photographer and the photographed object.[24] In this sense, photography fit the disciplinary site like a glove. Photography made it possible to gather knowledge about

---

23. On photography and statistics, see Benjamin (1978). On criminological uses of photography, see Sekula (1989). On psychiatric uses of photography, see Huberman (1982). On military uses of photography, see Virilio (1989).

24. Out of this conception developed the positivist rhetoric of photography, which reached a climax in Barthes's book by virtue of his expression: "It was there" (Barthes, 1980).

"the social body" of the individual. Its fixed format, the rhetoric of authenticity it made possible ("It was there"), the consistency of the process, its mechanical and standard means of production and reproduction, the camera's accessibility and virtuosity (which doesn't demand a long period of specialization)—all these made the task easier and its performance efficient and systematic.

The characteristics listed above made it possible to arrive at photographic results that, on the one hand, maintained some standard qualities, while on the other hand preserved the uniqueness of the individual and the exclusivity of the event. The data provided by the camera are easy to classify, categorize, collate, and cross-reference. Photography indeed grew along with its own archive. Photography as archive offered central governing positions to manage this body of knowledge. The police investigator or the doctor are seemingly situated in a control tower, in the center of the archive, with all the data at their fingertips or at least provided with the means and authority to collect the necessary data. Here, too, as at any other disciplinary site, new knowledge is manufactured from prior knowledge. The police investigator can measure and compare profiles, run through all the suspects documented in the archive like in a movie, and draw the necessary conclusions.

The perspective from the tower or from the control room at the photographic archive is shaped by two modes of disciplining photography. On the one hand, the photographic act is subordinate to the act of a subject who governs its visual field and testifies to it; on the other hand, photography produces testimonies that are gathered in an archive, whose logic is, in principle, similar to that of other disciplinary sites. However, photography, like the disciplinary site, has from the start incarnated both governmentality and critique—both the common, unique space of the direct point of view and its cellular breakup into private units.

Beside the two disciplining photographic practices arose two critical practices. The first wishes to introduce the camera into prohibited visual fields that attempt to remain concealed from public view and bar the camera's entry. To take one example, press photographers' coverage of the Intifada was often a kind of critical act, involving illegal entry into areas defined by the army as off limits. The second practice seeks to undermine two basic principles of archive logic—(1) a central point of view (panoptism) and (2) a homogeneous table and single classificatory scheme. It accomplishes this by "subversively" creating countless private archives that disrupt the panoptism of the point of view and the homogeneity of the classificatory space. The multiplicity of points of view and the various photographic angles make it possible to better utilize qualities inherent in photography, such as the manipulation of exposure or enlargement.

Alex Levac, *Bus Line 300*, black and white photograph,
1983

Here's another example, again taken from Israeli press photography. Following
the 1983 capture of a Palestinian terrorist group that hijacked a bus, the army
spokesperson announced that all the terrorists who'd participated in the action had
been shot to death in the firefight between them and army forces. Many press photographers were present in the area at the time. One of them, Alex Levac, exposed
in his laboratory a picture showing one of the terrorists being led off alive by two Israelis. There was no doubt that someone had subsequently murdered this man. The
exposure led to a political scandal, to the establishment of a commission of inquiry,

and to an upheaval within the Israeli security service. Here, too, photography used and realized the rhetoric of freedom of speech and the public's right to know. This is photography as testimony, as a critique of power and an opportunity to restrict it. In both examples, the individual photographer can assume a critical position toward the centralistic supervisory position. But even the photographer's critical position, like Foucault's conception of the critic analyzed above, is constructed into the disciplinary logic of supervision and management, as a site in which the subject is governed and yet governs his own actions.

THE ETHOS OF THE CAMERA

All of this refers to the camera's action in the intersubjective space of discourse and action. The camera operates within power relations in the space of governmentality and critique: the subject who uses the camera confirms himself as an "author" of a photographic enunciation. But the camera has another ethos as well—its very own ethos, the ethos of an instrument that interpellates the subject and is part of a network of blind objective presences. Desubjectivization here consists of going beyond the subject and transitioning to the object and its special ethos. In the context of the present discussion, this transition to the object means a transition from Foucault to Baudrillard.

Foucault poses critique as opposition to mechanisms of governmentality—mechanisms that produce subjects. Baudrillard poses critique as opposition to mechanisms of "realizing the world" that bring material and social reality under control by means of observation and action: "All of modernity has as its purpose to bring about the rise of this real world, the liberation of man and of the real energies. . . . Today, the world has become real beyond all our hopes. A shift has taken place in the real and the rational data thanks to their own realization" (Baudrillard, 1995, 96). Foucault and Baudrillard counter the subjectivization of the individual and realization of the world with resistance in the form of desubjectivization. With Foucault, the struggle to desubjectivize (to restrict the subordination of subjects by governing systems) takes place in the intersubjective space of discourse. For Baudrillard, desubjectivization is not a struggle but an unintended process that takes place in a space composed of networks of objective presences and that results in the total renunciation of the illusion that either subject or free will exists. These differences between Foucault and Baudrillard can be formulated in terms of the differences between the intersubjective space of discourse and the space composed of networks defined above.[25] Different

---

25. These differences also express themselves in the conception of time, as I attempt to show below when I return to the scene of Rabin's assassination and analyze the videotape that "documented" it.

contemporary intersubjective spaces are conducted along a temporal one-way street, moving from the "before" to the "after." The space composed of networks of objective presences, on the other hand, is multidirectional; its temporality cannot be governed or managed. Anyone who momentarily imposes an intersubjective space on it and attempts to act within it is subject, at the same time, to the changes that take place in the network.

For Baudrillard, the work of critique takes place in the process of desubjectivization itself. But he attributes this process to the world and to the objects that make up the world. According to Baudrillard, each object has a destination, a function it is meant to fulfill, but its destiny is exactly opposite—to deviate from that destination, to divert it, to betray it, to cease carrying out the function entrusted to it: "This is their [the objects'] destiny, in the sense that this is what always happens to them; this is our destiny, in the sense that this is what always happens to us" (Baudrillard, 1988, 80). We are at the mercy of objects that do not fulfill their task, that betray their purpose time and time again.

A destination exists in a given "container" of time. It is the end of a preplanned itinerary, a telos that endows every station on the way to its realization with a meaning. The road to the destination passes through a homogeneous time-space unit that can be observed, either to supervise it or to criticize and restrict such supervision. By contrast, destiny is the implosion of all purposes, an involution of time, an event that transcends any prior control or possible observation. Between destination and destiny there is a constant state of lack of focus, an incongruity, such as that between reality and thought: "A certain type of thinking has solidarity with reality. It emerges from the supposition that there is a referent for the idea and a possible ideation of reality. . . . The other form of thinking is eccentric with regard to reality, alien to dialectics, alien even to critical thinking" (Baudrillard, 1995, 140). The destination cannot govern destiny; thought cannot overtake reality. In both cases, the focus can't be sharpened. So, too, with regard to photography.[26] Sometimes the camera may

---

26. In Foucault, on the other hand, the dialectic of the visible and the invisible is maintained, as well as the view that isn't fixated on a field of observation. The nature of the unseeing can potentially become realized and turn into the seeing. In place of this, photography makes it possible to think about relations of absolute transparency: everything is present and nothing is hidden, in principle. This is true of death, too, which is not only the result of what Foucault calls *biopower* (a binary system of thinking of things in only one of two ways—to take or to give life). Death itself undergoes spatialization and networking, and terror can overtake it at any point in the network, without limitations, without relations of visibility and invisibility, without designating power as a potential and then realizing it. In this sense terror is transparent. When it appears, it is present. It doesn't act within the dialectics of present or potentially present. It doesn't need to penetrate the borders of quarantined sites. Terror is like a virus that spreads throughout a system.

follow reality, and sometimes vice versa. The camera has a defined purpose, which the photographer attempts to realize. But it also has a destiny, of which the photographer may become the victim. In the intersubjective space, the camera that is operated from the position of a subject follows the event. At the end of the day, when the pictures are printed in the newspaper or placed in the album, two points of reference in time are created: the event and the photograph. In the space composed of networks of objective presences, subjects don't really govern the camera they're operating. The camera is always already there as part of the network in which the event will take place, and it is capable of reversing the points of reference in time: the documentation can reveal the event that destiny has summoned for the camera there situated. (This was the case of Ronny Kempler's camera, which documented Rabin's assassination.)

These relations—between thought and reality, destination and destiny, event and photograph—are not conducted solely in intersubjective space, where subjects' organized points of view may suggest that everything is under control. But when individuals assume the observer's position by overseeing a visual field, suddenly they find themselves not only observed by other subjects (a reversal of intersubjective relations) but also activated by something else—something that attracts, seduces, or repels. In this situation the governing relations between subject and object are reversed. The object is a presence that can have no point of view attributed to it and that cannot be subordinated to a point of view or synchronized with the path leading to the destination. For this a subject is required, but the subject is now being conducted according to the order of things. Therefore, the reversal of relations between object and subject makes it impossible to assume a homogeneous space-time, in which things flow according to the inclination of time, preparing themselves, as it were, for history's point of view, represented by the authorized power or by its critics, which will weave it into a seamless story. But the historian, news reporter, politician, and critic are fixated on a photographic screen as on an intersubjective space, in which the active presence of objects, their allure or repulsiveness, and the presence of the camera itself cannot be seen. They seat themselves in photography's darkroom, running and rerunning their films of reality to interpret it, seeking to endow it with a form that shall eternally conceal the various and peculiar forms it has taken, before their very eyes.

THE SUBJECT OF HISTORY

The subjects of history, of the media, and of critique are constituted in an intersubjective space of discourse and action. In that space, critique belongs to the critics.

However, their critique also takes part in a space composed of networks of presences, but there it appears as part of the configuration of aesthetic relations that shape various networks of presences. These relations change in accordance to movements in the network—which are expressed by changes in the densities of the various points—and are diffused in various ways from points of view in the intersubjective space. Sometimes these movements are diffused as seeming waves of critique without critics. The presences are points of no view, relay stations bound to be activated by the network in which they are intertwined. They are liable at any moment to turn into signs that exist in a space of intersubjective interpretation. The assassin Yigal Amir was a critic who sought to act solely within the intersubjective space. Whereas Yitzhak Rabin—chief of staff of the Israel Defense Forces (IDF) during the Six-Day War, defense minister during the Intifada, and prime minister during the Oslo agreements—was at the end of his days the product of a critical field devoid of critics.

Yitzhak Rabin was one of the creators of an intersubjective space of discourse and action—the occupation of Palestinian territories—and one of those who attempted to impose it on a given territory as the only legitimate space of discourse and action (and quite often succeeded). The intersubjective space that was constituted under the occupation functioned as a grand disciplinary site: it could be observed and controlled. However, this space—which for many years was governed with a high and mighty hand and which has known much bloodshed, misery, and injustice—could never have been reduced to the tangle of networks of presence, of which it was also composed. After twenty-seven years of occupation, at the start of his second term in office as prime minister, Rabin began to advance the peace process, the destination of which was to end the occupation. This change in Rabin's position can be depicted as the adoption of a critical position with regard to the discourse, of which he himself was one of the creators. The change in Rabin's position was depicted by many in terms of a personal process of maturation, a sort of late blooming that led the man to view the world differently and to seek to change it in light of his new point of view. The competition over the narrative of Rabin's development—as an authentic author or as one galvanized to action under the influence of others—is a competition among various authors in cultural fields of production (politics, literature, art, and so on). In each of these fields an exacting history is conducted that knows who did what and when and who was influenced by whom and in what. These descriptions preserve the distinction between the point of view and the object of critique ("reality") in a way that makes it possible to stabilize and fix the one or the other and write their history, so that the critical positions in regard to it can be measured. These descriptions also assume a causal sequence, stretching between the point of view to the world adopted by the individual (Yitzhak Rabin) and the re-alization of the plan incarnate in this point of view, along with direct interference (the purpose of which is to change the world in light of that point of view).

In place of this, Yitzhak Rabin can be described as someone whose point of view did not become fixed and who did not fix a defined object for observation and manipulation, which could be managed otherwise or criticized. What has been de-picted as a change in the intersubjective space—Rabin as the man who imposed the occupation and as the man who imposed liberation from it—seems the result of a re-treat of the panoptic point of view and of the will that was purported to be omnipo-tent. This retreat implies a recognition of the limitations of active subjects and of the power of other networks, of which he, the prime minister of Israel (seemingly a pref-erential point of view), was merely a part. It seems that Rabin acted with the under-standing that it had become impossible to continue conducting Israeli policy as if the world were made up only of an intersubjective space of discourse and action.[27] In ret-rospect, Rabin seems to have acknowledged the tension between his role on the stage of history as someone imposing his preferential point of view on an intersubjective space of discourse and action, and the role this point of view plays by dint of being a presence in networks of presences, which neither Rabin the man nor Rabin the prime minister could always observe or manipulate as he pleased.[28] In the State of Is-rael's and the Palestinian Authority's intersubjective space, the Israeli army is being replaced by Palestinian policemen, and torture chambers are being turned into mu-seums. The hegemonic historical or political discourse represents these actions as "making peace" or as "the end of the occupation." But each such action is inspired by one of the organizing visions of the stage of history but doesn't lead to its desig-nated destination on that stage. Each such action also produces movements in vari-ous networks of presence, movements with a destiny of their own, which sometimes converges with their designated destination—and sometimes doesn't. We may ex-amine them as actions toward destinations; we may analyze them and adopt a criti-cal position toward them. We can also view them as aesthetic configurations of random movements in various networks that enable goods, ideas, people, and things to move through space. These movements create opportunities for the production

---

27. I'm not speaking about Rabin's intentions but about the meaning of his acts.

28. It is important to note that the State of Israel, near the time of the assassination and shortly there-after, executed two Palestinians. The purpose of these acts was to get rid of the authors of terrorist actions carried out against the state's citizens. The assumption that underlay both these executions was that elimi-nation of the authors would lead to elimination of their "works."

of new intersubjective spaces, in which some have realized the governing position and some have realized the critical position. After the fact—always after the fact—whoever has exploited one of these opportunities and adopted one of these positions finds it necessary to justify the specific aesthetic configuration in which he finds himself intertwined and to describe it in consequential terms of action and discourse. From this justification arise both the ideology of established power and the ideology of critique.

As described above, Yigal Amir sought to withdraw from a few networks, those from which liberation was apparently more meaningful to him for the purpose of assuming the critical position. To realize this withdrawal, he actually had to withdraw as well from intersubjective spaces that constitute links in those same networks. On the evening of the assassination, even when Yigal Amir encountered various networks of presences, he transformed each presence he encountered into a sign from heaven and interpreted movements in the network as divine proofs. He arrived at the plaza with a pistol in his pocket. Approaching the plaza, which was already crowded with a hundred thousand people, he saw this mass and comprehended it as the boundary of his belonging. The demonstrators appeared to be a sign of his nonbelonging: "I roamed through the crowd and saw the emptiness. I didn't understand this language. It was Arabic. And then I went to the parking lot area" (Amir quoted in Zvi Barel, 1996). At the plaza, Amir received confirmation of the foreignness of the mass, of his own alienation; confirmation of his being detached from any network, of being there alone with his destination.

From the moment he withdrew from the various networks, from the various intersubjective spaces in which he was acting, his destination led him onward. The destination was no longer the product of a feverish mind but an actuality that gradually became manifest in a demarcated location. This destination had previously escaped the regulatory mechanisms in the intersubjective space and was immune from the supervisory gaze of policemen and friends alike. From Amir's standpoint, his purpose—Rabin's assassination—was the pinnacle of critical practice with regard to history—history as a clear visual field, which provides select individuals with the opportunity to realize their point of view in action.[29] At the same time, history (or God, as its metasubject) transforms the hero, the select individual, into an instrument for the realization of the purpose. In his view, Amir is a critical subject because he sees what others cannot see; he is a hero because he's willing to forfeit his life to act

---

29. See Derrida's discussion of the force of law (Derrida, 1990).

according to what he sees. But what he sees and does turns him into an instrument in the hands of the "real subject." For him, the struggle to assume the position of an autonomous subject isn't the be-all and end-all of being critical. Being critical means assuming the position of an autonomous subject to be worthy of the mission entrusted to him from outside, canceling the autonomy of the human subject before the divine subject: "I said, if God (*Hashem*) wants, then I will do it and go and exact vengeance."

Amir wanted to eliminate Rabin—whom he considered the "author" of a false peace—and believed that Rabin, like himself, was not enmeshed in the mass crowding the plaza: Rabin, too, stood outside the networks of presences and was acting from the position of a subject desirous of omnipotence. In his testimony, Amir reported that he removed his yarmulka on arrival at the plaza in order not to be identified as a rightist. He sought to evade recognition by the crowd, which classifies individuals as presences belonging to the right or left, to such or other high-risk group. In place of this, he sought to position himself as a central protagonist on a stage of history that he himself had conjured. He made the crowd transparent and excluded it from his visual field, the visual field of history, which seeks to impose an intersubjective space on the entire network. It was an alienated, foreign crowd that spoke a language he didn't know. Facing this crowd, moving aimlessly about the plaza, Amir delineated boundaries of subjectivity, boundaries between the self and the other. In his visual field there was room for Yitzhak Rabin (flanked by Shimon Peres), for the "people" as a historical subject, and for himself. Amir delineated boundaries for these subjects, attributed an interiority and a history to them. From his standpoint, these subjects were sort of virtual disciplinary sites whose actions could be managed, who could be educated and led to the most worthy realization of their purpose.

According to Amir, he and Yitzhak Rabin are the authors of actions, things, and thoughts. Rabin, as author of the peace—as the man who managed it, supervised it, and led it to what Amir identified as the "sin of the Golden Calf"—is responsible for the actions of the people. Amir, too, like Rabin, is a loop of subjectivity, no longer merely another nameless individual, one among the mass, but one capable of being the author of actions—perhaps even acts of redemption, if he should be so lucky. Amir also assumes the omnipresent point of view of he who sees and knows all—who stands above the people, who knows them, who can judge their sins and mete out punishment: "My feelings died three years ago. I saw my people going to rack and ruin, like a mother who sees her children being killed. One must protest in some way" (Amir quoted in Yarkoni, 1996). In the space of discourse and action established by Amir that evening at the plaza, there stood only Yitzhak Rabin and himself—the one seeking to govern the people with an understanding of the boundaries of governance, the other seeking to redeem the people from this governance. Amir imposed on both of them a fateful encounter—taking place as it did in the glaring light, under the watchful eye of a divine supervision, suspended above them as in the day of judgment.

To prepare for the big day, Amir trained himself to conquer emotion and devote himself to the purpose at hand, toward the realization of the project. He disciplined himself as an exemplary model, as one who knows to differentiate between emotion and intellect, as he said during his trial: "Certainly I didn't act out of gut feeling. One doesn't perform a mitzvah out of gut feeling. I do it because it is moral. When I was arrested at the site, I did not resist. I had performed my duty" (Yarkoni, 1996). Three times previously, Amir had arrived where Rabin was located with the purpose of assassinating him but failed to do so. Heaven placed signs in his path only when he had arrived at a reflexive and critical maturity, only when he had succeeded in transforming himself into an exemplary model of the people's discipline. This model was opposed to the deterioration of the people and of Yitzhak Rabin—whom Amir described as a subject gone sour, who'd become weak and given to harmful influences (such as Peres's). In Amir's eyes, the multitude of police officers at the plaza became transparent. From his point of view, he could recognize only Rabin, the police as divine messengers protecting Amir (from the policemen themselves, who might have identified him), and the camera, or divine supervision, which would recognize him as having interpreted the signs correctly. Amir wanted to eliminate Rabin from the arena under the eye of divine supervision.[30] Amir related that he didn't know whether the police would allow him to remain or recognize him as dangerous and remove him from the scene. After standing in the lot for ten minutes and not being ordered to leave, he interpreted this, too, as a sign, and thus posed himself once more as an interpreting subject facing the signs sent to him by divine supervision: "I said to myself that if a policeman should make me leave the spot, it would be a sign that the right time hadn't arrived yet. I spoke with one of the policemen about Aviv Geffen[31] to neutralize the possibility that he would make me leave the spot" (Amir quoted in

---

30. It is hard to avoid a comparison between the story of Cain and Abel and the arena sketched by Yigal Amir, in which he and Yitzhak Rabin competed for God's love and acknowledgment of their actions. Rabin, who was the more beloved, became the object slated for removal by Amir, who was subsequently "accorded," as one of the judges put it in the verdict, a mark of Cain to bear on his forehead for the rest of his life.

31. Aviv Gefen, a young Israeli singer who sang that evening during the peace rally.

Brener, 1996, p. 9). This sign joined other signs, such as the fact that he was permitted to wait approximately forty minutes in the lot where the prime minister's car was parked, without being evacuated beyond the police fences like the other civilians. He sought to achieve divine recognition of his act: "I am not sorry for Rabin. I wanted heaven to see that someone from the people did this."

FLOODLIT ARENA

Amir acted in the light of day, in a visual field with total visibility: street lights, cameras, police, reporters, security men, a crowd, and divine supervision, of course, which oversees all actions. Amir did not seek to hide: he acted in a space that was all light. He was master of an omnipresent point of view and an omnipotent position of action, and therefore he could take and give life. To Peres he gave life, from Rabin he took it.[32] Death in broad daylight is nothing new in the space of networks.[33] In such catastrophic cases, individuals who come to harm have no specific name or address; the determining factor is their location in the network. They happened to be at the site of the event. Death that does have a specific name and address is also not a rare occurrence—underworld killings, for example. But death eventuated in broad daylight that has a name and address known in advance: this indeed is a rare thing. Even more rarely does a critical interpreter take the authority to pronounce such a sentence of death and carry it out by himself, in the city square, where it can be seen by all on the way to redemption.

In Amir's visual field, he and Yitzhak Rabin faced each other; beside them were the people, between perdition and redemption; and the eye of divine supervision was the interpretive law. For Amir, his vision existed independently of the assassination site in the plaza. One might say that he was searching for a location for a screenplay that already existed in his mind. He previously tried two other locations: the Yad Vashem memorial and a new highway intersection inaugurated by Prime Minister Rabin. Finally he chose the center stage of the public plaza and of history, where Rabin already stood and would be replaced, in a single act, by Amir himself. The crowd watched him, cameras were everywhere, and, above all, the eye of divine supervision observed him. Until the moment of the assassination, the intersubjective

---

32. Amir reported that he could have attacked Peres before Rabin arrived. But since he knew that he wouldn't be able to waylay both men, he preferred to wait for the more worthy and precise—from his aspect—target.

33. Usually this form of death takes the form of catastrophes, such as suicide bombings or the artillery bombardment of Lebanon, which are characterized by their contagious action with regard to the crowd as a network of presences.

space of discourse and action, in which Amir was destined to be the prime minister's assassin, was devoid of a defined place. At the moment of the assassination, this imaginary space became palpable in the arena by the plaza.

THE AMATEUR'S VIDEO

The assassination site—the perfect arena, which interpellated Yigal Amir on the evening of November 4, 1995—also interpellated another individual roaming the plaza that evening, filled with a premonition of impending disaster. He sensed "a feeling in the air that something might go wrong, I have no proofs or evidence. . . . There was tension, I had a bad feeling."[34] This was the amateur photographer, Ronny Kempler. He was also intertwined in the network of the mass, but, being equipped with a video camera, he also had a point of view on the crowd. He saw the rally through the camera lens, by means of which he imposed an intersubjective space of discourse and action on the plaza. Kempler later related that that evening he imagined his movie—the movie of his life. In his mind's eye, he directed a movie about the prime minister's assassination eventuated before his camera at a peace rally in the plaza. Kempler assumed the position of neutral observer, who with his camera brings samples of reality directly onto the private home television screen. He sought to document another rally, which would join the collection of movies he'd photographed over the past year, featuring political figures.

Kempler did not interfere with the events. But, all the same, he did have in his mind—so he said—an exact screenplay, in which the prime minister's assassination was eventuated before his camera. Throughout the rally, he roamed the plaza with his camera and guided it toward the final scene: political figures pass in front of the camera lens one after another, until the prime minister is captured in the frame. The final scene was planned down to the last detail. He would film the prime minister leaving the frame. Instead, the video ended uncunningly with another disappearance: the prime minister vanished from Kempler's view not only as a result of being shot but also because Kempler flinched and ducked precisely when his camera was supposed to record the prime minister falling to the ground. A double retreat: two points of view retraced from each other precisely at the moment of impact when the sound of the bullets connected them in time. Kempler was convinced that destiny had toyed with him. Yet his hand on the camera—moved, perhaps, by destiny—had toyed with Yigal Amir as well. More than once during the film, it seems that eye

---

34. This description was given by Ronny Kempler on the day his video was shown on Israeli television.

contact was established between Amir and Kempler. For a span of fifteen minutes, Ronny Kempler stood with his camera in an observer's position overlooking the very site that was to become the scene of the assassination. As in any suspense film, an exposed back in the first act means murder in the last act. The assassin, as well, had been already caught by the lens, captured in the center of the frame. Amir wanted to be seen, at any cost. His actions were directed toward the greater eye of the divine supervision. By chance Kempler provided him with one such eye. And Kempler's screenplay became (cinematic) reality.

The Israeli media tended to present the videotape as a testimonial document.[35] Kempler's attitude toward it was much the same. The film was comprehended as documentation photographed from a point of view that was external to the event and that focused on the scene of the assassination. The images that flickered on the screen functioned as signs that experts of various kinds, either more or less authorized, were invited to isolate, arrest (*arrêt sur image*), and focus with attendant enlargement. The movie returned to the event the dimension of darkness it had lacked—the dimension of opaque signs that must be deciphered. The movie made it possible to create a space of discourse in which every element is a sign that requires interpretation. Every movement perceived on the television screen or in its space of discourse—a space that included Yigal Amir as chief protagonist—became the end of a causal sequence that had to be reconstructed and deciphered. Yigal Amir was caught in the act. He did not attempt to hide; he did not act behind the scenes. But the visibility of the assassination, its senselessness and lack of purpose, was what everyone sought to deny or disavow to discover what "really" lay concealed behind it.

The videotape plunged everyone—investigators, reporters, the home audience—into the darkroom of history. The movie could be rerun back and forth to show how security plans collapsed, how Yigal Amir sat in one spot waiting for the prime minister without anyone paying attention to him or moving him from his place. The movie demarcated clear boundaries for interpretation and also determined what was worthy of interpretation. This framing focuses observation on what is seen on the screen while the camera itself is reduced to an instrument in the hands of the observing subject who documented the event. Implicit in the video's presentation to the public was a two-stage conception of time that unequivocally differentiated between the event (which "was there") and the documentation that recorded it for posterity. In this view, the assassination, product of a distinct causal sequence that was connected with Amir and

---

35. Kempler's tape was broadcast on Israeli television, with extensive commentary, a month after the assassination—a delay that has never been explained.

certain political conditions, had presented itself to Kempler, who—with his camera—was depicted as having been positioned outside the event. Anyhow, the discussion focuses on what the camera shows. The interpreters are trying to extricate additional signs from the film. Observation will lead to a story similar to Kennedy's assassination, perhaps. However, Kennedy was shot from concealment, and the story of his assassination is full of enigmas.[36] Yigal Amir shot Rabin in view of the camera, in view of the security men and the police officers. The presence of these latter was a part of the visibility in which it was possible for Amir to carry out the assassination. Generally speaking, visibility was a protagonist in Rabin's assassination.

The causal readings, by their very nature, ignore the actual "eventuation" of the event, its unique and purposeless departure from any prior causal order and from any pattern of meaning that can be produced for it in retrospect. Thus the TV audience was invited to be immersed in a murky film with quiet abstract pictures (that can hardly be deciphered without the help of experts or digital treatment) flickering before their eyes.

Let us move slightly away from this view of the television screen and reposition Kempler's camera at the site of the assassination as the one that saw Amir and was also seen by him. This is not the camera that bears witness to an event from outside but the one that frames the stage ahead of the action and creates the space in which the assassination was eventuated, outside any known causal sequence. Hence the camera is not an instrument in the hands of a subject who controls it but an object with an independent existence and a destiny of its own, which is capable of contaminating the destinies of others who are caught in its path.

Amir, as I already mentioned, wanted to be seen, at any cost—even at the cost of failing in his mission. Yigal Amir's being visible to all was not dependent on Ronny Kempler's accidental camera. Amir's actions were directed toward the greater eye, the eye of divine supervision, the eye of history. By chance Kempler provided him with one such eye. Television, which day in and day out crams history into a single small screen, provided him with another eye. The assassination was visible, it refused to function as a secret, as an antisign, an ultimate act purporting to distance any interpretation or interpreter not versed in the decipherment of signs from heaven. The signs were seen by Amir and guided him to carry out the assassination, and signs made it possible to produce Rabin's assassination as a "bigger than life" tragedy. Signs were recognized and, seen in retrospect, were already in place, in view of the

---

36. On Kennedy's assassination, see Oliver Stone's 1992 film *JFK*.

camera and in view of the assassin, who was first to interpret them and transform them into the background to his action.

Attempts at decipherment require testimonies, solid evidence to prove causal links, which the state, the law, and the media can better administer and govern. The camera's entry into the arena, I argue, detaches the event from the intersubjective space and its own causal order. It frames the event's rupture of the causal order and makes its fatality more palpable. But fatal, entirely coincidental links, devoid of intent or purpose, have no place in such explanations. They cannot be observed, spoken of, or interfered with. They avoid any regime or management. Such is the coincidental and surprising connection created between Ronny Kempler's camera and Yigal Amir's pistol, Kempler's identity as the photographer of the assassination and Amir's identity as the assassin—the connection that gives rise to the model of the event as meaningless, though possessing an aesthetic form all the same.

The explanations of Yigal Amir's motives searched for a source or reason that could be identified, such as Halakhic decrees by fundamentalist rabbis or, in more general terms, "the atmosphere of incitement"—the Halakhic discourse or turgid air as conductors of murder. Any connection between such as these and the event that took place in the plaza—the moment when Yigal Amir played the role of assassin before the camera and pulled the trigger—is very loose, if it exists at all. Many have spoken in its behalf, but nobody has yet managed even to describe it in persuasive fashion, let alone prove it. Such ideological or religious motives can also be attributed to many of Yigal Amir's friends, who underwent a course of "training" similar to his. Nevertheless, at least to this day, none of them has been suspected of assassinating or attempting to assassinate a prime minister. Neither has the examination of Yigal Amir's psychological profile rounded out the picture or singled him out from among all those who grew up with him in the same ideological environment. Words, however great their potential for incitement, do not generally translate, just like that, on one autumn evening, into pulling the trigger. Lea Rabin, the prime minister's widow, claimed there was no reason she should see the movie; after all, she "was there." She had been an eyewitness to the event. In saying this she identifies herself with the photographer of the movie: two eyewitnesses to the same event. But Kempler, who dropped the camera a moment after the shots were fired, who raged at destiny for choosing him to photograph the assassination, was not just an eyewitness to what "was there." The camera cannot be reduced to the status of a provider of testimony. It always also generates—not by itself, of course—the very events it has come to document. The camera's entry into the arena detaches the event from the intersubjective space and its own causal order. For viewers watching the tape on television, the camera didn't provide any new causal explanation: it merely framed the event's rupture of the causal order and made its fatality more palpable.

Kempler is one of the heroes who were present at the site of Rabin's assassination. Seconds after the shooting, after Amir played the role of assassin in a movie written and directed by Kempler, the latter tried to break away from the camera in horror. It was an instinctive reaction similar to pulling one's hand away from red-hot iron, attempting to interrupt the circle of mutual recognition that had brought Amir and Kempler there, face to face—the assassin and the photographer of the assassination. When interviewed, Kempler did not dismiss the possibility that Amir might have noticed him: "Could be. He was here a long time, and I was here a long time. I had a bad feeling." (Kempler quoted in Anat Meidan, 1995, p. 7). The arena was constituted; the camera framed the exposed back and created the space in which the assassination was eventuated, outside any known causal sequence. Whoever analyzes the movie within the framework of a linear conception of time, within a two-stage framework of time, positing first Amir the assassin and later followed by Kempler as the photographer of the assassination, still believes that events are prior to the camera and take place apart from it. The moment Kempler meets Amir, he is always the photographer of the assassination. At that moment Amir is always Rabin's assassin. The moment of mutual recognition between them—the coincidental encounter that brought both heroes to the same crime scene—is what fixed their identity, as a result of their mutual constitution, as photographer and assassin.

In the act of assassination, Amir transformed Rabin into an absolute presence, an object. Amir, who had realized—much too seriously, one must add—his critical position (critique as desubjectivization), found himself in the final analysis shackled, in both the literal and theoretical sense of the word, to a reality composed of networks of presences. This is the reality in which the action of subjects doesn't take place independently of the action of objects, and the latter may even be better able to act. The reality in which Yitzhak Rabin was intertwined as an object turned on Yigal Amir and organized itself with great rapidity, contrary to any expectation Amir might have expressed when he sought to master it. Rabin was deprived of the opportunity to continue maintaining the position of subject and to act from that position according to plan. However, his lethal transformation into an object, a fetish, a ghost who continues to haunt Israeli politics, only intensified the effects of his presence in the networks in which he'd been previously intertwined as well.

THE FLOODLIT ARENA [OF MURDER]

Aïm Deuelle Luski, *The Arena of Murder,* photograph
produced by the north-west-south-east camera, 1996

The network negates the subject's point of view, voids its position, and murders the object as a stabilized and silent presence, with regard to which the subject can constitute itself. We live in a world where the object has a destiny of its own and can influence other destinies. The subject cannot overcome it.

THE PHOTOS

The north-south-east-west (NSEW) camera was developed by Aïm Deuelle Luski and presented for the first time in Nir Nader's and Erez Harodi's exhibition *The Gallery of Education.* The camera consists of a simple wooden box with four openings made out of crossed razors, each in the middle of one of the box's sides. The box is placed in and covered by another box, which allows for a controlled exposure of the openings. The four openings are exposed together, and light enters the inner box from four directions at once. It falls on two sides of a negative that form an angle of 45 degrees in relation to the openings. The camera was developed for taking photographs of the border zone between East and West Jerusalem, where the demarcating line between the Palestinian and Israeli city has been gradually erased in the course of (then) twenty-seven years of Israeli occupation. I thought that the NSEW camera could serve to illustrate the unique, unsynchronized encounter

Aïm Deuelle Luski, *The Arena of Murder,* photograph
produced by the north-west-south-east camera, 1996

Aïm Deuelle Luski, *The Arena of Murder,* photograph
produced by the north-west-south-east camera, 1996

THE FLOODLIT ARENA [OF MURDER]

Aïm Deuelle Luski, *The Arena of Murder,* photograph
produced by the north-west-south-east camera, 1996

among the four points of view presented in this chapter—of the victim, of the assassin, of the amateur photographer, and finally mine, in the author's position. I
asked Aïm Deuelle Luski to operate the NSEW camera at the scene of the assassination. The four photographs contain segments of visual information about the
plaza, juxtaposed in a vertigo of points of view.

CHAPTER 9

SAVE AS JerusalemS

1

Jerusalem, as everyone knows, is a name of a city. But what is this city whose name is Jerusalem? That is a more difficult question. There is an earthly city whose name is Jerusalem, and there is also a heavenly one. There is a Jerusalem of stone and a Jerusalem of paper, a Jerusalem of iron, and a Jerusalem of gold. There is a Christian, a Muslim, and a Jewish Jerusalem. Evidently there is also Jerusalem as the capital of a Palestinian state, which is but a dream and a symbol of a national struggle, as well as Jerusalem as the capital of the State of Israel, which claims today to encompass all the other cities in one city "united forever."

"Jerusalem" is the hero of this chapter—Jerusalem in quotation marks, as a name for a heterogeneous ensemble of spaces, events, and meanings. This ensemble includes the struggle over the city's geographical and historical borders, its transformations along these two axes of time and space, the mapping of the city, the nature and structure of its urban networks (both physical and virtual, those that are contained within it and those that cross it and spread far beyond its geographical borders), and finally, the politics of naturalization and citizenship in and of the city, the city as a subject, and the subjects of the city. I try to argue that any discussion of "Jerusalem" must encompass all these aspects at once and account for their interrelations. To understand the (human) reality of the city, one must understand the (discursive) reality of its name and through it ponder relations between maps and warfare, between history and strategies of producing truth and subjectivity, between the inscription in concrete space and transcendent temporality. I try to touch on this complexity by way of theoretical interpretation of Foucault's conception of space and spatialization, focusing on the notion of heterotopia (a space composed of different and contradictory layers). I relate this interpretation to an analysis of the administration of Jerusalem's urban space and to two artistic projects of Israeli artists—an itinerary traced by Sigalit Landau from the Israeli Museum to the Palestinian neighborhood El Azariya and an interactive map of one of its neighborhoods prepared by Aya & Gal.

During the three decades and a half of the Israeli occupation of East Jerusalem the organization of space and the distribution of representations in the public space of Jerusalem have been in the hands of one authority, one body determining the rules of the place—the rules according to which Jerusalem is governed and preserved as an archive of past and present. The occupation is also—always—an occupation of representations. Palestinians were deprived of most resources and positions that enable the representations of (their) past and the production and distribution of images of (their) city. A recent demonstration of this fact was the yearlong celebration of the supposed three thousandth anniversary of Jerusalem organized by the municipal authorities with support from the state and Jewish organizations abroad. The entire event, the history it unfolded, and the future it promised was wholly biased, representing mainly the Jewish point of view of the city and eliminating the present national conflict. The opening ceremony took place in the Palestinian village of Silwan, located in the valley between the Old City and the Mount of Olives. The moment was one of elation and joy for Israelis and one of intrusion and threat for Palestinians, who protested at the end of the ceremony by flying balloons colored in black, green, and red, the colors of the Palestinian flag. For a few, ephemeral moments the Palestinians occupied a nonlocated space in the city's heaven in which they could inscribe their own images and representations. But neither then nor now could they actualize their representations in a public space. The Palestinian residents of Jerusalem have no archive in which documents and images from the history of their city can be compiled, stored, classified, and displayed at will, and there is no Palestinian agency that claims the authority for stating and enacting the rules for a Palestinian representation of the history of Jerusalem.[1]

This is a not uncommon description of the Palestinian situation in Jerusalem, and its importance for the political struggle against the many evils of the Israeli occupation of the eastern part of the city cannot be denied. And yet, politically useful as it may be, the description is questionable. One may ask, for example, What exactly is this space administered by the Israeli government, how homogeneous it is, and to what extent is it indeed governed and controlled by the Israeli authorities alone?[2] One

---

1. This is a general and generalizing claim. It characterizes the condition of the Palestinians as being deprived of their own place, which means, among other things, the archive as a possible Palestinian place. The fact that there may be some archives in which documents about the Palestinian past are stockpiled does not contradict the exclusion of Palestinians from the archive as a possible place of their own. See also my discussion of the structural subjugation of the Palestinian narrative to the Zionist one (Azoulay, 1996). On the archive as a place, see Derrida (1995). For the conflict between Israelis and Palestinians over the organization of the public space and collective memory, see Bishara (1992). Bishara relates the exclusion of Palestinian traces from Israeli public space to the Zionist ideology of "rejection of the Jewish Diaspora." The Diaspora Jew and the Palestinian are two "others" that the Israeli Zionist discourse systematically excludes.

2. This text is an attempt to think about Jerusalem outside and against the binary logic imposed by the occupation, which necessitates a seemingly clear-cut opposition between conquerors and conquered, unification (imposed by the conquerors), and partition (demanded by the conquered and a few among the Israeli left). As two opposed political solutions, unification and partition adhere to a sacred national space in common. Those who enforce a united city are ready, if not willing, to continue the oppression and discrimination against the Palestinian residents in the name of a sacred Jewish national space. Those who struggle for the partition of the city have as their goal a Palestinian nation-state with its own sacred national space. Instead of this binary logic, this text tries to describe the city as a complex mesh of networks, spaces, and times, which are not given to any clear-cut binary division. The political demand to put an end to the occupation is not abandoned, but the conception of the occupation as an entity with clear-cut "ends" is questioned.

may ask whether this description, just like those it seeks to replace, does not deny the heterogeneity of the different spaces gathered under the name "Jerusalem" and reduce it to a homogeneous, single space—the national one. For if one considers Jerusalem only as a site of a national struggle, then its space must follow the rules of a single master narrative that contains two adverse versions and two possible ends, or "solutions"—either a domination by one nation and the subjugation of another (whose traces in the city are wiped out much like the remnants of an old tenant) or a partition of the city that actually doubles the national space. I try to show that in both cases the national space is made sacred and is privileged over all the other spaces of the city, in which there actually exist, and could have existed, complex interrelations that can't be reduced to a model consisting of two parties that are external to one another.[3]

I start with a very short version of such a unidimensional history of an ethnic and religious space, which I then try to somewhat reformulate. When the Muslims conquered Jerusalem in the seventh century, they had to remove vast quantities of accumulated garbage that covered the Temple Mount compound. They then built the El-Aqsa Mosque on the site. The Crusaders conquered the city in 1099, slaughtered Jews and Muslims, removed all signs of Islam from the Temple Mount site, and transformed the mosque into a Christian basilica. One hundred years later, Jerusalem was again purified when the Muslims returned and removed all crosses and symbols of Christian ritual. Descriptions of Jerusalem from the eighteenth century tell of a neglected city in ruins, overflowing with garbage. Extended Ottoman rule had neglected the acts of purification. Afterward there was an Egyptian occupation, then Ottoman rule again, followed by British, Israeli, and Jordanian rule, each occupation accompanied by removal activities. The Israeli army conquered East Jerusalem, including the Old City, in the 1967 war. Immediately after the conquest of the Temple Mount, the Israeli army set about "cleansing" the buildings and the minarets of Arab Legion soldiers and then vacated and razed an adjacent Mus-

---

3. The distribution of means and opportunities to create other spaces or link into them is not equal among Israelis and Palestinians. For example, a precondition for links to, and mobility within, globalized spaces is the modernization of physical space, which has usually taken place only when and where this space has been nationalized or at least has become an object for the administration of a nation-state. Without a nationalized space of their own, the Palestinian access to the spaces of globalization is restricted and mediated through different Israeli agencies. Miyoshi (1997) points to the continuity between old forms of colonialism conducted by different nation-states and postmodern forms conducted by transnational corporations. Even if these corporations call into question the very idea of the nation-state, they can emerge only within its framework. See also in this context Sassen's analysis of the way the global economy is anchored in postmodern, highly developed metropolitan centers (Sassen, 1997).

lim neighborhood. The David Tower Museum, founded in 1988, was the climax of a conservation practice that effectively aimed at cleansing and purifying. The story of the city of Jerusalem, as written inside this museum, is a result of the cleansing of the story from any disturbing details that might trouble the causal order that enables the occupation to continue.[4]

But does the city exist only in one ethnic, religious, or national space? Does it really respond only to one (hi)story? The common description aimed at banishing simultaneity and heterogeneity and imposing—each time anew—an image of one hegemony, can be told differently, using a less common description that attempts to illuminate the simultaneity and heterogeneity existing—despite the main history—within the city. Jerusalem's first museum—the museum of the Greek Orthodox patriarchy—was established in 1858. In 1902, the Franciscan Museum was established in the Church of the Flagellation. In 1905, Bezalel's museum was established with the goal of collecting Jewish cultural treasures from all over the world.[5] Indeed, this collection was the basis of the Israel Museum, which opened in 1965. In 1923, the Supreme Muslim Council established the Islamic Museum. In 1938, the Rockfeller Museum was established in East Jerusalem, its main goal being to house archaeological treasures. Each of these museums represents its own point of view, a point of view that determines the rules of the place and its exhibits. The establishment of a museum marks a threshold consisting of hoarding treasure and controlling the entrance gates regarding what is let in. But the museum is part of a discourse within and through which its status, position, and authority are determined. The severe procedures of selection that a certain museum exercises reflect only the rules and constraints of the discourse within which it operates; rejected objects may still flourish outside this discursive space and its museum incarnation. When a museum exercises more than one discourse and is more loosely anchored in any of the discourses it exercises, it may allow more objects to pass though its space and employ multiple heterogeneous space-time frameworks—those that it crosses and those that it frames.

---

4. The history on display in the museum at the moment completely ignores the partition of the city in 1948 and the Jordanian control of the city for nineteen years. The city is presented as a site and an object of conflicts among the three monotheistic religions, while the national struggle over the city recedes into the background and is depoliticized.

5. The aim of the Betzalel Museum, as in other Zionist museums established in the first half of the century (such as the Ein-Harod Shrine), was to gather "the treasures of Jewish culture" of all times and places. The construction of the realm of knowledge and objects does not differ in principle from similar constructions taking place within the framework of the history museum. However, in a way that reminds one of the classification of animals in Borges's Chinese Encyclopaedia, one of the categories, "the Zionist Museum," tries to include the entire table of categories and threatens to undermine its logic of classification.

This was the situation of the museums described above in 1948, at the time of the foundation of the Israeli state. These museums existed side by side in the space of simultaneity and heterogeneity.

The first description follows a "sequential," diachronic pattern and presents the history of the city as a continuum of stories of occupation, defeat, and domination. Each story replaces its predecessor and suppresses its claims to shape the city's present. The second description follows a spatial and rather static pattern and emphasizes certain privileged sites without the specific narratives associated with them. In the diachronic, sequential description, time and space are taken to be empty, homogeneous containers of events that the historian collects. In the spatial description, space and time are taken to be clusters of intersections, links, and transmission points in a way that allows the simultaneous coexistence of heterogeneous frameworks of spatialization and temporization (for example, of the museum as a cultural site, of the objects and artifacts displayed in it, and of the visitors who pass through it).

The spatial description may be read, of course, as but another ring in the diachronic chain of domination stories—in fact, as the culmination and resolution of the ongoing conflict, leading to a kind of urban harmony in which the peaceful coexistence of different points of views and competing positions is made possible. But such a reading would miss the essential difference between the two descriptions. The sequential pattern rests on the logic of detachment and purification: each new ring in the chain seeks to replace its predecessor and either removes or incorporates its traces into its new regime of identity. The spatial pattern, on the other hand, rests on the logic of simultaneity in the *present*, without governing the elements that comprise it.[6] In other words, subordinating the spatial logic to the logic of the sequential pattern eliminates the difference between the two descriptions, establishes the sequential pattern as a metanarrative, and imposes a homogeneous conception of space-time.

For this reason, the spatial description is presented here as neither the culmination of the sequential narrative nor as its replacement. At most, the spatial description provides a sketch for an attempt to deconstruct the logic of the sequential description. Space, under the former description, is fragmentary, multiple, extending beyond the physical and the visible, and never fully subject to the domination of its masters or even of those who claim to map and represent it adequately. Among the many subjects and objects that inhabit it, it has also an agency of its own. The

---

6. See Benjamin's discussion of space and the present: "History is the subject of a structure whose site is not homogeneous, empty time, but time filled by the present of the now [*Jetztzeit*]" (Benjamin, 1978, 261).

spatial narrative proposes a grid, a network of interrelation, a structure of junctions in which not all possible passages and connections are manageable or can be brought under control according to a preconceived plan.[7]

The diachronic, sequential narrative exists within—but is not controlled by—the spatial description, as a possible link, another junction, a way out to another dimension, a passage to and from (hi)story, being always more and less than the story that unfolds it. Space is organized in many ways, and it is impossible to describe it as a product of the acts and conscious intentions of urban agents—civilian, military, or paramilitary—that claim to administer it. Space is not an object, a container, and these agents can never really become its master, for space is not written in the language of agency and authorship and does not respond to its syntax and semantics. Both space and the agents who use it are part of the networks in which they are enmeshed, in ways that undermine their professed identities and fool their explicit intentions, turning them all into knots of acted-upon actions. I try to exemplify this through the case of "the Green Line," the borderline that tends to reemerge when spatial agents try to wipe it out and disappear when they try to reinscribe it.

In November 1948 Israel and Jordan signed an armistice agreement and drew a dividing line. Both parties considered the line in the nature of a temporary concession and hoped that the political reality, which it created, would soon change. At the talks, their representatives insisted on drawing the line with two different pencils. Abdallah El-Tal, the Jordanian, used a red pencil, while the Israeli, Moshe Dayan, used a green one.[8] The map was of small scale (1:20,000), and the two lines together had a certain width, which meant in reality a long stretch of no-man's land, 60 to 70 meters wide and many kilometers long.[9] The line crossed streets and even houses, thus enlarging the area of friction and conflict between the two parties. The two leaders tried hard to keep their agreements and disagreements in check, believing, so it seems, that they were capable of bringing everything under control, letting nothing evade their planning. Unfortunately, the result was just the opposite, and all along the dividing line—that narrow and long no-man's land created by a pencil—emerged an unexpected, unplanned area of conflict. It was as if the pencil took revenge on the hand that wielded it as an innocent, indifferent, and available means of

---

7. The distinction drawn here is indebted to the one formulated by Deleuze and Guattari, between smooth and striated space (Deleuze and Guattari, 1980).

8. On drawing the borderline, see Benvenisti (1996).

9. Beside this accidental no-man's land were other no-man's lands that were created intentionally. The parties agreed not to agree about these territories and to postpone the division. Thus the map of division actually reflects the reluctance of the two sides to come to terms with the division of the city.

control. A year after the agreement, a fence was erected along the dividing zone. None of the parities liked the idea of such a conspicuous delineation of the borderline, so the fence was officially named "a fence for the prevention of infiltration." Infiltration had to be fought without a formal recognition of the transgressed boundary.

2

In 1995 Sigalit Landau was invited to present her work in the Israel Museum. The exhibition dealt with the logic of the museum space—the white, modernist, neutral space that purifies itself constantly—and its intricate relations with the complex urban space of a city like Jerusalem. The exhibition included a video film by Sigalit Landau that takes place along two axes—an interview with the person responsible for museum hygiene (which is supervised at its entrance gates) and documentation of Landau's (staged) ejection from the museum into a garbage container, traveling inside the truck to the Palestinian village of El-Azariya, where she is tipped out together with the garbage. The video film and the exhibition initiate a discussion about sites (museum, garbage dump), the borders that mark them (walls, military closure), exit openings (garbage truck), manifest and latent networks that connect sites (garbage removal), and purification and sterilization procedures (the scientific discourse). The video starts with an interview with David Bigeleisen, supervisor at the Israel Museum. "My handling of the trouble you've brought into the museum," he said to Sigalit Landau, in regard to her request to bring a mushroom into the museum, "consisted of isolating your trouble inside a transparent bubble. You didn't want to kill it, you wanted to maintain it inside the museum space, in order to keep it alive. By bringing such a thing into the museum space you are endangering the museum space."

At different levels in Landau's exhibition, the cultural discourse dealing with the museum, purification, and control of the entrance gates is confronted by the parallel or complementary discourse about purification, a national discourse. This complementary discourse is an allegory of the purification that accompanied each conquest of the city since its establishment and now accompanies the Israeli occupation and the power relations between Israelis and Palestinians imposed by it.

The space of Landau's exhibition looks like a violent encounter between a modernist discourse about purification and art, significantly expressed by the museum space, and a colonial discourse about "cleansing" and exploitation. Various objects help to mark out territorial divisions of the space and are positioned as dialectical images—dialectics without the following stage, without sublation (*Aufhebung*).

Sigalit Landau, *Harabait* (Temple Mount) (general view), 1995

Thus, for instance, on the left side of the metal door that has been transformed into a tent shelter stand two hollows produced by the application of heat, looking like the imprint of an atomic explosion. These two mushrooms of destruction at the same time transmit a message of warmth and shelter, as might be expected from a protective structure, or presence of the "Rock" (the foundation of the Temple Mount), whose reconstructed impression is positioned in the center of the show space. The crater under the Rock is composed of green computer mouse pads, physical data taken from the virtual world is a world that can be reorganized at the push of a

Sigalit Landau, *Harabait* (Temple Mount) (detail), 1995

button. The pads have been exposed to food, drink, and time and have become a fun-gal culture—a living world of color, shape, and organic health. The fungus is banned at the museum gates: it is exhibited in a hermetic case, where it is identified with filth, rejection, and infection. But only a few kilometers away, in El-Azariya, the site of the municipal garbage dump, the fungus is perceived as harmless. It lives there, breathes, and decomposes the garbage that others dig into and earn a living from.

This is the face of the occupation, like a zero sum game: there plenty, there need. What is prohibited here is allowed there, and vice versa. The museum removes its garbage to El-Azariya. El-Azariya is situated in a Palestinian area where, from time to time, prolonged closure is imposed by the Israeli army. The garbage dump has be-come a source of income for many who have lost their source of income in Israel as a result of the closure: "There are Palestinians who work in the garbage in order to survive. Since the closure, there are several hundreds who stand there each day wait-ing for the garbage to arrive from Jerusalem, from the Jews. They are looking for aluminum or something good to sell, sometimes clothes. I went and took pictures, and they didn't believe it, they thought I was exaggerating. So I went and conducted a full investigation—why they come, what they do. These are simply hungry people

Sigalit Landau, *Harabait* (Temple Mount) (detail), 1995

who've been going there for several years already, although we didn't know about it" (Zigari, Kol Ha'ir, 17.7.96).[10]

Sigalit Landau's exhibition took place at the Israel Museum in 1995, the twenty-eighth year of the Israeli occupation of East Jerusalem. During those years, the organization of space and the distribution of representations in the public space of Jerusalem have been in the hands of one authority that determines the rules of the place—the rules according to which Jerusalem as an archive of past and present is governed and preserved.

At the center of the exhibition space, near the reconstructed rock, there is a bar of soap in the form of a computer mouse. This is a reminder that holiness is a virtual affair. There is no ownership and consequently no change of ownership. Instead of changing hands (that is, ownership), one may rest content with hands-on commands like computer commands: Open Temple Mount, Delete Temple Mount, Replace Temple Mount. With a computer-mouse-shaped soap in hand, Temple Mount can be held in the hand. With a push of a button, one might Copy Jerusalem or Save As JerusalemS, saving all of Jerusalem's "other spaces": "I went with a lump of clay to try to capture the shape of the Rock because taking pictures is banned there. This is really an amazing place. It is difficult to get up there because prayers take place there

SAVE AS JerusalemS

all the time. The whole idea of the exhibition was to provide an alternative, to explain to people that they are going to return the eastern part of the City to the Palestinians, to build a replacement and recognize that the Israel Museum could be the replacement: This is a mount and this is a mount."[11]

3

Heterotopia (*heteros topos*, other place/space), says Foucault in his article "Of Other Spaces" (Foucault, 1993), is a site that is designed for human activity, well demarcated, both spatially and temporally, and is characterized by the simultaneous coexistence of two or more spatial settings. Foucault mentions a few examples—the museum, the cemetery, and the holiday village. Foucault's examples (closed and demarcated sites created by humans), I argue, prevent one from fully realizing the power of the heterotopic idea. These examples restrict the concept of heterotopia to the point of view of sovereign subjects who define the rules of the game in heterotopic sites.

Heterotopia concerns the users of a site and not only its spatial organization. Spaces may be multiplied, and the simultaneous presence of the individual in these different spaces may be multiplied as well. The individual may be a citizen in civic space, an address in virtual space, an outlet in a network, or a body in a physical environment. Moreover, heterotopia is no longer just a matter of well-demarcated sites. The whole world, or at least large portions of it, has become heterotopic. Heterotopic spaces are not mastered or administered by the subjects that inhabit them; their rules are not determined according to their will. If the world is heterotopic, or if being-in-space means being-in-heterotopic-space, going into and out of "other" spaces is a matter of making and unmaking links and contacts, hooking or unhooking appliances, being in touch with someone, being exposed to the gaze of someone, being in reach of something.

Let me now go back to the passage from Foucault's (1993) "Of Other Spaces" concerning tension between the paradigm of time (history) and the paradigm of space—and the transition between them.[12] History is a diachronic paradigm characteristic of the nineteenth century; space is a paradigm characteristic of our own age. That transition itself is still described by Foucault (who is usually associated with the spatial paradigm) in terms of the diachronic time-space paradigm and the historicity that it entails. Furthermore, Foucault reduces temporality to historical

---

11. Conversation with Sigalit Landau, June 1996.
12. For a detailed discussion of this topic in Foucault's article, see chapter 5.

temporality and actually dissociates spatialization and temporization. His genealogical researches, which undermine the concept of historical time as an ahistorical container indifferent to the stuff it contains, still write the history of space within the framework of the diachronic paradigm. In "Of Other Spaces" he mentions some of the main stages in the history of space without thinking about the spatial dimension of this history itself, once again assuming space to be a homogeneous trunk in which some stuff—a variety of spaces in this case—is being accumulated. But time is a rhizome that springs out everywhere, and the rhizome has no trunk, historical or otherwise.[13] One may domesticate some chunks of time, call them by the names of periods and ages, and divide them into centuries and decades, and yet each one of these chunks may root itself in a different spot on a ground that changes continuously and loses its coherency due to these multiple temporizations that cut through, cut across, and interweave space in so many different ways. Space and time are always in the plural.

But for Foucault the history of time is still written in the singular. For this reason, perhaps, his analyses of social formations stopped at the disciplinary society. Disciplinary society is characterized by sites well demarcated by a single, recognized, and visible borderline in which all the participants in the power relations share a single geographic and architectural space. In the second half of the twentieth century these sites existed and flourished, but new technologies and new economic and geopolitical relations allowed them to be woven into and crossed by a variety of other spaces, to be shared differently by different inhabitants of the site, and to be opened and responded to in different, differentiating ways to their gaze and movement. Mobility in these new other spaces is not measured by the ratio between traveling time and traveled distance but by other means, such as the ratio between time and the number of links crossed and created or the ratio between a site's surface and the intensity of temporizations that cross it. The forms of space-time in the late twentieth century were characterized above all by new and intense means for temporizing space and spatializing time (such as access to air time for reaching more listeners in a wider zone or access to historical time through visiting "historical sites" or digging deeper into the ground of archaeological sites).

Gilles Deleuze (1992) touches on these issues in a small essay entitled "Postscript on the Societies of Control." There he describes the new social formation that replaces the disciplinary society in the West, briefly mentioning its new

---

13. The notion of the rhizome is borrowed from Deleuze and Guattari (1980).

spatiotemporal dimensions: "Control is short-term and has rapid rates of turnover but also is continuous and without limit, while discipline was of long duration, infinite, and discontinuous. Man is no longer man enclosed but man in debt" (Deleuze, 1992, 6).

Mastery and domination are not inscribed in space, and physical borders are no longer a main mechanism of control. Man is no longer "man enclosed" because the boundaries of domination have become complex and undetermined: they are disseminated everywhere, and yet they are mostly invisible. The seemingly inevitable link between a physical and a conceptual limit has been loosened, and the positioning of an individual in any particular place in social space is no longer necessary. Man, Deleuze claims, has become "man in debt." Debt may be disseminated over different spatiotemporal frameworks. It is not physically associated with the individual who is in debt (as was the case when the individual was enclosed) but is linked to his or her address in so many virtual and nonvirtual spaces.[14] In such a world, not only are time and space multiplied and fragmented, but individuals are fragmented and multiplied according to the number of spatiotemporal frameworks within which they are linked. Individuals do not act on a world but are part of an action that they never begin and their organs (hand, eye, mouth) are not means for a purpose or expressions of subjectivity but are links in unanimous chains of action and reaction. Together with many other instruments and objects, hand, mouth, and eye enable the functioning of systems (observation, communication, production) that in their turn make these organs effective and useful to the individual to whom they supposedly belong.[15] A short discussion of the hand and its spatial environment serves here as an example of these new spatiotemporal dimensions.

The hand is a link in the network. It belongs neither to a sovereign citizen nor to an instrument that is supposed to serve the citizen. It is the hand of the neturalized[16] citizen, the heterotopic citizen, the one who becomes a citizen of liminal zones, of intermediate spaces, a citizen of passages, a citizen in passing, one who is always in the process of becoming a citizen. Such a heterotopic citizen tries to create an intermediate environment "inside" the networks of social interaction, knowing all too well that there is no place "out there." The heterotopic citizen lives in the

---

14. For more on the relation between time and debt, see Derrida (1991), especially the sections on Mauss's analysis of gift and giving.

15. In *Discipline and Punish* Foucault speaks about handwriting as an apparatus for the constitution of subjectivity (Foucault, 1975b). For more on the hand, the eye, and the mouth as instruments and their role in the construction of subjectivity, see Azoulay (1997c).

16. The word *neturalize* and its derivatives was coined by Aya & Gal by replacing nature by *network* in the verb *naturalize*.

immanent tension between two elements that structure the field of social action—(1) the position of the subject within a defined field of discourse and action, which allows them to judge and act with a certain authority and claim to knowledge (these are remnants of the disciplinary society) and (2) the unavoidable intertwining of the subject's acts within conflicting networks of interaction that lie beyond their control, undermining their plans and intentions and constantly robbing their actions of meaning.

When this is the nature of our most basic spatial condition, the spatial inscription of sociopolitical demarcations, boundaries, and borders cannot be presented any longer only in terms of territory and territorialization. The individual, too, cannot be "contained" within the space occupied by his or her body. The limited space of the body is multiplied in these "other spaces" and is represented or has correlates in these spaces. But all these spaces are always somehow "out of joint": there is no exact overlapping, no one set of spatial coordinates that contains them all. All these other spaces are populated with persons, bodies, objects, instruments, and appliances. They are interwoven in different, partly intersecting and partly unrelated networks of speech, vision, and interaction. And in the constant shifts and transitions among these spaces the hand provides the ticket, the license, the right of passage. It serves as a gatekeeper and a bridge, it crosses and builds distances. In short, it allows space to become spatialized.

When the concept of heterotopia thus applies to space and also to those who use space, it is indeed possible to overcome the constituting subject, which Foucault targeted as something to get rid of to escape the strictures of historical discourse. By extending heterotopia to include space users and by understanding the hand as an agent that is not subject to the logic of subjectivity, I can question or even deconstruct the claim of the national constituting subject in the city of Jerusalem. I follow different hands in the heterotopic urban space of Jerusalem to escape the hold of that national subject over the city and undermine its attempt to gather the multiple segments of a fragmentary, heterogeneous, urban space and incorporate them into its own, single-voice history.

4

Before the conquest of East Jerusalem, the Israeli and Jordanian parties to the conflict recognized the armistice line, usually called the Green Line, as an international boundary only de facto, but never de jure; their city was one and was only temporarily and brutally divided. In June 1967 the Israeli army crossed the Green Line between Jordan and Israel and conquered East Jerusalem (along with the rest of the

West Bank).[17] The unrecognized borderline was unilaterally erased by Israel, and ever since then the entire city has been in Israeli hands, which alone have handled all its municipal affairs. Shortly after the war, in defiance of international law, Israel annexed East Jerusalem along with other territories surrounding it. After June 1967 the Green Line was systematically erased from all official maps and gradually disappeared on the ground as a result of massive urban development. Erasing the line was the form of its inscription, and massive urban building projects were soon planned and performed to further erase what the initial erasure had inscribed. When Israel tried to erase the borderline unilaterally, the city was actually divided for the first time in consciousness, not only on the ground, and a dividing line that both parties recognized—one party to wipe out its traces and the other to reestablish it—was inscribed.

Following the occupation of East Jerusalem in 1967 and as an expression of its claim to sovereignty over the entire city, Israel annexed the occupied part and granted its 66,000 Palestinian inhabitants the status of permanent residents, giving them the option of becoming its citizens. As permanent residents, they had to swear allegiance to the Jewish state, the political incarnation of the Jewish national subject. Not surprisingly, very few Palestinians (no more than two thousand) accepted this offer of a change of sovereignty and quick naturalization. As a result, unification again divided the city into classes of inhabitants. Most Palestinians are not citizens in their own city. Their status of permanent residency continues to be conditional: Palestinians who leave the city for a long period of time for purposes other than education lose their right to live there (B'tselem report, 1997). Legally, they have become foreigners who immigrated to their own birthplace, and their right to stay there is not automatically granted to their children. Thus the unified city is based on a system of nationalist apartheid in which non-Jewish residents are systematically discriminated against in terms of rights, housing, urban and economic development, and education.[18]

The ambivalence and indeterminacy of the Green Line that divided the city between 1948 and 1967 embodied the heterogeneity of the city and the fact that it in-

---

17. "Temple Mount is in my hands," shouted the commander of the conquering unit into his field radio, coining an idiom that has become a symbol of the Israeli conquest.

18. Much effort is invested in maintaining or inventing the Jewish "character" of the city, especially in building new Jewish neighborhoods all around the eastern part of the city. In the last few years there were discussions of several plans for the development of Jerusalem, all of which support the Israeli policy of Jewification of the city. Speaking before architects about the annexation of an undeveloped area on the western outskirts of the city for the purpose of building new Jewish neighborhoods there, Mayor Ehud Ulmart reiterated this policy: "We have to influence the patterns of growth in the city so that they would fit the desired character of the city" (Zandberg 1997). The "desired character" means maintaining its Jewish majority, of course.

habits simultaneously heterogeneous spaces and times that cannot be reduced to a single geopolitical space or contained in a single historical span. The conflict was inscribed onto the surface of the city, and its resolution was visibly postponed. Direct confrontation between the hostile parties was deferred, allowing for a certain coexistence between conflicting fantasies and narratives. The different heterogeneous segments of which the city consists—national, religious, and ethnic groups, forms of life, collective memories, and collective dreams—were not forced into a hierarchical system, and no primacy could have been granted to any of them.

Such a hierarchical system was an inevitable consequence of the Israeli occupation and annexation of East Jerusalem and of the official, imposed unification of the city. The hierarchical system has been maintained within a fixed demographic framework. A special governmental committee for the development of Jerusalem found in 1973 that the population ratio was 73.5 percent Israeli Jews and 25 percent Palestinians, and the official policy of all Israeli governments since has been to maintain this ratio by various means. Massive development of Jewish neighborhoods and Israel's legal administration of the city have created a continuous, even if fragmentary, Jewish area in and around the city and have cut deeply into the Palestinian settled areas, shattering the Palestinian presence in and around the city into isolated fragments.

There are three main mechanisms for maintaining this population ratio, as well as the Zionist image of Jerusalem:

- *Cartography*   The Israeli sovereign draws the city maps and uses cartography as a means of maintaining its demographic balance. The annexation of East Jerusalem and its surroundings incorporated as much land as possible for future Jewish development and as few Arab suburbs as possible. Later changes in rather flexible municipal boundaries brought more Jewish neighborhoods into the city. Today 411,000 Jews and 166,000 Palestinians live within the jurisdiction of the city of Jerusalem. But a different map, which would have taken into account the dynamics of Palestinian life in and around the city and the geographical reality in the Palestinian sections of the city, would have yielded a very different demographic ratio.
- *The legal apparatus*   The conditional residency granted to the Palestinians enables the Israeli authorities to control the demographic composition of the city on an almost daily basis.
- *Planning and housing*   The ratio of new housing for Palestinians and Israelis is one to eight. Palestinians are denied permission to build much more often than

Israelis. Between 1967 and 1995, 64,000 apartments were built in Jewish neighborhoods (half of them on confiscated land that mostly belonged to the Jordanian government), and only 8,000 were built for Palestinians.[19]

The Israeli occupation and administration of Jerusalem is based on a misleading ambiguity between representations (maps, statistical tables) and the represented objects (urban space, population). On the one hand, the occupation regime uses the clean, objective language of scientific discourse and assumes its distinction between objects and their representations. On the other hand, the same regime takes an active part in the production of both the represented objects and their discursive representation, as if there were nothing to distinguish between them.[20] When the data gathered "in the field" do not yield the desired map of Jerusalem, the map changes. When the reading of the map yields data that smack too much of apartheid, the data change. Jerusalem too, that most metaphysical of all cities, has witnessed the loss of the clear metaphysical distinction between the original and its simulacra, between territory and map, between the "thing itself" and its representation.

However, this is not a result of the fragmentation of the visual field and the field of action or of the dissemination of the forces acting in Jerusalem. On the contrary, it is the result of Israel's domination and overdetermination of these fields of vision and action. What seems for a moment as a postmodern practice of representation—a free and open market of identities, territories, maps, and narratives, a real fair of simulations— appears on closer scrutiny to be the result of conscious manipulation of the data, the map, and the territory, of rigid control of the different markets, and of massive intervention in the various practices of exchange. Israel administers the city to fit its desired map, and it draws the maps to fit its desired city. As a result 70,000 out of the 170,000 Palestinian permanent residents find themselves living in suburbs outside the official territory of Jerusalem, and they are gradually losing their status of residency.

At the basis of Israel's illegal policies in Jerusalem lies the faith that the Israeli state and its agents are at one and the same time an incarnation of a universal principle of transcendent subjectivity and the most powerful expression of one particu-

---

19. The data are taken from B'tselem Reports, an Israeli organization for human rights in the occupied territories (B'tselem Reports, 1995, 1997), and from the daily press.

20. The Israeli policy and plans for the development of the city have always given preference to political considerations over urban ones. The construction of new neighborhoods immediately after the Six-Day War was planned to eliminate the traces of the Green Line. The annexation of new areas all around the city was planned to make possible rapid growth of the Jewish population. The ongoing discrimination in the allocation of construction permits to Arabs and Jews has been a clear attempt to force Palestinians to leave the city.

lar national subject. Israeli governments have acted and spoken as the sole legitimate representative of the Jewish people and their holy city. They have acted as if they believed that the world, history, and their neighbors are but clay in the hands of the potter, the Israeli sovereign, and that they can impose their will on reality and mold it singlehandedly to their own view. "Let there be no Green Line," they have declared: "let the city be united." And the divided city has become one. Jerusalem thus becomes the arena for the manifestation of two aspects of subjectivity: (1) the subject as an origin and an expression of mastery over others and (2) subjectivity as self-mastery and self-determination. Presented from the perspective of this double subjectivity, the Green Line appears as a scar in the heart of the holy city, and the city itself appears as an entity that has existed continuously, with no interruptions, throughout three thousand years of history. The city has sometimes been desolate, of course, in ruins, and fifty years ago it was divided, but there has always been one discrete entity, they claim, which has undergone destruction and division. However, the Israeli attempts to present a unified city never succeeded in erasing completely the real and imaginary line that still exists in some other spaces separating two hostile communities, two peoples, conquerors and conquered.

So many hands have a stake in the city of Jerusalem. So many people and groups are fighting to lay their hands on the city, to manipulate its past and future, digging its ground to find new data to support these conflicting claims, reconstructing the evidence and preparing themselves, and their city, for the day of judgment. Hands intermingle with and interfere in the work of other hands. Hands build energetically and destroy, no less energetically, what others (and they themselves) have built. Hands draw maps, open some paths and close others, inscribe some dividing lines and erase others. Above all, hands try to mold the city's image and superimpose it on all other competing images.[21] These latter hands are an extension of a national subject, acting as if there may never be another chance to do whatever isn't done today in this city where time stretches to eternity, and almost all this work is being done in the name of a *past* and for the sake of a certain *future* in a diachronic time conceived as a homogeneous, empty container in which events are chained uninterruptedly from the depths of the past to the most distant future.

---

21. The hectic work being done in Jerusalem is only partly overt. Much of it is clandestine, concealed from the public eye. Some hands work gently, others are violent, but everyone seems very busy, and everything seems awfully urgent. Everything must be done before it's too late—before further urban development takes place, before too many Palestinians infiltrate the city, before more land is confiscated by the Israeli authorities, before the peace talks resume, before the next war, or before the Messiah comes.

But what about the *present?* When one cares only for the past and only for the sake of a future, the present tends to disappear. When one ignores for a moment both the past and the future, this hectic urban scene I have just described is suddenly emptied of all national and religious narratives and transcendent subjects that animate it. One can see the city as a multiplicity of heterogeneous spaces and irreconcilable points of view. All one can see are busy hands, gentle and violent actions, rapid, seemingly arbitrary changes in the city's surface. People work, travel, stay home, surf the Internet, turn on their televisions, zap from station to station, watch a local network, then watch a global one, go shopping at a shopping center, get stuck in traffic jams, sit in a bar or a coffee house, visit friends, go to the movies or to the theater, play with their children in the streets or in public gardens. These sites of social life change from area to area, from neighborhood to neighborhood, differing among themselves not only according to the great division of the city between East and West Jerusalem. The way the Israeli occupation divides the city is not unambiguous. Today the city seems to function as a single urban unit. For the innocent, or ignorant, eye, the few checkpoints manned by a few policemen and soldiers scattered here and there on the outskirts of Arab neighborhoods, as well as the ruins of some old military posts, are the only visible, often misleading witnesses to the Green Line. The checkpoints are especially ambivalent signs. As a symbol of the passage from the Jewish part of the city to the Arab one, they certainly defy Israel's policy of unification (though Jews and Arabs clearly have different access to and mobility through these checkpoints). For the purpose of security they are quite ridiculous, since the imaginary dividing line may be crossed at numerous other points. The national logic of unification creates the need to control passage from the Arab part to the Jewish part of the city, but too strict a control contradicts the unifying imperative. In fact, the checkpoint is a symbol of paradox for the Israeli domination over Jerusalem, where the unifying efforts only deepen the dividing forces that resist unification. Recently, a possible ethnic solution to the paradox has been tested by Israeli authorities—an ethnic purification of the city ("the silent transfer" as this process was termed by the B'tselen organization). Such a purification would enable a peaceful coexistence of the spatial and (Jewish) sequential narratives of the city. If the city became entirely Jewish, it would be possible to subject the spatial narrative to the sequential (national) one, to transform Jerusalems into "Jerusalem—a city united forever." In the meantime, the checkpoint functions as a filter, but various spaces leak through the holes, link into other spaces, escape all efforts at unification—diachronic or synchronic.

The refugee camps on the city's outskirts bear witness to the most difficult, brutal, and painful aspects of the occupation of Jerusalem. Most Jews who inhabit the western part are hardly aware of the camps. In the seams of the city, however, in neighborhoods like Pat and Beit-Tzaffafa, the differences between east and west are not that visible, especially for one who is not a resident of the area. A visitor may mistake the Arab houses of Beit-Tzaffafa for the villas of the occupiers and mistake the eight-story building project in neighboring Pat for the housing estates of the occupied. As a matter of fact, the difference in height is just one more example of the evils of the occupation. High-rise construction is permitted only in Jewish neighborhoods; the Palestinians must solve their problems of density and overpopulation in other areas, outside Jerusalem.

The professed policy of the Israeli state since 1967 has been to turn Jerusalem into a Jewish city. The unification of the city has not been a political utopia that is meant to serve all parties involved. Its aim has not been to build bridges between hostile nations and religions. It is, rather, a unilaterally metaphysical fantasy projected by Israelis onto thousands of years of the history of Jerusalem. But the city is harsh and stubborn; it does not respond in kind.

The "Jewification" of Jerusalem follows a logic of "catch as catch can." Every area under the city's municipal jurisdiction that has not yet become Jewish is a target for a second conquest that would make it Jewish or at least more Jewish than it is now.[22] The Jewification of the city, which is closely related to its unification, seeks to increase the Jewish areas of the city at the expense of the Palestinian areas and thus gradually to homogenize the entire urban space, imposing on it a national Jewish identity. However, the practice of "catch as catch can" yields opposite results. Instead of expanding the homogeneous Jewish areas, it creates more and more heterogeneous areas, which are complex and fragmented, containing more zones of friction and conflict. The entire city has become riddled with enclaves. Israeli authorities imagine themselves to be the subject and master of the city, responsible for the production and management of its space and its borderlines, capable of administering trends of mobility, routes of passage, movement of populations, patterns of construction and modes of exchange (of instruments, artifacts, smells, news, weapons, health, friendship, and love).[23] But despite all the means and measures of

---

22. Seventy square kilometers have been annexed to Jerusalem since the Six-Day War (B'tselelm report, 1995).

23. The description presents a complex picture of the relation between occupiers and occupied without, however, erasing the differences between Arabs and Jews and the ability to multiply spaces created by the Israeli occupation. The entire urban infrastructure in the Palestinian sections is conspicuously less developed than the infrastructure in the Jewish sections, and the gap keeps widening. But the multiplication of spaces is not merely a result of a more or less developed infrastructure.

control, surveillance, and repression at their disposal, which keep the Palestinians in a kind of a third-world enclave, circulation and exchange take place constantly in ways that defy the nationalist rules set by the Israelis.[24]

The circulation of goods, messages, images, and people takes place in "other spaces" that are not necessarily subject to the rules of the national space determined by the Israeli authorities. Apart from and besides the authorized routes, communication, circulation, and exchange take advantage of the many loopholes scattered all along the borderlines in Jerusalem. These loopholes are not accidental gaps but the very stuff of which those lines consist. Due to the presence of these loopholes, the border may interpellate all its users with a double message: "Respect me," and "Transgress me." It may declare at one and the same time, "Here is a border" (discriminating between Israelis and Palestinians), but "There is no border" (for the city is united and welcomes all its residents alike). This Janus face of the border appears in the national space but also in economic, educational, and other daily spaces.

Israeli authorities act as if they believe themselves capable of controlling which face of the borderline will appear where and when. But the borderlines have a life of their own and users of different kinds who use and abuse them in many different ways. Thus, for example, Israel has built Jewish neighborhoods as enclaves in the midst of Palestinian areas in a step-by-step attempt to accumulate more and more urban territory, hoping that somehow the new enclaves will form a new border. However, the rapidly growing Jewish enclaves have turned the Palestinian neighborhoods, too, into enclaves that continue to spread (through mostly illegal construction of new houses) and often trespass borderlines, erasing some and inscribing, or threatening to inscribe new ones.[25] Whereas Jewish neighborhoods were supposed to purify the national space, fortify it, and demonstrate Jewish sovereignty in it, they too often serve opposite ends. Instead of purifying space, they emphasize its heterogeneous nature; instead of fortifying it, they create more areas of friction and increase the threats to the safety and well-being of those who dwell in and around

---

24. The border that Israel imposes on the Palestinians does not function according to the intentions of its authors. It acquires new meanings and functions through the interpretations given by those who use it. Conceived as a means to limit, it actually functions as an amplifier of production (Foucault, 1976). Instead of closing more tightly the gaps in the boundaries separating Jews and Palestinians, it creates ever more and new gaps, and instead of consolidating governmental control, it dilutes it (see also Lyotard, 1979, sec. 13).

25. The man responsible for Jerusalem in the Palestinian Authority, Faisal Husseini, prepared plans to strengthen the city's eastern ring. These plans are like a negative of the Israeli plans for the same area. Israel is capable of blocking Husseini, of course, while the reverse is not true, and yet Israel's capacity to implement its plans does depend, among other things, on Palestinian reactions to those plans.

them; and instead of demonstrating Jewish sovereignty, they create more opportunities to challenge and question the claim of the sovereign.

Straightforward Jewification seems politically impossible under the present circumstances. Therefore, the urban space is planted with as many Jewish spots as possible, in a way that makes any neat division of the city between Jewish and Arab practically impossible. Israel has set the ends and chosen the means to realize them, without understanding, however, that the means are not solely determined by the ends that they serve or by the ruling subjects who impose them. Israel's policies in Jerusalem have brought the city to the verge of a spatial unification of such a heterogeneous kind that no transcendent temporality could chain it in a consecutive chain, no single narrative could contain it, and no political subject could master it. Unification—if one still wants to use this word—takes place in such a space by way of numerous links and a constant weaving and unweaving of knots in an undefined network that escapes the rule of any sovereignty that claims transcendent, ahistorical authority.

5

Is it possible to avoid one single narrative that has primacy over others, one single narrative that channels and directs the multiplicity of actions for the purpose of one preconceived or predetermined telos (a telos that seemingly lies outside the field of social action and endows it with meaning and justification)? Does not such a reading of the city (which seeks to interpret the present as an ensemble detached from the past and from the subjects who claim to act in its name and insist on its representation) produce one more single narrative? Aren't these two readings—one that obliterates the past and one that obliterates the present—rather similar? The two strategies—a spatial strategy that ignores the past while focusing on the present and a sequential historical strategy that ignores the present while focusing on the past—do not exist as ready-made artifacts, ready to be picked up and used to shape reality according to one's will. Opting for one of these strategies would not change the heterogeneous nature of reality. When one of the two strategies is enacted successfully, it may strengthen one competing element at the expense of the other, but it is incapable of eliminating the latter. No strategy, however successful it may be, can homogenize the heterogeneity of the city.

Yet between the two strategies lies a radical difference. The first, a spatial and "presentist" strategy, reads the city as a heterogeneous multiplicity of relations—economic, political, religious, ethnic—that cannot be reduced to the national narrative. When the national narrative is thus completely ignored, the national subject that animates that narrative is deconstructed, its transcendent status is denied, and its legitimating power is annihilated. The claims of nationalism are so radically denied that national narratives are not allowed even the existence of one type of force, relations, and legitimacy, among the many of which the heterogeneous space consists. This strategy is self-defeating. Instead of *recognizing* the existing heterogeneous multiplicity and conceiving the national narrative to be one element of this multiplicity, it seeks to eliminate unwanted elements and *produce* an abstract, "better" multiplicity. Thus the present is endowed with an abstract heterogeneity that ignores nationalism, its embodiment, and its role in urban life and space. As a result, this abstraction actually works to create a new chain in the sequential narrative in the form of a multiple spatialization that would be the new historical agent that replaces the national subject, the old hero to be driven off the stage. But even if it were to be triumphant, the spatial strategy does not have either the means or the motivation to eliminate the national subject, the many forms of its narrative, and its various agents.

The second, more common strategy is the one enacted by the Israeli government. The heterogeneous multiplicity of the city is made subject to the Jewish national narrative, to the mechanism of its exclusions, and to the constraints of its temporality, which stretches from antiquity to eternity and is constructed in cycles of (Jewish) destruction and redemption. Within this framework, Jerusalem is "a city united forever," temporarily spoiled by elements that introduce divisions and fractions. Unity is understood as "united under Jewish sovereignty," and the threatening elements are interpreted accordingly, in nationalist and ethnic terms. Hence unity implies, to some at least, Jewish purity and requires efforts at purification. Dividing elements are impure elements, and they must be removed. Jerusalem as "a city united forever" can maintain its unity only under the perspective of eternity, and if purity has not been achieved yet or cannot be achieved due to present circumstances, it is certainly aimed at for some point in the city's eternal future.

6

A few years ago Aya & Gal, two Israeli artists who live and work in Jerusalem, launched the project of NETuralization. For Aya & Gal, neturalization does not take place in a state, does not involve laws of immigration, and is not related to national identity. In their project, neturalization contradicts the conventional laws of naturalization in the modern nation-state. The procedure that baptizes one as a citizen in the nation-state is, first of all, a means of determining the identity and status of an individual and a certain relation between the individual and the political sovereign. For Aya & Gal neturalization means just the reverse. Neturalization is a process, not a procedure, it exists for the duration of this process, not striving to achieve any end. Alluding to Deleuze one may say that for Aya & Gal's neturalization is an action of the order of *becoming*, not of the order of *being*, and it actually consists of active de-naturalization—not to be a citizen but to become a citizen. One intentionally becomes a stranger in known, common situations, strips oneself of one's identity, or navigates one's way in purposefully strange environments in which one exercises a gradual accommodation. Aya & Gal's neturalization process deconstructs, or dissolves, the unification and seeming coherency created when a certain dominating point of view—the point of view of the national subject, for example—is imposed on a heterogeneous reality. It is placed between different regimes of power and knowledge, partially escaping the control of each, exposing the bold stitches with which the dominating regime is trying to hold together a heterogeneous reality. Aya & Gal's project, I should add, is in no way a practical proposal, a politically conscious attempt to come to terms with the problem of naturalization in general or with the civic status of Palestinians in Jerusalem in particular. Nevertheless, it can be easily related to these problems, and to the specific situation of Jerusalem. Speaking about their work, Aya & Gal said:

Schematically, the neturalized citizen lives in two separate worlds. The act of neturalization puts him in a liminal position, which he could not hold in any other way. He becomes a neturalized citizen when he dons the suit. But it can be any form of separation, although separation isn't exactly the word. We are not attempting to disconnect him from this world, but neither is there any attempt to fix him in the other world he's being offered. The intention is to place him for a moment in a nonterritorial position, it being unclear where the world begins and where it ends, and what his data are. (personal communication, 1996)

One day, Aya & Gal's neturalized citizen got into an automobile. His body was encased in a layer of skin made of latex. He embarked on a drive around the YMCA tower in Jerusalem, one of the elevated points in the city's center. The car rolled through the streets of some neighborhoods of West Jerusalem, an area that has become the heart of the city after the "urban surgery" performed by Israel after 1967. The car was actually moving like a spider in the middle of its web. The YMCA tower enjoys a panoptic view of the city. It is an elevated, privileged point of view that may symbolize, in our story, Israeli domination of the city. Only the Israeli authorities do

Aya & Gal Middle East, *The Neturalized, Local
Observation Point*, 1996

not need such an elevated point today, for they are equipped with so many other instruments of surveillance and control (some of which I have mentioned above).

One neturalized citizen sat in the car that morning. He sat in the driver's place,
a place intended usually for sovereign citizens trained by the state to drive through
its streets, the place of a person worthy enough to navigate on his own, choose direction, have intention. But the place awaiting the citizens is in fact the place of a
missing accessory, the accessory that when connected to its place can propel the car
and drives it properly. The state has forged this accessory—a free yet obedient citizen—in its factory but hasn't yet cast it inside the automobile. The automobile can
set out on its way only after the citizen has sat in his place. Inside the car that toured
the Rehavya neighborhood that morning sat a neturalized citizen. His sensory environment was dulled by the layer of latex and honed by the electronic eye that saw for
him. A video camera that was attached to the steering wheel documented every turn,
every stop. On sharp turns the neturalized citizen's legs were captured by the camera lens in an overview, looking down from the steering wheel. The video camera is
the eye of the automobile, and the neturalized citizen with eyes in his head but with
his head covered in latex uses the camera as his own eye. This act of neturalization
was the basis for the creation by Aya & Gal of an interactive map that later became,

Aya & Gal Middle East, *The Neturalized, Local
Observation Point,* 1996

Aya & Gal Middle East, *The Neturalized, Local
Observation Point,* 1996

SAVE AS JerusalemS

Aya & Gal Middle East, *The Neturalized, Local
Observation Point,* 1996

in turn, an invitation to the spectators (users of the interactive map) to become neturalized. The invitation is addressed to the one who uses the map. As the artists put
it: "The neturalized-citizen operates all intersections. When you watch a movie, you
watch somebody else doing something. When you touch the mouse, it's as if you've
shut the car door and driven off. You are inside the network, you and the network are
one and the same thing. Whoever comes to see becomes part of it, whether he wants
to or not" (all quotations of Aya & Gal from a conversation with the author, 1996).

Aya & Gal projected their interactive map of Rehavya's streets in the YMCA
tower and later in the Documenta exhibition in Kassel. Spectators are invited to enter a sealed space, sit down, take hold of the mouse, and set out on a journey of navi-
gation. They are invited to become neturalized for a moment in the network of streets
while driving by means of a mouse. The seeing car provides them with new fields of
vision that do not allow whoever is driving at the moment to assume the position of
a hypothetical detached spectator. The interactive map projected on the wall is the
opposite of a territorial advantage (like "the view from above," for example) as a
means of control over space. In this map, the overhead view from the tower is replaced
by the systematic view of the photographed map, which has been composed of hun-

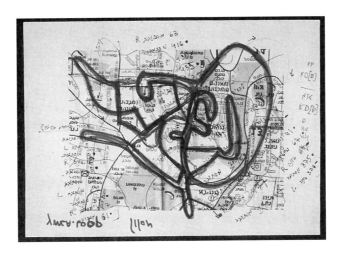

Aya & Gal Middle East, preparatory maps for *Local Observation Point,* 1995

dreds of segments filmed by the video camera while driving through the city streets. A conventional city map guided driving through the streets of Rehavya.

In the photo below, one may discern the spider web formed around the YMCA tower. The web emphasizes the hierarchical dimension contained in the map—a panoptic view at the center, not far from the prime minister's residence, and a winding drive through the streets that surround it. The transposition of the drive from the video to the interactive map was mediated by a nonhierarchical map made entirely of strings of numbers. These numbers enable spectators to drive through intersections and road junctions. Each number signifies an intersection or an encoded link between several intersections, and thus all intersections in the numerical map are linked equivalently to all other intersections. "The project at the YMCA is another type of observation," say Aya & Gal. "Let's assume that a spy takes the CD of the interactive map to Syria and wants to identify the escape routes from the prime minister's residence, located in this area. He can do it interactively. He can decide that he wants to drive left. You film a movie, and scan the information, and the question is how you splice it and organize his navigational possibilities. From an innocent movie of the streets of Rehavya, such as any tourist could take, it can turn into top-secret information. The way in which it's arranged turns it into an interactive

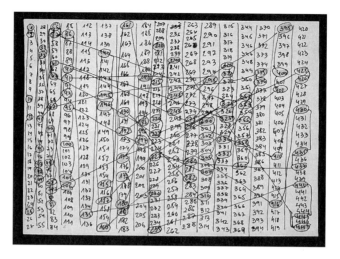

Aya & Gal Middle East, preparatory maps for *Local
Observation Point*, 1995

map that had better not fall into the Syrians' hands; it's already in the same class as
an aerial photograph" (personal communication, 1996).

7

The hand is an important part of the body. It is an agent of action, an instrument for
the realization of one's will and intentions. The hand is not conceived as a free agent,
of course. Its activity is "in the hands" of the one whose hand it is, its master. The hand
is a unique manifestation of its master's identity, personality, social status, and manners, an expression of his or her inner nature. For two centuries at least, this same
hand has also supposedly represented its master as a legal person, equal to others, and
expressed his or her right to be represented as such. For more than two centuries, in
Europe at least, this hand has reached out every once in a while to the voting booth
and given expression to its master's reason and free will, his ability to make a reasonable decision.[26] This is the hand of the citizen. In modern political systems voting has
become the main instrument of political representation, and the citizen's hand has become the material seat of his or her political freedom. The voting citizen is a subject

---

26. *His* ability first (the rich before the poor) and only later *her* ability (the ladies came last).

who gives expression—by means of a simple, handy gesture—to his or her inner, private will, thus turning it into a public voice.[27] Together with the eye that sees and the mouth that speaks, the hand takes part in the interplay between interiorization and exteriorization, subjectivity and citizenship, freedom and equality.[28]

But the hand, whether it belongs to a citizen or to an illegal resident, to a sovereign or to a subject (subjectus), does not simply belong to its master. The hand (and the same goes for the eye or the mouth, of course) is a mediating agent of actions whose origin and end lie far beyond the control of its master, the one who acts. The hand is an instrument for the realization of working plans inscribed in the networks of interaction and communication and in other instruments of all kinds distributed around civic, geopolitical, and virtual spaces. The hand is not a free agent and not the obedient agent of a free subject. It is controlled by different networks and various objects, continues their work, prolongs or extends them, and signals their presence. The hand is almost always a necessary organ of a certain instrument, an important switch in a network. When the modern citizen appeared a few centuries ago, the hand was still a major organ for using force. Today most Western citizens keep their hands near their pockets, manipulating buttons and plastic cards with them, moving timidly and politely among instruments in a very limited area, yet reaching very far indeed. With a slight move of a hand so many gates open wide, vast distances are bridged, and foreign worlds become accessible. Yet once inside the webs of technoscience and the networks of the media market, that same mighty hand is interpellated, constrained, and manipulated by powers far beyond its control, obeying a logic we have not yet begun to understand. But one thing is clear: there are no subjects in this web, transcendent or otherwise, and no sovereignty either.

---

27. In assemblies as well as in voting booths, by raising a hand, casting a vote in the ballot box, or pushing a button, the hand expresses an inner will and a public opinion, taking part in decision making, in the process of collective self-determination, and in the formation of the general will.

28. The hand of the Israeli citizen is the hand of the sovereign. The sovereign—as defined by Agamben—dominates and imposes the law on the outside, on the other, on the abnormal, on the exceptional. He who demarcates, determines the threshold, distinguishes the excluded from the included (Agamben, 1997). Palestinian hands are not like this. Their hands do not represent their "owners," the persons to whom they belong, as legal persons equal to others, as citizens who have the right to be represented. At most, the Palestinian hand is an overt expression of the origin and identity of the one to whom it belongs. It is a means in the hands of the Israeli sovereign, who may use fingerprints for the purpose of identification and identity as the mark and cause of discrimination. Palestinians' hands are part of a space in which identities are determined not according to what one does but according to one's origin. In Jerusalem, a Palestinian hand may remain "within the law" if it is the hand of a manual worker who serves others, or it may transgress the law in protest and rebellion by throwing stones or Molotov cocktails, brandishing posters, or drawing graffiti on walls.

The industrial revolution and later technological developments created new conditions for the hand's movements and activity, transforming the spatial relations within which it is entangled. Once an organ for carrying objects in space, the hand has become hooked to vehicles, an organ of transportation and commuting in real and virtual spaces. The hand has become capable of taking on acts and roles once associated solely with the leg, freeing the entire body for all kinds of new activities. Means of transportation have been improved to such an extent that the distance and time of traveling leave less and less of an impression on the body and mind of the travelers. However, our daily environment is populated with instruments ready to hand, especially designed to fit one's fingers, enhancing their movement to become ever more controlled and precise. Gadgets of all kinds interpellate the hand and call on it to operate them and through them to activate the entire systems to which they are hooked. The hand has become the servant of two masters: of the person in whose body it is an organ and of the networks of interaction and communication to which it is hooked through all kind of instruments.

This double mastery over the hand means, in fact, the deconstruction of a single sovereign subjectivity, liberation from the interiority of the subject, from the tyranny of the truth of the self. But to realize their interactive freedom, citizens must escape this regime of modern subjectivity in which the hand is often enlisted to illuminate the interiority of the individual, to coax it and install it as the sole master of the body. Once liberated from the tyranny of the subject and the logic of subjectivity, citizenship turns into a habitual and continuous act of neturalization, a form of deviation from permanent citizenship, a kind of reverse naturalization: "Usually," say Aya & Gal, "[the position of] the spectator [in art, in culture] has no interactive dimension. The spectators just see everything through their eyes. Seeing is completely detached from action. The neturalized citizen has an interactive dimension, but he is generally blind. The blindness stems from the fact that he is never sure in which space he is present. He is in a transient position—neither here nor there" (personal communication, 1996).

In postmodern, multiple space, every place "takes up place" in countless maps, pictures, and networks. Every point in "real" space in principle becomes present in other spaces of at least two different types—the spaces in which it is represented (by means of photos, maps, and so on) and the virtual spaces of interaction and communication (which locate the point alongside other points, connect it to them, or separate it from them). Real or virtual, a place in a postmodern, multiple space is nothing more than a connection and crossover point from place to place.

The spaces of interaction and communication cannot be reduced to a given physical territory. They are not coterminous with any such territory, and neither do they cancel it out. The industrial and technological revolutions that made these changes possible have caused irreversible damage to the metaphysical conception of place as possessing value, essence, meaning, and a peculiarity of its own. I would like to suggest that the French Revolution balanced the damage to the metaphysics of place to a certain degree by inventing the citizen. The citizen is an address—and an intersection—in the virtual space of the republic, into which all the other spaces are supposed to devolve. If the citizen is an address, the person lives at this address. The Man inside the citizen ensures—according to the metaphysics of the sovereign subject and its modern state—that the address will not remain a virtual address. Man ensures the metaphysical rights of the citizen—to be the possessor of an essence, value, and peculiarity, to be the origin of acts of interaction and communication, to be the source of their meaning and value.

The invention of the citizen was in fact the invention of a new place—the human being. The citizen described in the *Declaration of the Rights of Man and of the Citizen* was depicted as someone who is supposed to defend the human being, natural rights, and liberty by means of membership in a sovereign political community. For its part, the humanity of the person provides the citizen with an anchor for a universal pretension to possess rights and experiences that precede the political order and that cannot be abrogated by it. The Man who found expression in the *Declaration of the Rights of Man and of the Citizen* is a "natural" human being whose body is his own property, who has a right to that body. He is endowed not only with freedom of movement and speech but also with freedom to operate the instruments at his disposal. Right ascribes concrete acts and alienable objects to an inalienable transcendent subject. Hence the person who dwells in this body and operates these instruments conceives of them as alien, subject to his or her authority. The freedom to operate and the desire to make use merge into the regime of a subjectivity that is beyond the world of appearances.

The concept of Man mediates between the citizen as an address in virtual space and as an individual, concrete place in real space. The citizen's possessions—the body being his real estate—are a real place that in principle cannot be appropriated. The assets can be replaced in accordance with market conditions, and thus the body is left as the fixed residence of the sovereign citizen. This place and the space in which it is planted compete with the virtual space in which the citizen is only an address, an intersection, and a crossover point. There are at least two orders of space involved here. A growing colonization movement of the individual and of the world takes place in both. Both are characterized by a claim to totality. Each has a tendency to deny or ignore the other space. The entire world turns into a heterotopic space.

Aya and Gal's NETuralization project makes it possible to reinterpret the concept of heterotopia in a way that distances it from the examples provided by Foucault but somehow maybe returns it closer to the logic of the concept. There is no heterogeneity of time and space if the human being still remains their sovereign and if he or she is maintained as a coherent entity that occupies a homogeneous territory. The heterotopic dimension of the world is a daily occurrence that takes place at surface level, in the abrasive meeting between spaces, in the small gaps in between, in new configurations. Heterotopic Neturalization is neturalization in no place at all; in other words, it takes place on the boundary between places. It is an act of individuals that only seldom exceeds the boundaries of private action to take place entirely in that undefined space that is open in principle to everyone and in which each individual is nothing but an address. This act of Aya & Gal is another attempt—perhaps as hopeless as its predecessors—to escape homogenizing and arbitrary networks of exchange and communication without falling into the closed world of the subject and the spaces managed by the state and its apparatuses.

8

I am not trying to suggest that the world of technoscience—with its virtual spaces, random events, and inevitable catastrophes—is necessarily better than the modern world in which identities are fixed and pinned down to nationalities and territories. Neither would I agree to the metanarrative implied by such a suggestion and especially not to its *either-or* logic. I have assumed that the postmodern resident of other spaces is always already here and there, involved in and identified with both this and that, and that a unified, coherent world has been lost forever. Always serving two masters or more, residents may at best navigate their way between the different spaces, resisting all temptation to stick to the one and disregard the others, trying, as much as possible, to keep moving in between.

And Jerusalem? Jerusalem should be denaturalized. One should let it be what it really is—a complex of irreconcilable other spaces, a real heterotopia. One should free it from the hold of this or that transcendent, national subject. The sanctity of the city must turn into one more value of exchange in its many heterogeneous economies, a code for one more map of sites and itineraries. The condition for all this, of course, is the termination of the Israeli occupation and the granting of citizenship to its Palestinian residents. This citizenship should be equal, de jure and de facto, to the one that Israelis, who share the same geographic and urban space with them, claim.

This citizenship may be Israeli, but this means that Palestinians would have to acknowledge the Israeli occupation and accept the status of a minority in a Jewish state. The citizenship may be Palestinian, assuming that a sovereign Palestinian state emerges. In this case, the apparatus of the nation-state that has generated the occupation would simply be doubled and inscribed in two apparently separate, yet entirely nationalized, urban spaces. The establishment of a Palestinian state that would grant citizenship to the Palestinian residents of Jerusalem, which seems a more feasible solution, would probably solve the "national" problem within the national space, but no other problem. The separation of the two national entities would probably blur for some time the concrete links between the different spaces gathered within the two national spaces. From a minority, the Palestinians would become a majority in their own state, and they would be sovereign and autonomous in shaping their own identity.

But is this solution, which most of the Israeli left and most of the Palestinians are striving to bring about, an adequate remedy to the question of identity? Or is it actually a poison that will trap the Palestinian people for many decades to come in the space of a nation-state ruled by the drive to remove ethnic heterogeneity and achieve national homogeneity? The remedy is poisonous insofar as it requires Palestinians, in the name of their transcendent, national identity, to close the passages to the spaces in which they have managed to become integrated during these decades of Israeli occupation. The remedy is dangerous insofar as it requires Palestinians to cut their links to those networks in which they have managed to intertwine despite all the restrictions that have been imposed on them by Israeli authorities. The separation into two nation-states resembles surgery that takes place once, in the framework of a single body (space), a more or less traumatic event, after which most systems gradually recover and get back to normal functioning.

It is highly plausible that after such geopolitical surgery (the foundation of an independent Palestinian state), most systems of power and networks of economic, political, and social relations would sooner or later get back to their "normal" oppressive functioning in the local, national, and international spaces. The Palestinians would remain a minority dominated and exploited both economically and politically—only now they would be governed by two rather than one cluster of state apparatuses, and their inferior position regarding the Israelis (with whom they would still be entangled) would be reproduced. The Palestinians who stick to the solution of a separate nation-state give precedence to what Deleuze and Guattari have called the national axiom,[29] which is the system of the majority. As Deleuze and Guattari formulate it. "The response of . . . the axiomatic may obviously be to accord the minorities regional or federal or statutory autonomy, in short to add axioms. . . . This operation consists of translating the minorities into denumerable sets or subsets, which would enter as elements into the majority, which could be counted among the majority" (Deleuze and Guattari, 1997, 469).[30] Therefore, as far as national identity is concerned, even if a Palestinian state were to be created and the territory under Israeli control divided, it would still be appropriate, at least for some time, to think about hierarchized relations between a national majority and a national minority within a single space of national existence.

Another conceivable though less realistic possibility is that Israel will give up its definition as Jewish nation-state and become "the state of all its citizens"—Arabs no less than Jews.[31] But even then the threat of new and renewed colonial and postcolonial forms of domination would frame the Palestinians in a third-world enclave inside Israel and reproduce their inferior position in the many virtual spaces opened to Israelis in recent years through the high-technology industry and its transnational corporations. The new conditions would not emerge ex nihilo; they would transform present conditions in a way that would only intensify and emphasize the ugliness and injustice that thirty years of Israeli critique of the occupation have disguised because it was so utterly restricted to the national space.

Those who have hoped to purify their national space from "foreign" elements that are not "natural" to it would be surprised to find the excluded elements shaping from the "outside," even more powerfully, perhaps, what has remained inside. And those who have hoped to end the occupation by making nationality one (negligible) component of citizenship, instead of deriving citizenship from nationality, would lose the position from which it would be possible to resist the future exploitation and

---

29. This is the same axiom that guides Israel's policy toward illegal immigrants and guest workers. Israel uses guest labor "to free itself" from its dependency on Palestinian workers, thus damaging severely the already weak Palestinian economy. The 200,000 workers who have joined the Israeli labor market in the last three years are deprived of almost any rights, and their work conditions are worse than in any other labor-importing democracy.

30. In the words of Deleuze and Guattari. "Once again, this is not to say that the struggle on the level of the axioms is without importance: on the contrary, it is determining" (Deleuze and Guattari 1997, 470).

31. That Israel should become the state of all its citizens is a recent leftist slogan. But most people on the left who use it have only Israeli Arab citizens in mind and not the Palestinians under Israeli jurisdiction (who are supposed one day to have their own state alongside the state of Israel). The call for one democratic and secular state, which is truly the state of all its citizens—Palestinians from both sides of the Green Line—has been renewed lately by some Palestinian intellectuals, like Azmi Bishara, Edward Said, and Gada Karami.

oppression of Palestinians.[32] These would surely continue in a new integrated state, for the latter would be even more integrated into the global economy, and its minorities would resemble third-world immigrants in the metropolitan slums of the West even more than they do now.

Therefore, as utopian or disutopian as the two political solutions mentioned above may sound, they still do not mean emancipation or redemption, for there will always remain those other spaces in which one's hand is constantly busy serving anonymous masters, entangled in opaque networks no one will ever control. Thirty years of occupation—or fifty or a hundred, depending on how one counts—are imprinted in the Israeli-Palestinian space and in all those "other spaces" of the region. The traces of these years cannot be removed by a single political act or event, as path breaking, heroic, or momentous as they may be. The creation of a Palestinian state would not yield an "authentic" Palestinian existence or a "purified," more enlightened Israeli one. The various forms of occupation imprinted in the spaces of this region is something every political vision and act must take into account and try to reorganize to reduce the evils they produce more or less systematically. Reducing all spaces and networks into the framework imposed by two unified but all too similar homogeneous national spaces, dominated by two quite similar national utopias, would not help in achieving this goal. Instead, one should create as many heterotopic sites as possible and let them thrive at every juncture and point of passage where human bodies are or can be linked. One should "assert the power of the nondenumerable, even if that minority is composed of a single member. That is the formula for multiplicities. Minority as a universal figure, or becoming everybody/everything [*devenir tout le monde*]" (Deleuze, Guattari, 1997, 470).

---

32. On nationalism and citizenship, see, for example, Balibar (1997).

CHAPTER 10

THE PICTURE [OF THE BATTLEFIELD]

The development of technology is pure war.
—VIRILIO (1983, p. 54)

1

War isn't a matter of routine. What it involves is the disruption of routine. War "breaks out," it signals its appearance, it demands the declaration of its beginning and end. For an event to be considered a war, it must be relatively isolated, take place within a limited time frame, and express the pretension to victory of at least one of the sides. When events are prolonged beyond a reasonable time frame and appear to be incapable of resolution, we have recourse to the term *war of attrition*, meaning the mutual attrition by either side of the other side's strength. War is one expression of an economy of violence. It takes place between states, focusing on their armed forces.[1] An armed conflict between at least two sides is a condition for war. Occupation is another expression of the economy of violence. The suppression of the occupied side's power and the negation of its ability to fight (its ability to manifest its power) are conditions for occupation. In war, the physical territory is divided in such a way that the front turns into a stage on which the campaign is enacted. In the case of occupation, the entire territory serves as a stage. When a singular violent event between two sides that are involved in a state of war or occupation deviates beyond the stage intended for violence, it assumes a different name—sabotage, guerrilla warfare or terrorist action (when initiated by one side), and assault, retaliation, or accident (when initiated by the other).[2] The reproduction of the territorial relations and of the balance of violence is possible due to the presentation of these events as isolated from the "bigger picture," which delineates the stage and makes it possible to delineate it in this way rather than any other.

---

1. Usually the military brass or the media suggestively propose that certain events be termed a war, but only the state's agents are authorized to declare a war. When Jean Baudrillard declared at the time of the Gulf War that it hadn't occurred at all (Baudrillard, 1991), he was ridiculed or indulged. In the local context, for example, any possible war between the Palestinians and the state of Israel is likely to be decided in advance because it is reasonable to presume it will never be declared. A Palestinian uprising against Israel would be interpreted as another Intifada rather than as a war because of Israel's policy of granting only limited recognition to the Palestinians, which leads to not recognizing them as being authorized to declare war.

2. A complex economy pertaining to the management of violence distinguishes between war and guerrilla warfare, terror and preventive action, an assault and a terrorist action, occupation and an enlightened occupation, massacre and killing, accident and routine activity. All these terms serve as currency in an economy of bloodletting, and the differences between them reflect the intentions of the authors of these acts of violence and the linguistic and institutional machines they have at their disposal to manufacture their justifications. The agents of war would refuse to see the murder of "the engineer" (Yichye Ayash) as a declaration of war on Hamas, which led it to attack Israelis riding buses in their big cities. The agents of war will interpret a situation as war only if it revolves around a border and clear-cut territorial relations.

In a conversation with the former head of Israeli military intelligence, Major General (Res.) Shlomo Gazit, who was responsible for Israeli Defense Forces (IDF) informational activities at the time of the Yom Kippur War (1973), I tried to investigate the moment when a change in the field of vision or battle makes a difference and it is possible to determine that a war has broken out. General Gazit—and others besides him—"saw" the war in his mind's eye, he read it in the aerial photographs. Twenty-three years after the war, he interprets its signs like a doctor pointing to the symptoms of a disease.

A. A.: What was your field of observation when determining that the Yom Kippur War was or wasn't about to break out?

S. G.: The news of approaching war, which arrived "the night before," didn't come out of the blue. Notices and disturbing signs had been accumulating for ten days previously. The bulletin that was received on the eve of the war changed only one thing. It caused a shift in what was called the evaluation of the intention lurking behind the military maneuvers we'd seen beyond the borders. The bulletin didn't provide any new factual datum in the field of military developments. It just came and said that a combined Egyptian and Syrian offensive was to be expected toward the evening of that day. Our chain of communication was disrupted because the original bulletin didn't say anything with respect to the exact timing. At that meeting there was no longer any shadow of a doubt that war was to be expected before five in the afternoon. With respect to the hour, it was a surprise within a surprise.

A. A.: What was the radical difference between all the data previously accumulated and the bulletin that was received that night?

S. G.: The difference was that this was really war. The notices that had been accumulated previously provided the factual and technical background for the military developments without providing an explanation. The explanations were either accompanied by a question mark or accorded a lenient slant in the interpretation. Of course, we were mistaken in this matter.

A. A.: What were the signs?

S. G.: The main signs were the concentration of unusual forces on the Syrian front, the concentration of Egyptian forces at maximal strength along the Suez Canal, plus the incomprehensible news concerning the evacuation of the Soviet experts' families. I believe it occurred two days earlier. This was more or less the background.

THE PICTURE [OF THE BATTLEFIELD]

A. A.: And the bulletin, by contrast?

S. G.: It was from a good Arab source who simply came and informed us: "I know from a firsthand source that tomorrow (mistakenly, as I say, toward evening) a joint Egyptian-Syrian offensive against Israel is going to begin."

A. A.: How is the visual evidence confronted with the bulletin?

S. G.: It's not a matter of confrontation but of interpretation and explication. The facts themselves can be interpreted in different ways.

A. A.: Can you expand on the relation between signs and interpretation in the context of intelligence?

S. G.: The signs are something to which we ascribe meaning. In the intelligence discipline we distinguish between two things—between what's called feasibility and what's called intention. It's relatively easy for intelligence to obtain information about feasibility, all of it in the realm of physical facts, which can be obtained almost in a visual way by means of reconnaissance aircraft, satellite, or observations—the movement of trucks or surface-to-air missiles, an increase or drop in the communications load, radio silence along an entire sector. These are facts. It's almost like a stock market index: it tells us that the feasibility of a war being launched by the opposing side has increased or decreased by a certain number of points. It's a relatively simple matter, but it doesn't say anything. It says a whole lot, but it doesn't deliver the main thing, the explanation—because it could also be a training maneuver, a substitution of forces, or a defensive deployment for one reason or another.

The attempt to explain the intention from an intelligence standpoint can go in several directions. One of them is what happened to us on that night in October. A bulletin arrives from a very reliable source that tells you what lies behind the military steps taken in Syria and Egypt. When such notice arrives, we may either remain calm or go into a panic, but any doubts will have been laid to rest. A second direction is past experience, which in the case of the Yom Kippur War didn't serve us well. We knew that Egypt customarily performed such a military exercise every six months and that it was time for their routine exercise, and this was part of the Egyptian deception plan. The Egyptian army itself knew only that it was going to perform an exercise. It is reported that only sixteen people were privy to the secret of the war. All the others could do everything knowing it was part of an exercise that was due to end the following Tuesday. Past experience is one of the things that helps to determine intention, but it's very dangerous. It's the classic story of the boy who cried wolf. A third direction is an attempt to provide interpretation through a much broader analysis of the political and economic background of the circumstances. In principle, this is the most difficult part, and I'd say it's the part where intelligence almost all over the world fails: ascribing the wrong interpretation to a feasibility that you can more or less see and are familiar with.

A. A.: What determines the difference between a war, operation, assault, and so on?

S. G.: I don't understand the distinction in terminology. It's completely meaningless. The difference is quantitative. The Peace for Galilee operation is called an operation. I don't know whether it was an operation. Perhaps it began with the intention that it should be an operation, an intentional action limited in time and space, but as an operation it is currently in its fifteenth year. We are still mounting the Peace for Galilee operation. What's happening in southern Lebanon today is due to the forbear who fertilized the eggs of the Lebanese quandary. In my estimation, the IDF of today mounts hundreds of operations each year. An operational command dispatching two aircraft to photograph Lebanese and Syrian territory to study new deployments in the field: this constitutes an operation. According to plan it should last forty-five minutes and be concluded without mishap. The two aircraft will return and unload the cassettes of photographs, and that's it. But suppose that one of the two aircraft is brought down and we see a pilot or two falling in Lebanese territory. The IDF immediately prepares to rescue them. This may demand naval, aerial, or surface action or perhaps a combination of all three. The entire IDF launches an operation that may not necessarily end within hours. There may be an encounter with a Lebanese force, and then the whole thing begins to snowball. The original intention had been to mount a small operation of whose existence nobody was even aware. Operations of one type or another are mounted at least once a day, but in this case the chain of events may have turned into a war, and all this in an atmosphere of tension between Israel and Syria. On top of that, Assad reads us wrong, and Bibi [Binyamin Netanyahu] reads Assad wrong, and Clinton reads both of them right or wrong, and we find ourselves in a situation that nobody had intended and the result of which nobody can foresee. The distinction between an operation and war is meaningless.

A. A.: Someone nevertheless makes the determination?

S. G.: In IDF protocol there are operational commands but no war commands. For example, we have the operational command for launching the Six-Day War (1967).

A. A.: What does an operational command say?

S. G.: It says that the authorized echelons instruct a military force on land, sea, or air to perform a certain mission.

A. A.: If we read the command literally, it's possible to claim that there are no wars in Israel?

S. G.: No. That's not my intention. The operational command that launched the Six-Day War devolved with absolute certainty into a military campaign between Israel and Egypt, and this can be called a war. It did not expect the war to deteriorate into an all-out Israeli-Arab conflict, and it certainly didn't expect it to lead to the occupation of territory that would last thirty years and to everything that transpired between '67 and today. But the decisive majority of operational commands should be concluded without any special complication or escalation and without turning into any kind of war.

A. A.: So who does call operations by the name of war?

S. G.: The media.

A. A.: But the army also uses this term?

S. G.: The word *war* doesn't appear in the technical terminology. It does in the media. There's a war against traffic accidents. That's all.

A. A.: Is it the first shot that makes the difference between no war and war?

S. G.: Yes, it's the first shot. It was plain as day that Syria couldn't simply dismiss the downing of her MIG fighters ten days before the Yom Kippur War and that she would somehow try to settle the account. Everything began with an incident. Everything began in the Six-Day War because it's all part of the same dynamite-soaked atmosphere that had its start in the Six-Day War, as a result of which any match can cause an explosion or light a conflagration that wasn't necessarily anyone's object. We can go even further to the War of Independence, which in effect hasn't ended. It ended at the cease-fire stage, but the Israeli-Arab conflict of '48 hasn't been concluded. We could also begin a hundred years ago at the first Zionist congress.

A. A.: Why doesn't the downing of the MIG fighters signify the start of the war?

S. G.: In our terminology, it was a routine security incident. Look, today we are all searching for the soldier Dror Edri who is missing. Let's assume he's been kidnapped by the Islamic Jihad or by Hamas, and they'll demand a ransom for him, or it'll turn out that they've killed him. Ostensibly, this is a terrible incident with no connection to anything before or after it. But only ostensibly. Because this may have occurred in correlation with the anniversary of the signing of the Oslo Accords, and the organization may have wanted thus to demonstrate its opposition to them. So if we go backward, we again arrive at Herzl and the whole of Zionism. It is not war in the narrow definition of the word, or it is a small detail in the much larger framework of the Jewish-Palestinian war that began at the beginning of the century and that is much more important. This is a war, and in this play there are countless incidents, pictures, and acts.

A. A.: Are we at war all the time?

S. G.: This is one of Israeli society's most serious problems. Whether consciously or not, Israeli society ignores the fact that it's at war. It represses the fact that we are at war, and this is coming to you from someone who is a supporter of the peace process.

A. A.: Is it impossible, then, to describe war as the disruption of a state of tranquility or peace?

S. G.: Since 1917 or earlier, we have been in a constant war in which there have been episodes of cease-fire and calm. The world war lasted six years, but that doesn't mean there was shooting all the time. If the duration of the war was approximately two thousand days, those who were in uniform saw no more than 150 days of fighting. That's a lot, but it's not much as opposed to two thousand days of fighting.

A. A.: From which stage was the Yom Kippur War called a war?

S. G.: From the first second. From the moment the Egyptian and Syrian offensive began there wasn't a shadow of a doubt that we were at war. The concept of war is a literary concept. When you say to someone that it's a war, nobody knows what to do. So you've said it, but what needs to be done? An operational command says take the vehicle and do this or that. An army is an organization. It's an absolutely purposeful institution, and it doesn't deal with cultural philosophizing. At a certain hour you're supposed to perform and arrive at A, B, C, and D. The tasks entrusted to you are such and such.

2

"The eyes of the state"—the appellation applied by soldiers of the Golani brigade to Mt. Hermon—became a distinctive symbol of the Yom Kippur War. The land was personified, and its head—its most northerly part—was given a pair of eyes that were supposed to endow it anew with an overall view of the surroundings.[3] In 1973, Oded Yedaya, an officer in an elite unit who was present (whose view was present) at the conquest of Mt. Hermon, was a student of photography. Yedaya was afforded a different point of observation, most terrible of all—that of one who saw above the peak of Mt. Hermon, through and beyond what was seen by "the eyes of the state," that it could all have been otherwise. My conversation with Yedaya, today a well-known Israeli photographer, highlighted a different and complementary aspect of the war's regime of view.

A. A.: Was there a failure of the eye in the Yom Kippur War?

O. Y.: With respect to everything concerned with the view, everyone saw the movement of the forces. In this matter there was no sleight of eye. All the data said it was going toward war. But the intelligence service maintained its belief in the acquisition of oral information, too. They believed that they'd intercept commands over the radio. The intelligence community collects information from two sources—one of them sight and the other hearing. They didn't obtain the information from hearing because there was a deception. Our mistake as Israelis is that we always think we're very smart, but we fail to appreciate that the enemy may be smart too. They knew we were capable of obtaining oral information from them and that we were listening to the wireless. They simply decided not to pass down the war command, not even to the division commanders. The problem was the balance in the relation between eye and ear. They saw everything with their eyes and listened only to hearing. They were certain that the ears would know everything, but the ears heard only what the other side wanted us to hear. Thanks to reconnaissance observers, visually everything is seen.

A. A.: And what about the eyes of the state?

O. Y.: On October 8, 1973, an attempt was made to retake Mt. Hermon. As part of the same conception that we are almighty, the entire Golani regiment was sent to ascend Mt. Hermon. They took their APCs [Armored Personnel Carrier] and drove up. When they reached a third of the way up, the force turned back because the Syr-

---

3. In 1974, the Israeli artist Michal Ne'eman wrote the phrase "the eyes of the State" on two placards that she planted along the seashore in Tel Aviv, breaking down the consistent structure of a body with two eyes in its head.

ians laid ambushes and mowed down the first APCs. Contrary to fable, the Syrians fought. Northern Command didn't know what to do. They said that if Golani had failed, let's send the "magicians" [an elite army unit] to check what's happening on Mt. Hermon. I asked what kind of equipment we need. They said nothing except a rifle, backpack, and handcuffs because you're going to bring back a tongue.

A. A.: What does that mean?

O. Y.: I also asked what they meant. I thought that after being away from the unit for two years, I wasn't familiar with anything anymore. The meaning was to carry out a reconnaissance mission, see how they were deployed, and try to capture someone and bring him back so he'd talk. In the army things never work that way. There is no command telling you to go into a battle area and bring back a tongue. It's not that we didn't take prisoners. The main drill in the army and in the unit is that you're taught to attack and kill, not to attack and take prisoners. Each soldier has plastic handcuffs, but the drill is that you attack to kill. Obtaining information from the enemy is the work of the General Security Service and the Mossad. The army has never worked on taking prisoners and extracting information from them. Suddenly they decided otherwise. They didn't know where to get information. They were confused. They sent us, they didn't even know what to ask of us. And like good soldiers, we said we'd go.

An advance command squad was set up in the unit. They said that Uzi Dayan would sit in Northern Command and take charge of us. We arrived at Northern Command, and Uzi went inside and met the Command's intelligence officer. Uzi said, "Okay, we're setting out on our mission. What intelligence do you have? What do you already know about the area?" They said, "Nothing. You go and get the information." He said, "Wait a minute. You could have gotten an aerial photo the day before, information from observers regarding where the Syrians are located, something. If that's the case," Uzi said to them, "I'm taking my men home. I'm not going to send ten men on a suicide mission." After the operation on Mt. Hermon ended, it turned out how right he was. The Syrians' two battalions were scattered behind every rock exactly along the route we'd wanted to take. We would have been wiped out ten times over.

So the unit said, "If you want to capture Mt. Hermon, then let's plan how to take Mt. Hermon together." We began with an aerial photo. There's the Israeli spur of Mt. Hermon, above it the Syrian spur, and between them another hill along which the border once passed, for which reason nobody had ever built anything there. The

THE PICTURE [OF THE BATTLEFIELD]

guys from the unit said that according to logic, we should come from behind. Then the battles began over who would take what. The Golani regiment refused to accept assistance from anyone. After they'd failed, they had to take it alone, only them. They wouldn't budge. It's been a tradition since the Six-Day War that you march straight ahead again and again, and in the end you capture the mountain. Northern Command agreed to have us perform our reconnaissance patrol two days in advance of the offensive. We came from behind, not from the Israeli side, through the villages. The moment we began to ascend the mountain, of course, there wasn't a single soldier on this side. We captured the hill without incident. The Syrians were deployed on the western slopes in the direction of the planned Israeli attack. We had come from behind and captured the tripeaked hill, and all was quiet.

We told Golani over the radio that we could see it with our eyes, that it was possible to descend from the tripeaked hill and surprise the Syrians from the rear after destroying their command unit. Golani said, "No way. Don't you capture anything or do anything." They didn't want any help. We told them to pass our way, that we'd only provide them with guides and two scouts. Again they said, "No way." Their main contention was that any deviation from the drill or a familiar route might lead to confusion among their troops. After two nights, the night of the big offensive arrived. The paratroopers descended on the Syrian spur in helicopters and took it with only two wounded casualties. Golani chose brute strength. They took the most easily anticipated path that had been marked on the maps for a hundred years already. They advanced rock after rock, and I stood high above and saw it all. Many were killed there. Over the radio we heard how one after another was killed. Every hour we called and asked if they needed help. They replied in an angry tone: "Don't you dare move. Mt. Hermon is ours." Not even a diversionary operation. They wanted it to be only Golani and only their way. More than sixty soldiers were killed. The Golani regiment regained its pride. In the morning they asked one soldier how they'd gone on fighting after seeing half the regiment get wiped out, how they'd had the courage to advance. So the soldier said, "The guys told us to think about the fact that Mt. Hermon is the eyes of the state and that there won't be any state if it doesn't have any eyes." It was one of the most glorious and terrible nights in the annals of war.

A. A.: Actually, you turned into the eyes of the state, who saw them getting killed one after another. You were like observers?

O. Y.: We didn't actually see because it took place on the antipodal slopes. We heard everything on the radio. We were observers over the radio. We had several sets. We

Oded Yedaya, *Officers Patrol, the Hermon Mount, the Israeli Summit,* 1988

were plugged into the Golani network too. We heard how this guy was killed and how that force gave up. They could have ascended from behind in a more sophisticated battle rather than face to face.

A. A.: If so, why in fact did you ascend?

O. Y.: Exactly to bring back information from observation, whatever we could. We obtained the most relevant information, not a "tongue." We climbed to a point of observation from which the capture of Mt. Hermon was possible. It's not just an aerial photograph. We physically found the path. The entire Golani regiment could have ascended from there—alive.

A. A.: What do you see from the eyes of the state?

O. Y.: The entire country. You see all of Syria from there. On a clear day all the way to Damascus. There are warning systems of all types there, both hearing and sight. Mt. Hermon is a very strategic point. It is the key. This happened three weeks after Mt. Hermon didn't see the war, saw it but didn't hear it. It wasn't a problem of instrumentation. There has to be a brain behind the eye as well.

A. A.: If you'd taken photographs in the war, what would your frame have been?

O. Y.: There's one frame that stayed with me for many years, from the day after the battle on Mt. Hermon. It's in one of my stories as a trauma, too. The Syrian

commandos were scattered about the rocks. The Syrians saw that they'd lost and began escaping home, passing through the wadi between us and Golani. The cease-fire
hadn't yet gone into effect. The war was still going on. You're still trying to weaken
the enemy even though it's the end of the war. Here and there somebody would shoot
at them or yell at them to raise their arms. Some of them surrendered and came.
There were wounded men whom we tried to provide with first-aid. We had hardly
any food or water. It was freezing cold. I remember that one squad came right
through my sector. Two of them surrendered, and a third continued to lie behind a
rock. In war you either take prisoners or kill. You don't let anyone escape. There's no
question about that. Through the binoculars the distant and warlike turn into something human. I saw him. I don't know what he was thinking, maybe that we couldn't
see him. He evidently planned to hide until nightfall and then slip away to the Syrian border. I had binoculars rather than a camera. I identified his location. Then
there's this game of "I can see you, and you don't know it." I was with the binoculars,
and I directed the aim of the soldier with the rifle beside me until he hit him. Afterward, for years, you don't know if he did or didn't pull out a white rag. It's a sort of
frame I have in my head.

3

In late September of 1996, the Palestinians fought for the demarcation of a border
between them and the Israelis. The events that took place at this time aimed to
achieve what the "peace process" had failed to achieve—the demarcation of a border. The demarcation of a border means the end of occupation, the cessation of a
state in which one side restricts the other side's actions and determines that it must
obviate its power. A borderline is a necessary condition for war—otherwise the event
must be considered of a different order—just as war is a means of obtaining it. In a
conversation with press photographer Miki Kratzman, I tried to recreate two moments when a border appeared in a photograph. One is connected with the miniwar
that broke out between Israelis and Palestinians in the wake of the opening of the
Wailing Wall tunnel under Netanyahu's government, and the other is connected
with the departure of Israeli forces from the West Bank cities and the entry of the
Palestinian police as part of the Oslo Accords.

A. A.: When you arrived at the roadblock in Ramallah, did you know how to read the
arena of war?

M. K.: It looked like a battle area, but the division was unclear. For instance, it was hard
to tell where the Israelis were. The Israeli soldiers shot at the Palestinian policemen,

but it wasn't clear at each stage where they were shooting from. It wasn't clear to me, nor was it clear to the Palestinian policemen, but they ardently returned the fire. The Palestinians were roving about the area, and I didn't know from which direction they would shoot. Their moves were unexpected. I noticed that the same uncertainty I felt as a photographer moving among them also affected the Palestinian crowd.

A. A.: Where did you position yourself?

M. K.: I was in the midst of the Palestinians, but I tried to behold them from the opposite direction, as though from the Israelis' position. When they shot, I stood opposite them to photograph them. There was a very distinct territorial division with respect to where the civilians stood and where the soldiers stood. The civilians stood in sheltered spots all the time. The soldier, by virtue of being empowered within the population, dared to take a step forward each time to an exposed spot. It always looked as if he'd advanced one step too many. The confusion among the policemen was reflected by their movements, their lines of sight, and the lack of coordination between them. As you can see in the photo, they don't know where they're running. They looked to me like silhouettes flying through space and running without any connection to what was happening all around. In such a state of lack of awareness, I tried to capture the most illogical moments—for example, the figure of a soldier shooting with a cigarette in his mouth. Nobody fights with a cigarette in his mouth. Or two soldiers running in opposite directions; a soldier huddling beside an exposed wall, a policeman shooting over the heads of Palestinians who are huddled on the floor and watching him. Even they were in the grip of confusion with respect to the real danger, whether it was coming from their own policemen or from the Israeli soldiers. You don't turn your back on whoever is shooting at you, and that's what they were doing in that situation. These opposed directions of viewing interested me.

A. A.: Why did you choose to stand opposite them?

M. K.: To photograph them from the back would have looked unconvincing. They shot vainly, in the direction of places where you didn't see anybody. I'm convinced that ninety-something percent of their rounds were fired at nothing. They were in euphoria from operating their weapons more than from hitting anything with them. It all looked as if you'd taken people who'd been in the army for two days and told them to fight. There was no military drill. They looked and acted like civilians in army uniform with weapons in their hands. There was no logic to anything and everything they did, from somebody running and performing a Rambo-style barrel-roll in the street to

Miki Kratzman, *Ramallah,* 1996

people shooting and taking cover behind a bush. It's not wise to shoot from behind a bush, you'll be seen and shot back at immediately because a bush may offer cover but no protection. They are a newborn army. In one of the pictures you see two soldiers, each of whom is running in a different direction, giving rise to a sensation of disorder or euphoria. I know that in general when you shoot, everyone shoots in the same direction and you try to maintain a straight line, you try to be aware of each other; nobody runs ahead so as not to get into anyone's sights. Nobody runs unless it's done in orderly fashion. You change position, improve your angle. This was a Wild West show, every man for himself. In football it sometimes happens that one player or another decides to win the game on his own. He tries to pass everyone, starting at his own end of the field and ending up at the opponents' end of the field. The Palestinian policemen reminded me of something similar. It looked as if each one of them was going to win this war on his own. Each one of them advanced, shot off a burst, exhausted his clip, and retreated. There was no attempt to perform a flanking operation or to get organized in any way. It all looked very innocent—an innocent battle.

A. A.: Do they touch or hold each other?

M. K.: It's touch inspired by fear. It's like someone walking in the dark and putting his hands out in front of him in order not to bump into anything. This touching

Miki Kratzman, *Ramallah*, 1996

doesn't change anything objectively, but it exists, it's familiar, like a child holding on to his mother's skirt.

A. A.: When did you encounter the Israelis?

M. K.: The Israelis were far away. It wasn't a confrontation such as occurred in the Intifada where you see the enemy all the time: one of the two of them is the enemy, each is the other's enemy. Here people grabbed cover, people were at greater distances. The effective range of a bullet is much greater than the effective range of a stone or slingshot.

A. A.: What are you actually photographing here?

M. K.: The expectation of something bad. The one who's walking bent over is walking that way because he knows he could catch a bullet at any moment. Those who are yelling to him also know that he's going to catch the bullet at any moment. His slow gait is like someone trying to hide from something, but he's completely exposed to enemy fire. He advances slowly, like the sitting ducks in a shooting arcade or a mobile target. He knows he's being aimed at and that it's the shooter's decision whether to hit him or not.

THE PICTURE [OF THE BATTLEFIELD]

A. A.: Why do you photograph the woman?

M. K.: Because I know that in this dash someone is going to get hurt.

A. A.: What are the people doing there—looking for a better place to see?

M. K.: Civilians were milling about all the time, multitudes of unarmed civilians who stood behind the shooter's shoulder and gave him advice, told him where to shoot and encouraged him. Bullets were flying through the air all the time, and you couldn't tell where they were coming from. There was the noise of gunfire all the time, and civilians kept roaming about as if this was the best show in town. And occasionally one would die. There were lots of people there who wanted to see the battle. They ran because the shooting suddenly turned in their direction. They decamped singly. Each time one of them would run. While they ran, the policemen covered them. Among both the policemen and the crowd there was still an atmosphere of a war of stones rather than a real shooting war. In a war of stones when you're hit by a stone, it's not the same as being hit by a bullet. These people strolled from side to side, ran from side to side, as if clods of earth were being thrown at them. This is why so many were killed that day.

A. A.: The Palestinian police enter Nablus, and a terrorist wanted by the Israeli authorities enters your photograph. Could you recreate the photographic situation?

M. K.: In this photograph I surrendered to a different power, which constructs the frame. The man is standing and holding his M16, and he's determining how he'll look in the picture. As long as the camera was shooting, he wouldn't abandon his pose. On that day the wanted terrorists began to come out into the streets and publicly display their arms. The media rushed to them. Until that moment they had been undercover, and this was the first time they went on public display. He posed for the cameras. The situation flattered him, but it was also disturbing. He wasn't used to it. In this situation I sought out his gaze. He's like a man who's come out into the light from a dungeon, and he's blinded. You can see exposure isn't easy for him. His ambivalence is plainly apparent. At a certain moment his gaze registered impatience, the fact that he was sick of it. After that look I couldn't go on photographing. I had to put down the camera. His gaze was more powerful than mine. Like two people who stare at each other until one of them suddenly concedes and lowers his eyes. That's exactly what happened. In the looks we exchanged, he was the boss and not I.

Miki Kratzman, *The Withdrawal of the Israeli Army,*
Nablus, 1995

A. A.: How did you know he was a wanted terrorist?

M. K.: You see someone walking and there's five hundred people behind him, so you know it has to be some big shot. And he's toting an M16. That's not exactly regular issue among the Palestinians.

A. A.: What is the look you've captured in the picture?

M. K.: A look saying, "That's enough. Stop taking pictures."

A. A.: How does the evacuation of a town turn into a photograph? What happened in Nablus from the moment you arrived until you knew your camera had done its work?

M. K.: I drove to Nablus a little bit late. I went with the feeling that I was missing it all by ten minutes. I wasn't mistaken. As soon as I arrived, I realized that the last bus of Palestinian policemen had arrived several minutes earlier. I arrived after the euphoria. The main square was overflowing with people and the media. It was hard to take a picture without catching another photographer in the frame. I began looking for the quiet niches where nothing eventful was happening. I kept my distance from

Miki Kratzman, *The Withdrawal of the Israeli Army,*
Nablus, 1995

those who were shooting in the air, from those who were waving banners, to be alone with the photographic subjects rather than with more media. When there are lots of cameras, the decibel level rises, and all movement is greatly intensified. I wanted to avoid that, although the place was swarming with photographers. I didn't want to cause anything but only to capture it.

A. A.: Do you really believe you can escape the fate of the camera that creates the event?

M. K.: I'm unable to. But even in creating the event there are different levels. Ten cameras create more excitement than one. What happened in this photograph (see photo above)? I approached the soldiers because they looked like a wall. I waited for someone to pass, for something to happen. Suddenly this boy came from the right side of the frame, got stuck in the middle, and stared at me. At first it bothered me. Afterward I understood that there's a lot of power in it. I discovered the face peeking out of the background only when I was printing the frame.

A. A.: The boy stared at you?

M. K.: Yes. At the time of the photograph I didn't discern the type of hostility that I see afterward. It was a crazy event, full of people. The frame doesn't convey the madness that was going on there.

A. A.: When you come to an event, are you searching for a gaze?

M. K.: I'm not searching for it. I utilize it, and I'm aware of it. I would prefer that the photographed subject not respond to the camera. But the worst thing is when he responds to a different camera. I want him not to take notice of the camera at all. But if he's already taken notice of the camera, I'd like it to be mine.

A. A.: Did you know what you were looking for when you came?

M. K.: No.

A. A.: But you knew you were ten minutes late?

M. K.: Yes. Because such events always have some focal point. There are a few climactic moments. In the evacuation of a town it could be the arrival of the policemen, the departure of the Israeli soldiers, a procession, a parade, the dancing. Around all these events, or at their fringes, things happen. It also pays to be at the climactic moments to catch the interludes between them.

A. A.: What is an event?

M. K.: The military parade. It's a small event inside a large event.

A. A.: An event is something that is planned to such an extent?

M. K.: The planning is also a photographic object. The important thing in the frame is the relation among the components. A military parade is a classic example. The strictness with respect to order and systematization is in itself a photographic object. It doesn't matter which soldiers are standing there or whether they're children dressed up as soldiers. The parade interests me at the level of order.

A. A.: But in your photographs there's always another event that disrupts the order, that doesn't allow the planned event to appear?

M. K.: It's like a stone falling into water and creating ripples. I photograph the ripples and not the stone.

THE PICTURE [OF THE BATTLEFIELD]

A. A.: Your camera is also a stone. Maybe in principle you cannot photograph it?

M. K.: The analogy is incorrect. My camera isn't the stone that was thrown in the water. It's only a parallel to the stone. It's like the tremor after an earthquake. Its influence is marginal in relation to the central event. For the sake of the matter, if you've thrown a stone in water and there's a stick in the water that influences the ripples, then the stick isn't the stone. It's got an influence, surely. The camera has an influence, no doubt about it. But we try to reduce it to a minimum.

A. A.: So where's the stone?

M. K.: The event itself, these climaxes inside the happening, some of them planned and others not. These are the stones.

A. A.: A parade is a stone?

M. K.: Yes. It isn't the water. As a result of the parade all sorts of things happen. People come to peek. It begins with the Palestinian policemen pushing and shoving inside the parade ground to make room for the parade. It continues with kids who try to sneak inside to see the parade, with people trying to get hold of a high spot on the fence or in the windows of the buildings that don't have a better vantage point. And all these things that are happening all around are the ripples I spoke about.

A. A.: And are you interested in the ripples?

M. K.: I'm interested in everything. Usually, in the result, the stone itself is less interesting. It's not that I photograph only the ripples, but in the editing, in the screening, the stone usually comes out less interesting. I say "usually." For example, the soldiers' contemplation of the stone is much more powerful than the stone itself. When I take notice of the stone, I'm taking notice of the event at the level of time. There's a certain time and a certain place in which the focal point of an event subsists. That's the stone.

A. A.: You said "we" before. Who are we?

M. K.: "We" is the photographers.

A.A: Are you speaking in the name of the profession or in your own name?

M. K.: Pretty much in the name of the profession. In the name of the profession's better side. In the event at Nablus there were policemen, there were women, there were children, there were elderly people, there were birds, there were buildings, there were photographers. Each one contributed his share. That's all. It's like you're used to having policemen, to having whatnot, so you've got photographers, too. The boy who was there and raised the flag had an influence? The one who held a gun had an influence? The one who held a camera also had an influence.

4

In the photographs of Khaled Zighari, a Palestinian photographer and resident of East Jerusalem, the linear sequence, in which each chapter is replaced by the next in the series—Intifada, Oslo Accords, peace process—doesn't exist. First there was the occupation, then came the occupation, and still now the occupation continues; it seems that tomorrow, too, it shall remain. Many of the scenes photographed by Zighari during the past three years are reminiscent of what the Israeli press has printed in the past. Due to the absence of any public interest or perhaps because they don't accord with the times— the "peace process" period—his photographs today appear mainly in the Arabic and foreign press. The occupation hasn't ceased, and Khaled Zighari's pictures provide us with an opportunity to take another close-up look at it.[4] The scenes of occupation familiar to the Israeli public from the local press were photographed mainly by Israeli photographers. Some of them served as reservists before, after, or during the making of the photographs and were in effect part of the army of occupation, though at the same time they sought to assume the privileged position of the photographer—a position ostensibly removed from the event. Zighari's photographs, which record similar scenes, provide an opportunity to examine how the same reality gets organized differently when the camera that approaches it to see is in the hands of a Palestinian.

I dwell especially on two pictures. In both of them an Israeli soldier and a Palestinian subject appear. They are standing opposite each other, one on one. Each is deterring the other, signaling with his body that he is capable of using force, instantly, if the other takes just another small step. To this day I have never seen such power relations between an Israeli soldier and a Palestinian subject in a photograph. Evidently no Israeli photographer can capture their like with his camera. When the Palestinian photographer is at the Israeli soldier's back, and both the photographer and his subjects are surrounded by a Palestinian crowd, the soldier and the Palestinian are locked in a duel to deter each other. I asked Khaled Zighari to describe the situation with respect to one of these photographs:

---

4. An exhibition of his photographs called *The Exhibition of Truth* was held in Beyt Ha'am, Tel Aviv.

THE PICTURE [OF THE BATTLEFIELD]

Khaled Zighari, *Israeli Soldier and Palestinian,* 1995

Khaled Zighari, *Demonstration against Land
Expropriation, Palestinian Shouts at the Israeli Soldier
Pointing the Gun: "Shoot Me,"* 1994

K. Z.: The date was September 22, 1995. There had been arrests, some shooting, one or two people injured. Somebody said that they wanted to stab soldiers. So shooting broke out for no reason, and they continued shooting at the body that was lying on the ground. The Palestinian in the picture had blood on his hand. The gun was between the two of them. This was near the most important roadblock in Hebron, in the Old City. When there's any rioting, the roadblock turns into a pressure cooker, and there are lots of people. The soldier was unable to draw his rifle. In another picture, the soldier is holding the gun, and the Palestinian is wrestling it away from him. The Palestinian is making a gesture, and everybody's watching him. If the soldier makes a move, everybody'll swarm over him. There are ten soldiers and a hundred Palestinians. The Hebronites aren't an easy bunch. This was a time of riots, and they weren't easy either.

A. A.: What happened in this photograph, where the soldier aims the gun at the Palestinian's mouth?

K. Z.: It happened in Ramallah, on January 17, 1994. This was my first picture that packed a punch. Any knowledgeable photographer would choose this picture. The soldier draws his rifle for no reason at all other than to threaten the Palestinian and make him leave the demonstration. The Palestinian stands his ground and yells at the soldier. After I photographed it, the soldier butted me in the head with the rifle as a warning. A comrade of his, who'd seen me taking pictures, put his rifle to my head. I started yelling at the soldier and wanted to complain. I heard the officer of the battalion who was there saying, "For that we'll take him in the end." I didn't make any problems for them. When I was taking pictures and they drew their guns on me, I patiently kept asking the soldier to give me his personal details. There's the IDF spokesman [to turn to].

A. A.: Is that any help?

K. Z.: No. When I've got lots of problems, nobody helps me. That's why I said to myself that I've got a very powerful picture and I've got to protect it. I left the scene before it was all over.

A. A.: What is a "powerful picture"?

K. Z.: When there's a picture, it has to be on my film. The price doesn't matter. Whenever you've got a journalist and the authorities, there is going to be a little ruckus, and the authorities don't enjoy having a photographer in places they don't

THE PICTURE [OF THE BATTLEFIELD]

want. In the field, government credentials are no help. After they do with you as they please, they look at your credentials. In my list I've been beaten, injured, and held in custody thirteen times. I've been injured by rubber bullets at least three times, and one time I was shot in the shoulder with live ammunition. I was in Ramallah in '94. It was the date of my birthday. I was shot by a 9 millimeter pistol at a range of 5 to 6 meters. When I heard the shooting, I tried to escape into a shop. It was the first time I ever ran away from a picture that I didn't want to take. In the area where I was injured, one person was killed, two were critically injured, and five were wounded.

The truth subsists in my photograph. The most powerful picture conveys the truth. All these photos are truth. I didn't tell him to kill him or arrest him and I'll photograph you. Everything that happened is truth. I don't want anything bad to happen, but I don't like it to happen without my being there. It's worth a lot sometimes.

A. A.: Which photographer's credentials do you have?

K. Z.: I've got three certificates—one from the Israeli Press Office, one from the Palestinian Authority, and one from *El Kuds.* One for the Israeli authorities, one for the Palestinian authorities, and one for the Palestinian people. That's the best one I've got. It's for the people.

A. A.: What do you mean?

K. Z.: When I was a photographer for Reuters, the bus bombings in Afula, Tel Aviv, and Jerusalem took place. When a bombing occurs, a Palestinian photographer has got nothing to do. He can do something else, which is to get a picture of the perpetrator. It takes time to identify the perpetrator's body and ascertain the address, the family. In the case of Ra'ad Zakrani, the perpetrator of the Hadera bombing, I tried to obtain a picture of him at eleven at night. The area around his house was sealed off. The village had been placed under curfew. It wasn't easy. I tried to get into the village, from the main road. The soldiers brandished their rifles, they were in no mood to talk to anyone. I like having something that nobody else has got, having something rare. It's not that hard to photograph his picture, but it isn't easy to obtain the picture when the area is sealed off. I went through the mountains, from another village. From above I could see the house surrounded by soldiers. Ra'ad's sister told me, "You have to be inside our house," and she said she'd come and get me. We entered from the back, and we made a duplicate in five minutes. It was the first time I ever made a duplicate at night in five minutes. When it became known that we had a photograph, CBS and ABC called us. Usually you don't see the face of the perpetrator. If I didn't have my *El Kuds* certificate, nobody would recognize me, the Palestinian people wouldn't believe it. There was a time when Israelis disguised themselves as journalists and photographers when they were really security agents. With this certificate, when I speak nicely to them, they offer assistance.

A. A.: Who has an interest in publishing the picture?

K. Z.: There's a bombing, there are two sides, there are two pictures—a picture of the bombing and a picture of the perpetrator. The one doesn't exist without the other. Sometimes it takes a long time to identify whoever did the bombing. If they are identified, it's good to have the picture the same day. This way you've got the full story. If you cover the bombing, you've got to bring the testimony of the bomber and his family: why they dispatched their son, how long he'd been wanting to do it. They show the Israeli families. We have to create a balance between the two sides.

A. A.: What do you mean when you say that every photograph is truth?

K. Z.: I don't want to get in the middle between the two sides. When I've got the pictures, it provides me with evidence that it happened. The bombing happened, that's the truth. I know it was. How do I know? Because I've got the pictures. The bombing of the number 18 bus was the first time that a Palestinian was present at a bombing site. There were lots of security agents there. All Israel was there. My being there was unpleasant to them, to both the authorities and the Israeli people. There was one Israeli photographer who began to yell at me and shove me. He was endangering my life. I left the spot. At Yichieh Ayash's funeral, in the face of a half million Palestinians, we guarded the Israeli crews and were rewarded with stones. If there's an Israeli photographer about to be assaulted, I'm supposed to protect him. When settlers assaulted me in the road, I asked another Israeli photographer for help, and he refused to come to my assistance. He didn't take pictures when they tried to strangle me.

A. A.: What is the camera's role in such events?

K. Z.: When they pin someone to the ground and begin to investigate him, and there are ten of us photographers taking pictures of him, and there's also fifty Palestinians watching, it heats up the atmosphere. But usually, it's the soldier who began to investigate him. I say to the soldier, "You're on duty, and I'm on duty." I say to the soldier, "You begin, and I'll continue." I'm not heating up the atmosphere, and I'm not starting anything. Me, whatever I see I photograph.

THE PICTURE [OF THE BATTLEFIELD]

A. A.: Why is it important to get the picture?

K. Z.: In '94, when there was a bombing in Hebron, I tried to hide the film rolls. Two settlers were killed. We climbed a mountain across the way to take pictures. We were seen, and they came for us as if we'd carried out the bombing. I was a novice, and I didn't know that I could take pictures of whatever I want. I saw them, and I was afraid. I hid the camera and the film rolls. When they arrived, they told us to step aside. We stood on the wall, and they investigated us like wanted men—as if we were suspects. It wasn't that easy. We were on the mountain, and there was nobody there. They could do whatever they wanted. The soldier searched for our equipment and put a rifle to my head and asked me to speak with him in Hebrew. Fear wouldn't let me speak in Hebrew. He asked whether we'd taken pictures before or after the bombing and said, "We'll take the equipment and check." He took the film rolls and put a rifle to my head. I had one roll with me that I knew had to be protected. It's not a good picture. It was taken from a kilometer away. Everything appears so small, in all likelihood what you see is an ambulance and ten cars. It's not a picture, but it has to be protected. I protected it the way I did. I hid that roll. The soldier took all the other rolls, and to this day he's examining them. Another time, on the trans-Samaria road, I was returning from Ayash's house, which had been sealed. Two soldiers and policemen tried to take the camera away from me and didn't succeed. They were planning to shoot so that I'd give them the camera. I said to them, "You can take the camera only if you shoot me." I quickly clicked a few pictures. "You haven't got the right to do that to me. Take my personal details. Arrest me, but you won't take the camera." They busted my cellular phone so that I wouldn't talk to anyone. Afterward when I spoke with a different officer so he'd solve our problem, the first officer snatched the camera. I'm neither right nor left. In my line of work I do my job like a professional press photographer. I want a good picture, a picture that tells the entire story. I like the picture that speaks by itself, a picture that speaks.

A. A.: What did you photograph during the withdrawal from the towns?

K. Z.: The Israeli people don't like seeing their flag come down anywhere. I waited for nine hours at the Civilian Administration [building] in Jenin. I'm standing there like this. I can't move. I want a picture, and he knows what I want. He wants to take it down when I'm not there, and I want him to take it down when I'm there. I waited in the car. Suddenly at two o'clock at night I saw someone go up. There were no lights. I stood beside the gate. He had the flag in his hand, and I took a picture. That's what I photographed in Jenin.

5

The economy of violence today is increasingly conducted more in connection with the photographic economy than with the traditional economy of war. The camera designates the place of war. It is today one of war's most distinctive agents. And perhaps it is also a distinctive sign of the end of war as conducted in the form of a clear territorial deployment and its replacement by singular acts of violence, which are not necessarily less systematic. Wherever the camera is present, it frames the arena where war takes place. This is an arena whose dependency on a border is decreasing.[5] The borderline is determined in the place where the camera arrives to illuminate, restrain, restrict, monitor, and supervise. That is where the next bloodletting is declared, which will take place in light of the illusion that instruments that serve for the purpose of control and destruction can turn, by virtue of the intentions of those using them, into tools of salvation or critique.[6]

Horror is linked with photography, and vice-versa. In his book *La chambre claire*, Roland Barthes writes that in our culture "photography is the place of death" (Barthes, 1980). Paul Virilio put forward a more radical contention concerning televised photography in the 1980s: "Television cannot be art because it is the museum of accidents. In other words, its art is the site where all the accidents occur" (Virilio, 1994). One could make the further contention that unwillingly the photographer turns into a hunter after death. Sometimes the photograph is an action that takes place after the event. It perpetuates what can no longer be saved. Sometimes the horror is divulged slowly, after the photographic act, when the photograph provides the evidence to determine "A horror has taken place here." Sometimes the photographer (in the case of television) and viewer become witnesses to the horror, witnesses to the killing being performed in front of the camera in real time.[7] However, it also happens that the photograph is drawn to the horror even before it has occurred. The photograph seemingly chooses to record the heads that are going to roll before anybody has the slightest idea that a horror is going to take place here of all places. This

---

5. The systematic accumulation, on the part of government and military agencies, of photographs of Palestinians who have shot at Israeli soldiers diverts the war to a different arena.

6. I elaborate on this point from a theoretical aspect in the chapter on Rabin's assassination. The involvement of television cameramen in the war in the occupied territories (1996), the Rabin assassination (1995), and the bombing in Atlanta (1996) are just three recent examples of the presence of cameras at the site of the horror. In a more institutionalized way, the Gulf War, Somalia, and the Grapes of Wrath Operation are testimony to the assimilation of the economy of violence in the economy of the camera.

7. As happened in 1997, for instance, when a Greek Cypriot was shot dead in front of the television camera during his cousin's funeral.

occurred in the case of the soldiers who were killed in Lebanon in late 1996 and had been captured by Levac's camera only a few days earlier.

The photograph of *Bus Line 300* by Alex Levac (see chapter 8) is considered a historical photograph because of its revelatory action. It exposed, out of the darkness and into the light, a murder carried out in the name of the state and by its agents. Usually a historical photograph results mainly because a photographer "was there" near the event and with his camera at hand. The operation to rescue the bus from the terrorists took place under blazing spotlights, as in the framework of a General Security Service interrogation. The bus stood there somewhere in the dark night, immersed in a pool of light prepared by the "security forces." The lighting served both the photographers and the General Security Service. The former needed the lighting to take pictures. The latter needed the lighting to conduct the rescue operation but also to manufacture the darkness, which in principle it is incumbent on the photographer to expose. Photographers deal in exposure (to light). It is their true battlefield heritage.

In a detailed interview published in 1996, Ehud Yatom describes how he liquidated the terrorist who is seen alive in Levac's photograph. In the interview Yatom says that "the Bus Line 300 affair was a mistake from the start, because it was an open operation" (Yatom, 1996). From the point of view of the photographers, Yatom's insight was immediately reflected in the field a short time later, in the framework of the "security forces" pursuance of a policy to restrict the photographers' freedom of movement and action. This was tantamount to a policy of putting the lights out: less light on one hand, fewer photographers' eyes on the other. But the more the "security forces" tried to limit the field of vision, the greater became the photographers' challenge to penetrate it. This tango between the "security forces" and the photographers was typical of the field of vision that took shape during the Intifada.

A. A.: Can you reconstruct the photographing of Bus Line 300?

A. L.: I didn't know what I was photographing. I saw something of a blur. I saw two men leading away someone else. I took a picture of an elderly man with a beard who was being taken off the bus, wounded. After him I went looking for another frame. It was complicated to get through there. I stood alone, and I saw them bringing another wounded man. I said to myself, "Poor guy. Let's take a picture of him, too." There were no automatic cameras back then. I calculated the distance at more or less two meters with a closed shutter and flash, and I thought to myself that something's sure to come out. Even when the flash went off, I didn't know who it was. He looked to me like one of the wounded who was going to be given first-aid. I didn't know it was going to be last-aid. And then the two fellows who were holding him jumped on me and asked, "Give us the film, give us the film."

A. A.: What did they do with the wounded man while they were dealing with you and the roll of the film?

A. L.: I don't know. I didn't see. He was in such a state of shock. He certainly couldn't run away. His hands were tied. I was in no way willing to relinquish that roll of film. Any photographer who's worked for the press knows that when he's told not to take pictures it's an incentive to take pictures. When they demand, "Give me the film," you're not going to relinquish the film, not on your life. It was dark there. I pretended to remove the roll and gave them another roll instead and that was the end of the matter. Afterward the light dawned, and we took horrifying pictures of the two terrorists who'd been killed. We also photographed them taking out and dumping the bodies of the terrorists. They wrapped them in a blanket and tossed them into the truck. I've never seen anything like it. Afterward I thought, "What difference does it make? The man's already dead anyway." But I've never come across it.

A. A.: What did you see in the contact sheets?

A. L.: I gave the film rolls to the lab for development and went home. I was a wreck. A girl who was rather negligent was working at the lab. She didn't fill the developer tank to the top. The roll with this picture was on top, the highest. Everything below the legs didn't come out in development. If she'd put the roll in the other way around, then the heads wouldn't have been developed. When I saw the picture, I suddenly said, "There's the entire story right here."

A. A.: The photograph of Bus Line 300 is grasped as exemplifying the ability of a photograph to "change" something. Did anything really happen except for the darkness that descended over the activities of the "security services"?

A. L.: That wonderful picture of Robert Capa's in which you see the soldier: Did it change anything? Did anyone stop fighting because of that photograph? A photograph that changes things: what is it anyway? After this event it was no longer possible to approach any event—for instance, the bus of the workers at the nuclear plant or when the terrorists at Nizzanim arrived in boats on the holiday of Shavuot. They sealed off areas. During the Intifada it became a little more reasonable. Ever since Bus Line 300 at every event they've tried to arrange a "photo opportunity" for us, and nobody was able to take pictures spontaneously. It became boring because what can you possibly take a picture of when it's all over? I think that the press is to blame here to an unusual degree. For example, the press agrees not to publish overly violent pictures in which policemen are seen applying force. There's a sort of smoothing of the wrinkles, a camaraderie. The police will play ball with the photographers, the photographers will play ball with the police. There are only very few photographs that do something. The photograph of Bus Line 300 changed things. Television has a greater influence, maybe stills, too, but only as a cumulative effect.

A. A.: From what stems—your—belief in the camera?

A. L.: From the fact that after all Yatom didn't become a high school principal. That's already some small profit. I imagine that a few things have been changed. Maybe the procedures have been changed. You say to yourself that if people's morality will change, then you've gained something, but it's very naive to think that people's morality can change because of a photograph. I think that television has done a lot in helping us progress toward the Oslo Accords. One of television's climaxes was a little before Oslo. A Palestinian photographer from Jebalya in Gaza by the name of Majdi photographed a man throwing stones and getting hit in the head by a bullet. His brains flew in the air, and it was broadcast dozens of times on television. We're all terribly afraid of death. When you see death in front of your eyes and you're sitting in your living room, it brings it a lot closer to you. Maybe it was your son or your neighbor who shot him and blew out half his brain. I went and checked and discovered that he wasn't dead, that he was paralyzed. You see something like that, and it can't not do anything to you. You see death all the time, and when you see death happening in front of your eyes, it's incredible. These are strong photographs. If it's television taking pictures of it, it gives it a dimension of life. Stills freeze, it isn't live, it's stopped living. Still photographs have lost the dimension of vitality that television has. Television has some greater reliability because the picture moves, the color, the sound. There are a lot more dimensions than in a single still.

A. A.: Since the Intifada officially ended, it appears that the occupation is less photogenic or at least less attractive in the eyes of the newspaper editors. What do you photograph? What do your colleagues from the occupied territories photograph?

A. L.: A few days ago in *Yediot Acharonot*, on the front page, they published a photograph from Hebron of a haircutting ceremony at the Tombs of the Patriarchs. I know what I photographed in Hebron that day. They were conducting searches and emptying handbags. *Ma'ariv* or *Yediot* won't print these troublesome pictures. A boy getting his hair cut at the Tombs of the Patriarchs is nicer. I was in Nablus three weeks ago. There was a plenary session of the Palestinian Authority. I arrived at the building where the session was being held. Opposite the building a demonstration by the wives of Hamas prisoners held in custody by the Authority began to get organized. I just bent down to so something with the camera, and suddenly the women weren't there. When I raised the camera to take a picture, one of the Palestinian photographers nudged me and said: "Are you crazy, do you want them to break your camera?" There are places as opposed to which we look excellent. The Israeli press is stupidly complacent. Our colleagues are being prevented from taking pictures. Why is there no outcry to show solidarity with them? Nobody cares about anything. Complete apathy.

A. A.: In the case of Bus Line 300, you photographed death before it appeared. Do you remember any other such photograph?

A. L.: In two cases I photographed, I know that people were killed later. I took pictures of a Vietnamese Israeli guy who was riding security for a gasoline tanker. A week after I took his picture, he was shot while doing his security job.

A. A.: Why did you take his picture?

A. L.: Because he looked exceptional to me in that landscape. I thought it'd be good to have a picture. Maybe someday we'd need a picture of a gasoline tanker. Another picture, also in grave circumstances, was of the five soldiers who were killed in Lebanon. We also talked to them and played frisbee together. I photographed them on the day they went into Lebanon, and then suddenly the terrible incident in which they were killed occurred.

A. A.: I can't help mentioning the French television camera that interviewed the refugees in K'far Kana an hour before the massacre. Do you believe that the camera points out the heads that will roll?

A. L.: No. One shouldn't ascribe magical properties to it. It's a matter of probability. It's a small country. Things can happen. It's only a matter of probability.

A. A.: Then there's nothing magical about photography?

A. L.: There's some kind of power in photography. You are in effect organizing reality—not exactly organizing, but as photographers we isolate a certain moment that only the camera can isolate. Reality itself flows. The moment you've isolated that

Alex Levac, *A Gate on the Israeli-Lebanese Border,* 1995

moment, if you've done it well, there's magic in it. Because in effect you are telling the viewer, "Give me your hand. Go along with me, and I'll show you what I see."

A. A.: I'm reminded of the remarks made by Ronny Kempler, the photographer who was present at Rabin's assassination, who said he feels as if the hand of fate toyed with him.

A. L.: If it happened more frequently, I'd say there was something to it. I've never really gone into it too deeply. I was sad when I took the pictures of those guys. I told them, "Take care of yourselves." And they answered me, "You take care of yourself. We've got flak jackets." After they were killed, I looked at the frames. You suddenly begin looking for meaning in the picture. There's one frame that looks as if he's leaping to the sky. I photographed him from the back. You see him from behind jumping in the air. It's very peculiar that he's leaping to the sky. In the background you see the border, the security fence. It was also a terribly rainy day. There's no difference between the sky and the earth. I hate to say it myself, but the photo came out well, too.

A. A.: All the same, you do connect the photograph with death.

A. L.: The photograph sterilizes life. The freezing eliminates the life from the thing. Death is a frozen standstill. I often look at photographs from the turn of the century, World War II. I look at the photographs and I say, "They all died," and I can't make the connection. I see them as children. The moment you've taken someone's picture, you've completely isolated him from reality. You've given him eternal life, but on the other hand you've killed him. He won't move anymore, he won't sit down, he won't walk. Wherever you've left him, that's where he stays.

6

The Lebanese War assumed and continues to assume different forms—terrorist actions, cease-fire disturbances, conventional war, war of attrition, operations, penetrations, infiltrations, ambushes, forays, assaults, surgical operations. These different ways of legitimizing the economy of blood are a direct result of the economy of occupation being conducted in Lebanon. A short while after Rabin's assassination, Shimon Peres, who was then serving as prime minister and defense minister, launched a small-scale war within the overall war in Lebanon. This war was dubbed the Grapes of Wrath Operation. It was depicted as a "clean war," a technological war using surgical tools. Nonetheless, it will be remembered. It resulted in a massacre of civilians despite the use of new technologies, while its instigators "fell victim" (thus Peres and senior IDF officers dubbed the "mistake" at K'far Kana) to outdated technology. Two days before the massacre at K'far Kana I went to meet "I" (only his first initial has been authorized for disclosure) to speak with the eye of the commander of a Cobra helicopter squadron. I wanted to listen to his view, which sees a target in the place occupied by a person, and also to see what his eye is made of. "I" wears a helmet equipped with a sophisticated eyepiece. The wires emanating from it connect the helmet with the helicopter and turn the pilot into a part of his machine. When he trains the eyepiece in the center of the helmet, the helicopter sights move accordingly, and the missile cruises in the direction indicated by his eye, which amalgamates all the eyepieces into a single instrument, locked on a target. This unity is what performs the action. And "I" is only an eye in this framework. This instrument is tantamount to the realization of a familiar fantasy from the history of art, photography, and war—the dream of being only an eye, self-sufficient unto itself, an eye that can take both pictures and action, an eye that is also an arm, that closes in on itself as in a loop and destroys in its path everything that others have designated as a target for it. "I" belongs to an era in which he is both photographer and fighter.

However, he is constantly denying one side of himself. When he's the photographer, he denies his part in the fabrication of the picture and contends that he's only performing a sortie. When he's the fighter, he speaks like a photographer; he's not killing or destroying anything but merely taking aim to arrive at the right picture.

The publicity accorded at the time of the operation via television to the type of view exemplified by "I" looked like a program of training exercises designed to inculcate visual skills similar to his in television viewers. "I," so it appeared in those days, was the model according to which the state's security agents sought to pattern the eye of the television viewer. The training that a pilot undergoes over several years was telescoped into an accelerated course for viewers by the heads of the army. The viewer was invited to see how "clean" it all was, absolutely sterile. The targets are designated in advance, and all that remains to be done is to get them.

The first lesson—the obliteration of the second floor of a building in Southern Lebanon—was concluded without casualties, which was exactly the point. Through the eyepiece-eye of the pilot, real-time photos of the target and its obliteration were broadcast to viewers at home. Foreign networks nonetheless reported that someone had been killed. Afterward it turned out that a cook had stayed behind on the doomed floor. But this was only a marginal detail in a lesson to train the eye, and perhaps for this reason it was spared from the viewers. In the Grapes of Wrath Operation, the IDF established a surgical theater in Lebanon. Television established a special room for retinal procedures in every citizen's home. The coordination between these sites was excellent. The Grapes of Wrath Operation remained "exemplary" until that morning in Nabatiya. When the cannoneers joined the battle in the afternoon, with their brutal eye, the study material suddenly appeared irrelevant. The viewer's eye was no longer responding.

During the course of that war within a war, "I" set out each day to perform spectacular missions in Lebanon. Equipped with that sophisticated optical array, he set out to purge the territory, performing dozens of "sorties" whose goal was to destroy targets. It was reported that "I" "returned safely to base" from all the sorties. My conversation with him took place several days before the bombardment of K'far Kana. The organizing paradigm of his language was a panoptic point of view that facilitates control and purgation. This point of view was predicated on the sophisticated cameras he operated, which made it possible for him to believe that he does indeed have a panoptic viewpoint, control, and purgation capability. His panoptic pretensions were induced and guided by the panoptic pretensions of those who sent him and who, by means of him and his associates, oversaw a broader field of vision that included history, politics, resources, and logistics. Like a Russian doll, or alternatively like a telescopic lens, one eye (that of "I") was suspended within the field of vision of another "I" (which itself was suspended within the field of vision of the "I" above him), and so on and so forth. Battalions of eyes trained to see targets and shoot them.

The paradigm of the sophisticated, trained, professional eye—which can sift the wheat from the chaff, which knows how to designate and go after a target—is familiar to us from fields in which the push of a button destroys inanimate objects at most but never talking heads. "I" sounded confident that he and those under his command would accurately hit only their targets and avoid unnecessary accidents. A few days after my conversation with "I," over a hundred people were murdered in K'-far Kana in an artillery bombardment. I didn't speak with "I" again, but presumably he would have said that with his men in their Cobras, such accidents don't happen. With them, it's a matter of surgical elimination. Accidents, yes, on rare occasions, but not on such a scale. With them the objective is to purge, to destroy targets, not to massacre. Their strikes are accurate. A learned exposition of thermal optics might have served as the scientific basis for his contention. The massacre at K'far Kana, just like a "smaller" incident in which an ambulance and all its occupants were annihilated, are not accidents. They are events that make sense in the logic of the occupation of Judaea, Samaria, and Southern Lebanon. But these events also make sense in the logic of the weapons that generated them. Such accidents are of the essence to both the occupation and these weapons. Technology generates a space in which the border for which the agents of war are responsible becomes negligible in the framework of the overall bloodletting, which takes place in a large number of foci that aren't necessarily concerned with borders and territorial demarcations. An hour before the massacre at K'far Kana, a French television camera interviewed some of the refugees who were staying at the United Nations camp. The camera designated the heads that were led to the slaughter an hour later. The camera marked the territory that the artillery shells knew how to home in on. The camera and the missile were manufactured in the same factory, the factory for sophisticated precision optics.

A. A.: What do you see from your position in the helicopter?

"I": I see a target. On the way back, after the sortie, you might say to yourself maybe I saw slums, maybe I saw pretty things. In that stage during the sortie you see a target and all sorts of details that will help you find the target. If I see a citrus grove, to me it's not a citrus grove. It's a part of the means at my disposal to get to the target.

A. A.: And people?

"I": Some of the targets are people. The person is not in the sense of a person but in the sense of a target. He is regarded just like a target.

A. A.: Who sees?

"I": In the final analysis the vision is that of the pilot. You are required to see the target and decide that it is the target or alternatively that it isn't. What you see on television is that same pilot who placed the cross on the target by himself. After performing the entire procedure he's decided that this is the target. Nobody else can tell him whether it is or it isn't. In formation there are other helicopters with whose help you verify that you're talking about the same thing, that it really is the target. In the field the process is very short. You've got no time for discussion. It's a very short process that has to be performed rapidly.

A. A.: At this stage, do you already have a clear picture of what you're looking for?

"I": Sometimes it's performed in scrambling. Then you've got no advance preparation. You take off and receive the mission in the air. The mission is constructed in the course of its execution. There are two types of missions, planned or not. The first type is when you learn the target. The second is when you scramble and the mission and the target are structured in the course of execution. You receive the essence of the mission from all sorts of sensors.

A. A.: What are those sensors?

"I": The air force's control systems. They relay the battlefield picture to you over the communications, in professional operational terms. They wouldn't be understood by a layman's ear. There's a feeling of not yet having arrived at the action. You adjust yourself in anticipation of the next stage. You are not yet in the dimension of being there. Part of the preparation is to put yourself there and see what it'll look like and what I'm going to do.

A. A.: What is the track your eye follows from when you enter the helicopter until the shooting?

"I": Every operational sortie begins at the stage of entering a state of alert. Then there's a period of waiting, uncertainty in regard to what's going to happen. There's a stage of routine flight until the border is crossed in which no threat exists. Then you're still preparing yourself and musing about what lies ahead. You cross a line and

enter a threatening environment. The senses become honed, and everything is directed toward executing the mission. At this stage you fly the helicopter and make use of the navigational instruments to arrive at the target area and try to identify all the threats you're supposed to encounter and bypass them.

A. A.: And then, you've arrived at the target area.

"I": This is what's called in our professional terminology that you "acquire the target." It's a stage of acquisition that is, by the way, the difficult stage from the aspect of implementation.

A. A.: More than others?

"I": Out of a huge assemblage of details you've got to fish out the target, which is usually small. This is also the characterization of the operation—to strike accurately. The targets are selected very carefully. Out of all this complication, you choose the target. It's like a cone that's wide at one end and narrows. From the firing position the cone begins to shut, and then you look for the target. The targets are inside villages, in a civilian environment, in wooded groves. It's a stage that's difficult. You are motivated both to find the target and not to hit an incorrect target. Either one could be a failure from your point of view. Hitting an incorrect target is a double failure. As squadron leader it's necessary to see to it that all members of the formation are observing the same target, that they'll hit the same target.

A. A.: Do you have eye contact with "members of the formation"?

"I": That, too. But contact is implemented mainly with the help of a common language, terms that we define to ourselves before takeoff so that we'll have a common language. It's a language that is built up over time—terms that are developed and serve us during operational activity. Each one has firepower, and in the end, to gather them together, the common language is very important.

A. A.: Do you see what the "members of your formation" see?

"I": No. In principle no. He can look here, and I can look there.

A. A.: Do you coordinate by means of the words?

"I": The communication has a quality of its own. It determines how the mission will be performed as a formation.

THE PICTURE [OF THE BATTLEFIELD]

A. A.: Do you stay in the air for hours?

"I": In a sortie like this you might be given several targets—not an attack on a target when you leave here knowing what you're heading into, but when you get scrambled to the point where you patrol in the air and attack them. I've had occasion, for instance, to attack three targets in one sortie. At least two vehicles.

A. A.: Does vehicles mean vehicles in which there are people?

"I": Yes.

A. A.: Your language is completely clean?

"I": Yes. A vehicle is a target.

A. A.: Were you born like this?

"I": No. But since you've already asked, then we know that the target is a vehicle and that inside the vehicle is the target. If the man were to get out of the vehicle, then we'd attack him directly. These terms, I think, are part of the world called a fighter. We are fighters. And with us, after all, the entire country is fighters.

A. A.: Do you yourself take pictures?

"I": No. Everything's recorded.

A. A.: Do you watch the tapes again?

"I": Yes. You land, and we go into the debriefing stage. I see all the tapes of all the squadron and examine the leaders about the attacks.

A. A.: Does it remind you of computer games?

"I": No. Even when you're watching someone else's tape in debriefing, you've got the same feeling as he does, and then it doesn't look like a computer game. The term *game* doesn't exist.

A. A.: But the term *target* exists?

"I": Yes. You're in a, I'd say, I don't have the precise word, maybe, in a sort of other world, in a sort of other something.

A. A.: Is it difficult to recreate the progression back to reality?

"I": There's a stage at which you land and return to reality, especially when it comes to completely ordinary reality rather than that of war. You come back home, every once in a while, so everything's as usual. There's a difficulty in sharing the experiences, in experiencing the same things.

A. A.: I'm not referring to that progression but to the progression that connects back to people, to killing and to suffering?

"I": Yes. The progression of connecting a target to population and suffering happens. I want to say something that exists in the entire squadron, on the public level, too. There's an identification or understanding with the goals of this operation, and that helps a lot in dealing with the dilemmas that crop up—that is to say, not dilemmas, with situations. There's a high degree of sensitivity in the air force—beginning at the planning level and up to the controlling level and the squadron command—to not harming civilians. This is the spirit of the air force, and it's also stated openly as part of the goals—beginning at the highest level and down to the squadron briefings. In the final analysis when you're in the cockpit, when we're facing the target, you're working in front of screens and sensors for both day and night. By means of the sensors you identify the target, and after that you home in the missile on the target. Homing the missile in on the target is the easy part of the subject. It's the simpler part of the subject, the technical side of the operation.

A. A.: What happens from the moment you've located the target until the firing of the missile?

"I": I don't sit on the missile and arrive at the target with it. It's not a horse I'm galloping on and in the end thrust my spear. It's a technological resource that can sustain malfunctions, but they're at a low level of probability. These instruments' percentage of accuracy and their reliability are very high. There are sensors that check. The system tells you there's a malfunction, and then you don't launch.

A. A.: Do you locate the target on the screen itself or directly in "reality"?

"I": The locating is performed with the help of the optical system. Here [pointing to the tape onscreen] the waiting is for the arrival of a vehicle at a bend in the road. The missile has exited, and you continue to capture the target.

THE PICTURE [OF THE BATTLEFIELD]

A. A.: Is the vehicle in motion when the missile has already been launched?

"I": The missile knows to follow the cross [marked onscreen].

A. A.: Is it in "eye contact" with the cross?

"I": Yes.

A. A.: When you view the tape now, is it like the first time?

"I": No. It's the second feature.

7

On the day Hilmi Shawsha, an eleven-year-old Palestinian boy, was buried in the village of Husan, there were "clashes between the IDF and Palestinians." Siar Hilmi
Shawsha, the boy's father, told Amira Segev (1996, p. 3a), journalist of *Ha'aretz:*

I went with several dignitaries from the Palestinian Authority to the sector commander and
received his personal assurance that they wouldn't enter the village, that they'd keep their
distance. I said to him, "This isn't the first instance, and we all know how everything gets out
of control when you're inside. Keep your distance." He gave me his word of honor—not just
to me but to the dignitaries from the Palestinian Authority as well. Suddenly when we got
back from the funeral, and people were going to their cars, we saw soldiers between the
houses, beside my mother's house. Afterward everything began. Stones and grenades began
flying, an hour and a half of rioting.

What emerges from Siar Hilmi Shawsha's description is that on the day of the
funeral he wanted the village to be demarcated and sealed off from the Israeli security forces. Considering the common procedures of closure and curfew that the
army imposes on Palestinian villages, one might have imagined that Siar Hilmi
Shawsha's desire would have been reciprocated by the Israeli side, represented in
this case by the army. But is this really the case? The mourning father expresses by
his request his desire that the village remain off limits to Israelis—that those who
are identified with the hangman leave them to mourn in peace without inciting
them to provocation and violence. The army, on the other hand, would like to implement two procedures involving the application of force, two types of supervision. The first procedure is simple, and its purpose is to continue controlling the
village borders and supervising who enters and leaves (to this point the desires of
the boy's father and those of the army may coincide). The second is more complex,

and it expresses the pretension on the part of the "Israeli force" to being omnipresent and everywhere. This procedure is implemented by making the inhabitants' movements visible or able to be supervised, assessed, and judged—rapid and immediate judgment by any soldier who represents the force—as to whether they pose a danger or not.

I'd like to say a few more words about these procedures, these two types of supervision. The purpose of the first type—supervision of the stability and durability of the border—is to make certain that the separation is clear and unambiguous and that whoever the closure applies to doesn't invade the enlightened (Israeli) side and threaten it by his actions and sometimes even by his very presence. The second is a type of normalizing supervision whose purpose is to make the individual himself avoid deviant behavior—without requiring a show of naked force. Over time, constant observation of the individual's behavior is supposed to make him conduct such observations by himself and know, of his own accord, how to behave properly. The normalizing supervision, then, imposes much of the labor of normalization on the individual himself. This type of normalization works fine in school, in the army, and in the state. The condition for the individual's participation in his own normalization is his desire to become part of the social conglomeration wherein the normalization procedures take place. Alternatively, his participation is obtained as a result of the internalization of this desire as his own. The individual's participation in the process obviates or reduces the need for the application of direct force and turns normalization into a much less inclement process.

The Israeli army's pretension in applying the second type of supervision—the normalization of the Palestinian under conditions of occupation—is absurd and cruel. It is absurd because direct force can withdraw only when the individual trains to react with its presence as a sign—force transformed into power—and conducts himself in accordance with that sign. How can the Palestinian possibly internalize, as his own interest, the Israeli force's interest in oppressing him and establishing him as its own subservient and exploited other? It is cruel because the Palestinian, who cannot in principle internalize the Israeli force's interest as his own, induces the direct force to appear each time he fails to take its place. On each such occasion, when he induces the direct force to appear, he's punished. In other words, he is the reason for the appearance of direct force. On his part, the noble and enlightened Israeli is already willing to withdraw the force and to leave in its place only the emblems of force, to seep into the Palestinian's bloodstream and become internalized inside him.

The clashes that took place between the IDF and the Palestinians could better be described, then, as clashes between two contradictory types of application of force at the basis of which lie Israeli insensitivity to, oppression of, exploitation of, and disdain for the Palestinians.

Nahum Korman is a security coordinator for the Hadar Beitar settlement. His job is at most to defend the stability of the border between the village and the settlement and to prevent friction along the borderline. But Korman didn't suffice with this type of supervision. He, too, like the Israeli army, wanted to implement the procedures of normalizing supervision. He crossed the village borders in a hunt after Palestinian boys who had several hours earlier, so he'd been told, thrown stones at cars passing by in the road. He arrived not to defend a borderline that had been trespassed or the lives of citizens in danger but to fix what required fixing, to rectify the deviations, to punish the disturbers who had deviated from the limits of action allotted to them. Korman's visit to the village of Husan had an educational function. He arrived to remind the stone thrower that his action was further testimony to his incorrigibility, for had it not already been made clear to him in the past, in no uncertain terms, that throwing a stone was tantamount to striking at the supreme Israeli security interest? Since Korman's action in the village had an educational function, and since every Palestinian in the village has thrown, is throwing or will throw stones, Korman could apply his public punitive action to any boy who conformed to the abstract profile of a "stone thrower."

Korman arrived at the village to see, show, and be seen. His action was directed toward the public space so that both Palestinian and Israeli eyes would see what should be done to a boy who throws stones. It's hard to determine whether Korman meant to kill Hilmi Shawsha. It isn't hard to determine that Korman arrived at the village to teach a Palestinian boy a lesson in power relations. This is a lesson that is learned on both sides, in Israel and in Palestine. In Israel the Israelis are taught how to deliver the lesson, and in Palestine the Israeli who has studied the doctrine attempts to teach the Palestinian how to learn the lesson. This deplorable lesson isn't taught in straightforward fashion in the Israeli schools, but it is in principle accessible to every Israeli student (who will become an Israeli citizen) who wishes to study it. The lesson is learned in the body and internalized in its movements. Since it turns into part of the body language, it may be worthwhile to speak its language for a moment, to listen to the lesson. What is it saying? What is it saying to the Palestinian young man? The naked, direct, brutal, and violent show of force might have disappeared if only you, young man, could understand that the responsibility for its appearance rests with you alone. This force could have sufficed with its transformation into a sign or emblem, in the form of a permanent reminder, such as an elegant public building on the village's central boulevard. But it is you, young man, and only you, who are to blame for the redeployment of this force again and again in all its contemptible barbarity because it has no choice, young man; on account of you it appears. But Hilmi Shawsha was no longer there to listen to the lesson. Too quickly was the student extinguished at the touch of teacher Korman's studious hands.

8

Fantasy A. The area is clean, the vision clear, beams of light flood the field, which appears closely shaven. A prickly bristle is captured by the lens, designated as a target and destroyed. Each bristle is examined, and to it a machine is adapted to whom life has been granted to train in the focused discovery and extermination of a single species. Tables of species and varieties facilitate classification. Central borderlines, whose nature it is to determine who goes to which side, are placed in several fronts. Each borderline has an illuminated side and a dark side, an interior and exterior, an up and a down, worthy and unworthy, desirable and undesirable. Like trash, the unworthy or undesirable finds its way out, is compacted as by the action of an involuntary muscle acting not due to any command, trained to carry out its function like an automaton. The borderline is a substitute for the routine action of the muscles of the digestive system that mix the food and push it onward, toward the rectum and from there in its undesirable form help it to be expelled outside. The borderline doesn't act alone. Several muscles participate in the operational action, turning it into dry routine, its movements unfelt, like a monotonous progression of paired contractions and dilations repeating themselves and preserving the appearance of "no motion." The dark side on the other side of the border—in effect, behind the border—is relegated outside the illuminated field of vision most of the time, and it turns into a black and viscous crater that swallows the things that require an explanation, the causal relations that enable one side to be illuminated and the other side to stay dark, spongy, vulgar, lacking in nuance, subservient, and often even willing to serve. Instead of causal relations, sufficient unto the need are spectacular plans involving an increase in the magnitude of the light and its dispersal among the many. A ringlike expansion of the progression of paired contractions and dilations, a centrifugal motion of illumination. This movement is accompanied by instigated and involuntary frictional activities, commercial relations, violent moves, exploitative and coercive actions, murderous purges, acts of rape and plain spite that rehabilitate the border each time a resident of the dark side imagines that he's near the light.

The tongue is extended into the crater, and its phrasing is such that the occupants of the illuminated side are able to be the speakers of the different phrases. Turns of phrase are part of the economy of discourse that purges, cleans, improves, draws conclusions, economizes, preserves. They enable the institutionalization of drainage systems, the expansion of the trash disposal networks, institutionalized activities of preservation and education toward preservation as a value, the smoking and disinfection of the dumb and the conversant alike, the transformation of the conversant into the dumb, the removal of disturbing, destructive, and law-breaking elements. All come out of that same pretension that the light beam is being magnified, that eradication and purification are being allowed to happen of themselves, like the action of an involuntary muscle that knows its job, that desires nothing other than to eternally repeat the same action, to allow the eternal repetition to occur, to clear a fitting stage for the desperate cry, "Let everything repeat itself." As one young Palestinian says:

All my life I've lived inside killing, inside blood, inside what you call disturbances of the peace. I grew up in a refugee camp beside Ramallah, and there was nothing else to do there. I was born in Gaza at the Nusserat camp, and I was five years old when General Sharon decided to widen the roads, so that the terrorists wouldn't race through the alleys. I don't know what occupation is or what Jews are. I just remember that men came in the night and destroyed our house, put us in a truck and threw us out like trash in the middle of Ramallah. (Naji Nasser,[8] interviewed in Pe'er, 1996, 14–15)

The purgative muscular action has been assimilated into dry routine, which seems to be timeless, circular, lacking purpose or hope. But it is nonetheless subordinate to a vision projected into the future, which critiques the dismal past and is willing in the present to pay the price, always in behalf of a future that appears to be formulated like a series of contractual clauses toward whose realization it aspires. Acre by acre we shall purge the entire world, build roads, capture wanted men, enlarge our store of sterile areas.

Fantasy B. It, too, is concerned with the digestive system. Instead of getting rid of the refuse, burying it in one or another type of oxygenation facility, it would like to transform it into part of the exchange economy. Not just the tongue by means of its turns of phrase, but the crater, too—to stand at the edge of the abyss and discover that the water is shallow. The crater is not the exterior. The crater is not the unworthy, the undesirable, the inferior. Relationships that are not just linguistic can be

---

8. Naji Nasser, age twenty-four, was imprisoned for the murder of twelve collaborators and was released in the framework of the Oslo Accords. "You apparently don't consider me to have blood on my hands" (Pe'er, 1996, 14–15).

pursued with its occupants. Instead of burying the dead they can be recycled, injected into the circle of life like ghosts, turned into worthy corpses. Let there be an end to cemeteries that have relegated death beyond the pale. Every border that is examined and found to be arbitrary shall be replaced by a singular local border, one that doesn't lay claim to represent or speak in anyone's name, that isn't determined only by authorized agents, that seeks to undermine the authority of those who are authorized and behind which there is nothing but the border itself interlaced in a network of borders that squeeze in everything that ostensibly lies outside, in an involuntary motion. Mounds of trash thousands of years old are injected into the exchange relations of blood, capital, representations, money, and images.

Fantasy B, it is often stated, would like to get rid of Fantasy A. The former follows the latter chronologically and would like to take its place, to replace its method of spatial organization (which is based on a number of borderlines that separate different areas in hierarchical fashion) with a different method of spatial organization that has a framework where each point is in principle a borderline that has lost its limiting quality because it has also become limited by the lines and points surrounding it.

Fantasy B is akin to a corrective experience for Fantasy A.[9] The action from the inside out, which characterizes Fantasy A, hasn't ceased. On the contrary, Fantasy B has made it possible to multiply to infinity the sites at which it is carried out. In parallel, the action from the outside in, which characterizes Fantasy B, the corrective action whose purpose is to undermine the border that lays claim to separate the outside from the inside and to include the outside inside—it, too, takes place at countless points.

---

9. The fantasy pertaining to the recycling of trash that has established itself in the Western world in the last decade represents Fantasy B. Instead of throwing out the garbage, getting rid of it with no consideration for the state of the universe, many movements arose calling for the liberation of the garbage from its destiny to be buried in the earth. The classification of garbage as either recyclable or worthy of burial enabled many individuals to participate in a collective practice of moral self-determination out of a positive attitude toward what was grasped as the absolute other, toward the object. However, the recycling practice is motivated by a logic similar to the logic that motivated the practice it came to critique: out of an overall point of view of the entire world, an omnipresent and omniscient point of view, we advocate recycling only. Brigades of policemen will reeducate your children and fine you for delinquent behavior contrary to laws already engraved in stone. But in recent years this fantasy has proved to be more costly and damaging than the fantasy of garbage disposal and purification that preceded it. Nevertheless, to abandon Fantasy B today in favor of a return to Fantasy A seems impossible because merely the decision to retreat may demand such a price as to make Fantasy B more worthwhile. Thus arises a situation in which learned studies, based on the same data, lead to contradictory conclusions among the supporters of Fantasy A and Fantasy B, with no way to decide between them.

Small lanterns hang from the necks of people whose job is to cross, each time for a short while, the border between the illuminated side and the dark side, to cast a light and report on some of the frictions, to burn them in paper or record them on magnetic tape. They are the unwitting agents of the tongue sprung from the crater. They are motivated by the belief that the lantern may help those who live in the dark cloak themselves in a bit of light. They could be the emissaries of Fantasy A as well as Fantasy B. They are the implementers of a vision of a better world, which always comes crashing down in the face of good intentions—hostages of their instruments of sight and showing, instruments such as cameras or museums.

It's true that the world is *what we see*, but all the same we must learn to see it

—MERLEAU-PONTY (1964, 18)

Throughout the book I have tried to deconstruct Merleau-Ponty's phrase quoted above as a motto to this chapter. Looking at a series of events, cultural phenomena, and works of art I have examined the way the world is constituted as an object of a gaze. I presupposed that the gaze is not something given to the observer as a ready-made instrument but a faculty to be trained and cultivated. One is trained to see thus and not otherwise, to see under certain conditions of visibility, to see certain objects under certain aspects—the aesthetic aspect for example—and ignore other aspects. Some people are trained to see a walking man as a moving target; others are trained to read a photograph and never see visible traces of the presence of the camera and of the cameraman. In this chapter I propose an account of this presupposition. The museum is singled out here as a privileged site for studying the constitution of the gaze. But the aim of this account has a broader perspective. It is to reconstruct a general framework of interplay and exchange between the object of the gaze and its subject, conditions of visibility, and limits of the "sayable" (including traces of silence and concealment, of the unsayable and the invisible), and to understand how such a framework makes possible and delimits interventions in this complex web of interrelations.

Art is a part of the world; therefore, it would be correct to say that art is *what we see*, but, all the same, we must learn to see it. Learning to see art isn't simply learning to see, however, but is learning to see what deserves to be seen—learning to see properly. In other words, learning to see art means becoming a subject of art. This multifaceted learning involves mastering the field of knowledge called art and also training for art and recognizing its transcendent standing. I try to ascertain who *we* are, what *learning to see* is, what *art* is, and how its *transcendency* is created. The assumption that "art is what we see, but, all the same, we must learn to see it" carries within it an additional assumption: that art exists outside and prior to the act of learning it. These assumptions, I show in what follows, are produced and entrenched by means of institutions and practices of discourse. In other words, I attempt to show that training for art, like other activities concerned with art (such as display, research, and interpretation), gives rise to the assumption of the transcendency of art. The museum was established on the assumption that training people for art is a worthwhile task. Art exists, and the museum is the arena of choice in which to encounter and learn art. But this assumption ignores the fact that art—as an activity conducted in the public space—did not exist outside and prior to the museum and that it grew together with the museum, which devoted itself to the propagation and dissemination of art.

THE PLACE OF ART

The ability to be a subject of art—to assume the position of speaker from which one can see a certain object, talk about it, and intrude on it as an object of art—is dependent on training for art. From the most passive spectator who visits a museum once in ten years to the most creative artist who mounts several exhibitions each year: people in developed economies are trained to assume the position of speaker of art. Therefore, even artists noted for being distinctive modernists, whose concern is to deny everything that came before them and extract the norm of art out of art itself, started on their path with training for art. Both the producers and the consumers of art are educated to become subjects of art. Training for art is carried out in art schools, in enrichment courses of regular schools, by means of the media and literature, and by other visual means throughout the public space. Citizens train to find their way around and to orient themselves in the public space. They learn to classify the various visual statements (*énoncés*)[1] with which they are confronted there and to ascribe them to the market, politics, or art.

To ascertain the subject of art—that individual who is at the same time the product of training for art and the person accountable for this training—I suggest examining the divisions of labor in the field of art between the occupiers of different positions, as well as between what is allotted to view, speech, and action.[2] These divisions of labor—which are an outgrowth of the emergent museum of the late eighteenth century and of the development of art in the public space in the framework of the museum economy—produce and preserve a situation in which the museum space is the condition for the appearance of a statement as art statement. Any item exhibited in its framework never remains "the thing itself" (a lunch box, dollar bill, or fan) but always turns into an item with meaning, an item that signifies a meaning that is in principle absent from it. Beginning in the second decade of the twentieth century, when ready-made items were introduced into the museum, the artistic object has been defined as a separate and distinct object that creates or signifies a difference with respect to the world of objects from which it has been sampled. This

---

1. *Phrase* is the English translation for Lyotard's *énoncé,* and *statement* is the translation for Foucault's *énoncé.* I'm speaking about art as a discursive system whose unity is the work of art as a statement (see Azoulay, 1999).

2. On view, speech, and action, see Foucault (1963) and Ophir (1988).

difference is achieved as a result of the transformation that the object undergoes—its transformation from an object that is "the thing itself" (for instance, a single, specific cornflakes package) into an object that "points to" something other than itself (for instance, cornflakes packages in general, the culture that produces people who consume cornflakes, or consumer culture in general). This transformation, as I demonstrate below, doesn't take place in the object itself but in the conditions of appearance of the object in the discourse. In other words, the artistic object is produced by means of the discourse of its institutions and speakers, who acknowledge it as a distinctive object that "points to." This recognition isn't dependent on the appreciation accorded to the object but is achieved as a result of placing the object in the specific conditions of visibility that the museum space distinctively represents. The right, in principle, to reenact these conditions of visibility each time anew and to use them to make manifest anything and everything has turned into a basic right in the unwritten constitution of art. This right is generally formulated as the artist's right "to point to," and it has been the object of different contentions over freedom of expression in the history of the museum display in the past two hundred years. Attempts to limit the display of art have met with a counterresponse on the part of various agents of art as an attack on the artist's freedom "to point to" rather than as a struggle over dealing with this or that content or assuming a specific position.

This distinction between (1) the political position that may ostensibly *express itself* in an artist's work and (2) an artist's work as an *act* of pointing to a phenomenon has already been formulated several times in the framework of "struggles" over the freedom of expression that occur in the field of art from time to time in a rather noteworthy cycle. These arguments have an identical structure. This structure repeated itself, for example, during the Chelouche Gallery's 1991 exhibition of a painting by Israeli artist Arnon Ben David on which was written "Rabin is a murderer" and at the 1996 *Digital Stroke* exhibition of the graduates of Camera Obscura School of Art, when a work of computer art by Edith Cohen that displayed a portrait of Yigal Amir, Rabin's assassin, generated demands for its removal. Usually the contents of an exhibit or the position that may be inferred from it don't come up for discussion; the argument revolves around the artist's unequivocal, unlimited right to express whatever he desires because his work doesn't constitute a political *act* or statement but a *form* of artistic expression. For those who take part in it—actively and passively— the enactment of this ceremonial struggle over freedom of expression fortifies their belief that the routine of activity in the public space is one of freedom of expression, while their pretext for the struggle is a singular, blatant abrogation of that right. The reason they heed the summons to battle is exactly because it concerns the abrogation of routine. The rest of the time, according to this conception, communication in the public space is conducted according to rational procedures of debate and articulation, and the opinion or view voiced therein has a varying degree of importance and influence on "the common interest."[3] If the argument over freedom of expression is a singular and transient event whose aim is to foster and fortify the belief that freedom expresses itself and expression is free in the course of daily routine, then the museum is a permanent and enduring institution whose aim complements that of the struggle over freedom of expression. The museum denotes a boundary, a demarcation and separation between all the other objects and images scattered in the public space and those worthy of the title of art.

The exhibits that are stored away within the museum's walls and that enable different individuals to exercise their civil rights and obligations—such as conducting a rational argument over the right to freedom of expression—are in principle accessible to everyone. In actuality, they are accessible only to those who have learned to appreciate them. Entry to the museum is dependent on training for art. Education isn't a precondition because it can be effected in process: that's what the museum is for. But the museum and education are interconnected and are based on the assumption that training for art is worthwhile and inheres to the institution. Therefore, to examine this assumption, we must return to the change in the state of art and society that occurred with the establishment of the first museums. Their appearance is also connected to the appearance of art as an activity in the public sphere and to its constitution as a museal discourse.[4]

The first museum—the Instituta Ashmoleana, which is not a museum of art—was founded at Oxford University as an institution with pedagogical aims.[5] In the museum's charter, which was officially formulated in 1714, rules are defined concerning cataloguing procedures, the preservation of exhibits, entrance fees, and opening hours. This organized and institutionalized set of rules sought to eliminate any arbitrary dimension in the handling of exhibits and their public display. The museum included items of different kinds: archaeological remains, plants, animals, rocks, and birds. The various exhibits were collected in the framework of journeys

---

3. The structure of this struggle over freedom of expression resembles the structure of the "political scandal" as defined by Jean Baudrillard. The real scandal, says Baudrillard, is that there is no scandal. The function of the political scandal is to disguise the fact that there is no more scandal (Baudrillard, 1981).

4. After two hundred years, museum art—culminating in the art of the twentieth century, a large part of which is concerned with museum discourse or what is customarily termed "critique of its institutions"—has completely internalized its rules and devoted itself to its spatial logic (see Azoulay, 1999).

5. For the beginnings of the Ashmolean, see Bazin's book on museums (Bazin, 1967).

all over the world (including Russia and America). Journeys of discovery are concerned with the expansion of knowledge and with education,[6] and the establishment of the museum—which was intended to house the exhibits collected on these journeys—expresses the link between the act of display and the act of instruction or education.

In 1795, six years after the French Revolution, Richard Lenoir founded the Musée de l'Art Monumental. In the background an argument raged between those who wanted to leave the monument in its "natural environment" and avoid displacing it into the museum and those who contended that monuments were to be turned into state property, managed professionally, and exhibited to the public.[7] The questions concerning preservation—what to preserve, whether to preserve only the (politically) worthwhile or the entire past for its historic value—organize the debate along two axes. One axis poses a relativistic conception of taste, beauty, and the historical, while the second axis expresses a pretension to the universality of the judgment of taste and of the historical monument's value.[8]

These two axes of argument actually coalesce into a single issue: does the exhibit have value that is relative to its place and that will be lost due to its displacement, or does it have a universal value that it carries with it everywhere, regardless of its place or other circumstances? This issue, at either extreme of the argument, is actually based on a common assumption: that the object has immanent and authentic value. The way it is handled—whether left in its "original" context or removed to a museum exhibition space—must preserve and exhibit it "as it is." Both these modes of treatment seek to orientate themselves toward the exhibit as a closed, meaningful unit that cannot be interfered with or altered. The experts are supposed to know how to listen to the exhibit and to either be of service to it (museologist or restorer) or serve as its mouthpiece (historian or critic). Listening along with them should be all those who deal in training for art and whose stated purpose is to "bring art closer to the public" or to "bring the public closer to art." In the argument that arose at the end of the eighteenth century concerning how the exhibit should be handled, the in-

---

6. On the connection between journeys and education, see Abbeele (1992). The etymology of the Latin verb *educare* points to its meaning to lead or to guide someone—to convey people away from their prejudices (Abbeele, 1992).

7. On this argument, see Dominic Poulot's article on the emergence of the historical monument (Poulot, 1985).

8. On the argument during the French Revolution whether to destroy the royal treasures or preserve them as a (pedagogic) testimony to injustice, see Gaehtgens (1986). See also Kant's treatise "A Critique of the Power of Judgment," which sought to transform subjective into universal taste (Kant, 1991).

stitution won an advantage, and cultural treasures became the object of competition among museums trying to obtain them. The transportation of cultural treasures was part of the globalization process of merchandise in the Western world. During this process the museum entrenched its authority as an expert in the appropriate preservation and display of those exhibits that arrive in the museum already bearing their immanent value. The museum's authority and expertise were firmly established, then, and its function as a body that collects, preserves, displays, and mediates exhibits was acknowledged.[9]

The prevalent assumption is that the value of exhibits is determined by other cultural agents, with the museum at most complementing or validating the process of consecration. In other words, there is a structural division of labor between the museum and other agents. This division was determined at the time of the French Revolution more or less, and it can be discerned to this day in contemporary artistic discourse (see Azoulay, 1999). The museum itself conducts three institutionalized practices of representation that are the condition of existence of this division of labor: *reproduction, catalogue,* and *artistic discourse.* These practices of representation take an active part in confirming the exhibit's standing as a closed unit of meaning and in reproducing the relation between themselves and the exhibit. They endow the exhibit with an additional dimension, as precise and faithful as possible, but this dimension always stands in relation to the original unit and must therefore remain eternally damaged, lacking, and thwarted. The museum space, reproduction, catalogue, and artistic discourse are institutions that by their very nature engender the exhibit's standing as the original. But these practices and the museum space also function, as I've already noted, as a dwelling or instrument in the hands of the exhibit, and they present themselves as if they are subject to its mastery. According to need, walls shall be demolished or new ones built (to reorganize the museum space), photographic techniques will be improved or lighting systems installed (to preserve the faithfulness of the reproduction), enormous budgets will be raised (to produce a catalogue), or ancient writings and esoteric theories ransacked (the artistic discourse)—all to provide the exhibit with the appropriate conditions of visibility, display, and expression. *The exhibit commands.*

Thus, those who take part in the exhibit's production line (in the museum, reproduction, catalogue, or discourse) are unable to make a definitive statement such as, "I want the exhibit to look this way," but are limited to something on the order of,

---

9. The establishment of the ecomuseums during the 1970s was an attempt to revive the argument.

"To the best of my understanding and professional skills as an expert (museologist, curator, photographer, designer, or interpreter), the exhibit ought to look this way." The expert cannot take responsibility for the exhibit or the display beyond the professional responsibility of one who serves a different master. Thus art's transcendent standing is given additional confirmation. From the dizzy heights of its home far beyond, "art" lays down the laws of display. The museum is a temple; the curator, sometimes the critic, and sometimes the artist are the high priests; art itself, the idea governing the act, is the sanctity that is hidden from the eye, which all expect the exhibited work to reveal.

It is not the artist who is in command. For some time now, the artist's standing as the sole or final authority concerning the interpretation of his work or the determination of its boundaries has been much reduced. Saying that the artist is either the final authority with respect to the exhibit or he isn't there doesn't depend only on later theoretical insights and discussions formulated in the framework of a certain school of interpretation. This determination can be derived from the type of *phrases* of which the artist is capable. When an artist is asked to explain why an exhibit is laid out in one way or another, he never says, "I felt like it" or "This is the way I want it to be," but always comes up with a statement on the order of, "This is the way it should be" or "This is the correct way." In other words, the artist's position is linked to the positions of the experts responsible for handling the exhibit. All of these are supposed to remove the exhibit from the exchange economy, which is to say the latter cannot determine the identity, standing, and value of the former. However, this removal is what turns the exhibit into a distinctive currency of exchange whose identity, standing, and value are determined specifically by virtue of being removed from the exchange economy. The position of other agents who handle the exhibit is no different in principle from that of the artist. There are hierarchical relations among the different positions that change according to time and circumstance, and each time one agent assumes the position of the final arbiter authorized to interpret the object's will, all the others acknowledge the accurate listening ability of this agent who can decipher the object's will and who can determine the conditions for its authentic existence. Usually the artist is grasped as the one who can help in the most faithful—but not definitive—way in creating the precise conditions of attentiveness required for the object to be seen. In other words, the museum, whose function is to display objects to the view and turn them into exhibits, is actually busy listening to objects and helping them speak out: "The clinical gaze has the paradoxical ability to *hear a language* as soon as it *perceives a spectacle*. . . . It is analytic because it restores the genesis of composition; but it is the purest of all interventions insofar as this genesis is only the syntax of the language spoken by things themselves in an original silence."[10]

The critic or interpreter plays a central role in getting the silent artistic object to speak out and in creating its meaning, whether the interpretation is termed formal, political, or critical. The rigid division of labor in the field of art between those authorized to manufacture the visible and those authorized to speak for it is part of the array of knowledge and power relations that organize activity in the field of art. In the framework of these relations the hierarchical relation between the object and its interpretation is maintained, regenerating the object anew each time as the carrier of a hidden truth.

The museum was established to provide an eternal home for this truth. However, this innovation itself turned the work of art into a bearer of truth, the museum into the expert on how to handle and distribute this truth, and the individual into a subject of art. The institution's statement of intent is that art and cultural assets in general are supposed to be distributed at large and exhibited to all. The museum, unlike the private collection, is intended for the public. The democratization of the regime of the view—making art accessible, in principle, to everyone—was based on the formulation of civil rights at the end of the eighteenth century. The consumption of art became every citizen's right, and this activity was and still is presented as a virtuous quality. Every citizen was granted access to the museum and to a place reserved for him inside it. Visiting the museum turned into a sort of civil obligation and a necessary station in the course of his education.

The nature of art's accessibility to everyone was accorded a critical and systematic discussion by Pierre Bourdieu and Alain Darbel (1969) in their book *The Love of Art*. In it they analyze the patterns of art and museum consumption in Europe. The book examines the discrepancy between the democratic declaration on which the museum is based—art for all—and the specific cultural and social skills required by

---

10. This citation (emphases mine) is taken from Foucault's (1975a, 108) book *The Birth of the Clinic*. Foucault uses the concept of listening with reference to objects that can be seen in the clinic. This usage is completely accurate in the context of artistic discourse, as in such expressions as "the work speaks for itself" or "letting the work say what it has to say," which are quite common in the discussion of art. A work is measured by its ability to speak for itself, and when it requires a text, it is presented as having failed the basic litmus test. This cliché concerning the work that speaks for itself has cropped up repeatedly in the discussion during the past several decades and still occupies a central place in it. The pure view associated with the museum, from the aspect of structure and its standing in the discourse, is identical with the medical view that was constituted from inside the clinic. In the framework of any discourse, contends Foucault, phenomena are referred to objects that classify and organize them in tables, which enable comparison and examination. The museum organizes the field of scrutiny and guides the pure view in listening to the works.

individuals to exercise their right to consume art and take part in that specific discourse that encourages objects to speak out. "The museum," they contend in the concluding chapter, "gives to everyone, as a public inheritance, the grandeur of the monuments of the past, the means to splendorous glory of nobles of the past. This is an artificial generosity because free entry also means entry by request. It is reserved for those who have the ability to appropriate works, who enjoy a greater right to exercise this freedom that is accorded to them by recognition of this greater right of theirs—which is to say of their ownership of the means to appropriate cultural assets or, to use Max Weber's language, of a monopoly over the manipulation of cultural assets and institutional signs of cultural redemption" (Bourdieu and Darbel, 1969, 167).

WE

Bourdieu and Darbel's (1969) critique marks the beginning of the debate over the identity of the *I* who is everyone, the *we* who see the world but all the same must learn to see it. Bourdieu and Darbel point to one fallacious dimension in the museum's pretension of democratization. Ostensibly, citizens who wish to exercise their right to see can arrive at the museum's threshold and consume art in a free and democratic manner, along with everyone else. Indeed, they're invited to do so, but accessibility to the museum depends on prior knowledge, skills, capabilities, habits, and material and intellectual means that are not necessarily provided to every citizen. As Bourdieu and Darbel demonstrate, a supervisory, selective, and delimiting apparatus inside the museum classifies the candidates for inclusion in the game played on the field of art and chooses from among them those authorized to assume speaker positions in the artistic discourse (see Bourdieu, 1979). Bourdieu and Darbel's (1969) critique, which is aimed in the main at the class of art consumers, may be extended to the class of art producers. In either case we are concerned with the ability to become a subject of art. It is impossible to understand the identity of the "we" who learn to see without discussing the internal division of labor among its elements, which is organized through the intermediacy of the museum and in ways that reproduce this division in its framework. Each player in the field who assumes one of its acknowledged positions—artist, curator, collector, or spectator—is appointed over one segment of professional activity. In other words, the teacher should teach art, the artist should create it, the curator should curate it, the collector should collect it, and the spectator should contemplate it. Allowance is made for deviations, but only insofar as they constitute an infraction of routine. The act of deviation actually signifies that there's a boundary, that the boundary is now being transgressed, and that the demarcation of the previous boundaries will be highlighted anew on the conclusion of this transgression. The renewed demarcation of the boundaries means the preservation of the model of relations among the different positions, so that what is subject to the view, speech, or interference of each of those individuals occupying these positions will remain unchanged.

Future artists arrive at school to learn art. Actually, in school they learn how to generate themselves as the producers of the objects that will turn them into artists and how to talk about these objects so that they become noted artists. Even if teachers would like to renounce the conception of art as the production of objects, they will teach the future artists how to produce objects (or images) so that the students will be able to pass the obstacles in the course of study (end-of-term exhibitions, for example) and complete their final projects, which can't be anything other than objects ready to be exhibited.[11] The central theme of instruction consists of how to speak about "artistic" objects and images as distinct from objects that resemble them in the public space—how to speak about a flag, for example, as "not-a-flag" or at least as "not-just-a-flag" or how to speak about an advertisement as not-an-advertisement but as an advertisement that points to an advertisement. Even a curator who wishes to renounce the conception of art as the production of distinct objects is bound to curate exhibitions exhibiting objects that "point to." These objects will usually be taken from a store of such created by one of the "products" (artists) who have graduated from one of the institutions that teach art. So too the collector, spectator, and gallery owner all take part in this activity in a way that makes possible the continued existence of this same pattern of exchange relations and that reaffirms the standing and boundaries of the subject of art and the artistic object anew each time. In the framework of these exchange relations, each of those occupying the different positions acknowledges and affirms the other's position and thus also affirms the essence and character of the exchange relations and the exchange currency traded in their framework (the work of art).

Because each actor is appointed over only a single segment (of vision, speech, and interference), it is possible to transform the object of the exchange relations—"art"—into an absent signified, of which each of the works is a signifier. The signifier (the work) is always supposed to be interpreted and judged as a signifier of that absent signified. The transcendent signified determines the intertextual boundaries—the stores of signifiers against which the work-of-art signifier should be

---

11. The training is based on the act of being exhibited and requires it. Students must present their accumulated achievements and exhibit them as worthy achievements.

interpreted and judged. Due to its standing as a transcendent signified, art expropriates its signifiers from a sequence of connections and differences with respect to similar signifiers (flag, rifle, advertisement) and endows them with a standing that is in principle unique.

The museum, as I have tried to show to this point, transforms the image or object into an artistic statement. The object's transformation into statement by the museum is a necessary condition for its existence as a statement, but it is not a sufficient condition. For the object or image to attain its status as an artistic statement, all the subjects of art must agree in principle to interpret a specific signifier as art. Such agreement, however, is a condition for the constitution of the subject position in the field of art. When a spectator fails to recognize as art what has already been declared an art object, he will not be able to occupy the position of a subject of art. But it also means redefining the intertextual boundaries, positing the signifier (the work of art) in relation to other signifiers, and reading the signifier (the work of art) in connection not with the thing that is signified but with a principle ("art"). The detachment of the signifier from the signified—which occurs with the loss of the position of a subject of art or prior to attaining it—makes possible the formation of new fields of vision and the articulation of different relations among signifiers of different kinds. With the loss of the object's or image's unique standing as a work of art, the photograph of graffiti in Tel Aviv's municipal square and the computerized portrait of Yigal Amir that are exhibited in the museum are nothing but signifiers that empower signifiers that resemble them. They are in an "ecstatic relation" with other signifiers (images). An "ecstatic relation," according to Baudrillard, is not one of opposition but of saturation or deficiency in a sequence. One element expresses the saturation or deficiency of a certain quality in relation to another element possessing the same quality, an empowerment or diminishment of the quality that is common to both. Thus, for example, the photograph of the graffiti in the municipal square that was displayed at the 1996 exhibition *In the Wake of the Trauma: Graffiti from Rabin Square* is more authentic and larger than the original graffiti (which was exhibited at the Tel Aviv Art Museum). So too the computerized portrait of Yigal Amir that was shown at the *Digital Stroke* exhibition doesn't stand in opposition to any other image of Yigal Amir but functions as another signifier in the framework of the dizzying proliferation of Yigal Amir images. It empowers a quality that arouses in the viewer revulsion—or attraction—to Amir. However, by being located inside the museum it declares, "I am not Yigal Amir. I am not sanctifying Amir, I am not adulating him, I am art"—

"critical art," of course. The museum discourse attempts to mark this empowered image as completely distinct from the entire series of other images that exist "in reality" and thus preserve art's status as separate, distinctive, and transcendent.

The players in the field are busy with the products that enable them to display anew their position as subjects, as those who know the rules of the game and are adept at its moves. Thus, in response to the photographs of the municipal square commissioned by the mayor of Tel Aviv, the artist or art expert (the subject of art) will take a stand and say, "This isn't art." In other words, this signifier isn't authorized to be a signifier of "art" because the photographs, after all, were commissioned by the mayor, a political functionary who isn't authorized to baptize objects as art. Faced with the computerized image of Yigal Amir, the same artist or art expert (the subject of art) will take a stand and say, "This is art," because an artist created this image, after all, or it was hung in the museum by a curator. Both images—the photographed graffiti and the image of the assassin—don't present any new statement concerning the world. Both perform a rather similar function: they isolate an image that is prevalent in the public space and display an empowered reproduction of it in the museum. Neither image says anything about either the assassination or the assassin, simply because the image itself is not a statement. From the moment they enter the museum they are presented as statements about what is external to them (and generally what is external to the museum as well), to which they point. But in the framework of an economy of images that doesn't accept the rules of the game of the artistic statement, the image that points is part of the phenomenon to which it purports to point.

For a certain community whose members have been trained to be subjects of art, from the moment the object enters the museum the object achieves a preferred status as a signifier of art, inviting the judgment of taste to determine its standing in the field. Thus a particular work may be judged against the previous works of the same artist and a particular text may be viewed as a breakthrough from the aspect of its focus of discussion concerning a different artist. Such judgments constitute part of the museal exchange relations. These relations produce more and more objects that are collected into the museum stores and injected into the bloodstream of the art world. By virtue of being part of these stores objects become worthy of being learned: they themselves change from signifier to signified. They become objects that carry inside them the special meaning (or truth) that can be deciphered—partially, of course—only by the experts who know how to listen to this meaning and turn it into language.

TO SEE, TO LEARN TO SEE

It is possible to see in different ways: one can see graffiti as soiling a municipal wall, as a dirge, as a beautiful thing, as a thing whose place is inside the museum, as the voice of the people or authentic. In each of these examples the object of vision is recreated by a different mode of vision, a different mode of speech to formulate it, and a different range of action with respect to the same visible object. In each of these examples the object is recreated by view, speech, and action.

When manufactured as a work of art, the object exposed to view functions as a touchstone, like the high priest's breastplate. First it ascertains whether whoever sees the object recognizes it as a work of art. Those who fail this initial test drop out of the game and lose the position of speaker that they had or could have had. If they pass the test and recognize the object as a work of art, the range of *phrases* available to the viewers is delimited and organized by the transcendent signified known as "art." Having passed the test, viewers can go on to the second round.

Interpreters face the object that they have recognized as a work of art and now must become speakers of its meaning. Actually, they can succeed only if they fail. If they succeed in extracting the truth embodied in the work, then the labors of both the artist and the viewers are concluded once and for all. If interpreters can say what the work can say, then both the artist and his work become superfluous. If the viewers fail to extract the truth embodied in it, then they have succeeded. They have succeeded in providing additional testimony to the eternal gap between the viewer's work and the artist's work, which is the justification for them both. Interpreters show their concept in action and prove that, try as they might to marry their concept to the work, the work will always elude them. The position of interpreter can be occupied, even if temporarily, by any of the players in the field (including the artist). This is the position of critic,[12] the guardian at the gates who is supposed to guard against the invasion of works that can be reduced to entirely deciphered, pure discursive expressions. The critic, according to Kant (1996) in *The Critique of Pure Reason*, will maintain the internal order of his jurisdiction (reason) on condition that the state will award this jurisdiction an autonomous standing.[13]

---

12. In the Kantian sense of the term.

13. Pierre Bourdieu's (1979) book *The Distinction: A Social Critique of the Power of Judgment* attempts to put forward a revised version of Kant's critique of judgment. In the chapter titled "Anti-Kantian Aesthetics," Bourdieu (1979, 42) presents the ways in which high art (which is assessed by the power of universal judgment) defines itself in the course of defining inferior "barbaric taste" (which enables the contemplator to look at the picture and see what it contains). In their traditional roles the interpreter and critic are supposed to supervise this boundary and to prevent the intrusion of objects of barbaric taste into the jurisdiction of high art.

The critic, then, does a policeman's job by keeping out the works of art that contain messages that aren't universal and works that can be reduced to their concrete content. This job is the substance of the training for art. The critic hands in his ticket and presents a model for training. The citizen is invited to participate in the game. The principal weapon at the critic's disposal to guard the gates and maintain (together with the museum) the boundaries of the field of vision is the ability to get the work to speak out and to examine it in light of existing standards. The simplest way to do this is to criticize the work while "exposing" its inferiority with respect to those standards. A more complicated way might be to praise the work while pointing to the way in which it accords with and embodies the aesthetic standards. For instance, the critic can build an interpretative structure that contains only the formal values of the work and offer it to the viewer in a way that silences its particularistic contents and formulates only what can be universalized in it. One way or another, critics must guard the gates and thus ensure not only their position and standing but also the desirable division of labor between themselves and the "original" text (the work).

But critics are responsible people, and it is not for nothing that they're standing at the gates. The power they exert as guardians of the threshold is a type of struggle for autonomy; critics enlist to defend the boundaries of the field.[14] Critics try to guarantee freedom of expression and creativity in their jurisdiction when anyone attempts to abrogate it. They'll be the first to stand up to censorship if it attempts to remove any elements offensive to a particular public, to defend works someone wants to take down, to champion an artist whose freedom of movement has been taken away, or to battle the disqualification of controversial images. They will do all these things in the name of freedom of expression and creativity in the framework of the autonomous field of production, a freedom that has been achieved in full coordination with the "arts of governing" (*arts de gouverner*).[15] They will respond to this trespass as they would to the violation of an agreement. The "arts of governing" have promised freedom in return for control over the arts—the demarcation of art as a separate field. Critics are signatories to the agreement. They have been authorized

14. Critique—according to Foucault (1978) in his essay "What Is Critique?"—plays a double role. It is supposed to guarantee (1) that the truth and knowledge are produced freely in the public sphere and ensure that nothing economical or political intrudes on them and also (2) that knowledge is managed in an orderly fashion in the framework of the autonomy allotted to it. In fact, these roles are two sides of the same policing practice.

15. Foucault (1978) developed the concept of "arts of governing" in his essay "What Is Critique?" In it he speaks about the art of governing versus the art of not being governed, about *gouvernementalité* as a new form of control.

to defend this freedom against the outside and ensure control of the arts on the inside. They are supposed to guarantee the reproduction of the field of art by respecting the necessary separation between the work and its interpretation, between the original and the failures to conceptualize it, between the visible and the spoken, between the nonconceptualized sequence and the solidification of the work, between individual artists and the objects they produce. Critics are supposed to guarantee that artistic activity—and critical activity too, of course—doesn't remain in the "wild space out there" but is brought into negotiation with the rules that allow truth to be heard. Critics ensure that each actor occupies an appropriate position and that the division among the positions remains clear. They are the faithful servants of the discursive police, ensuring that the individual's truth will disclose itself from the work and that the truth of the work will never be able to be fully exposed by means of the discourse that seeks to interpret it.[16] Critics are responsible, then, on behalf of the discursive police, for creating the existence of the truth of the individual and turning it into a secret that will always exceed the words that seek to expose it. In the final analysis, they are responsible for having the artist produce the work, which enables the game to continue in an orderly fashion.

Critique plays a normalizing role in the agreement concerning control of the arts. Deviant messages that emerge from works produced in the framework of the field of art are always a pretext for opening the discussion of freedom of expression and creativity. The discussion almost always ends with the conclusion that order has to be restored—not the social order, which someone may have challenged, but the internal order of the field of art and the relation between it and the public sphere: let the artists produce art, the critics criticize, and the politicians deal in politics. In other words, the autonomy of art should continue to be defended. The lively debate over the messages of the works and the supervisory authority over them, successfully concluded "in favor" of art, succeeds, each time anew, in obscuring the basic questions concerning the supervision of the work and the supervision of the practice of critique. This supervision doesn't rest with the work's content or message but with its conditions of production, with the means of production, with the positions of production, with the means of distribution, with the conditions of distribution, with the conditions of visibility, and with the means of visibility. In other words, supervision rests with the speaker positions and not with the statements themselves.[17] To be "inside the

---

16. Any work whose secret can be exposed by translating it into a different language will lose its reason for being.

17. For more on art as a discourse, see Azoulay (1999a).

truth," as Foucault puts it, the speaker must obey the rules of the discourse that determine which positions one may speak from, what speech is permitted from there, and when it may be spoken. These supervisory mechanisms ensure the consolidation of a unified productive community, which is a "community of taste" in its own self-image and whose agreement over control of the arts extracts a loyalty to the "arts of governing."

This supervision is not a restriction of art (for art has chosen, in any event, to act in a restricted framework) but is the defense of an entire array of demarcations that make it possible, in a world that is poor in differences, to produce differences that have transcendent status.

ART

For the object to be more than just an object, someone has to operate it, get it to speak out, place it inside a story within whose framework it turns into art.[18] Art requires certain conditions of possibility in order to appear. These are historic conditions that are anchored in the logic of capitalistic consumer society and the logic of the museum site (see Foster, 1996a, 1996b; Krauss, 1990). They are necessary but insufficient conditions that guarantee that whoever assumes a position in the field will be able "to produce a difference" without being rejected by and evicted out of the field of phenomena that is being defined. If the object is accorded conditions of visibility, interpretation can enter the picture and illuminate it in a different light, "produce a difference," and interpret it as one type of art or another.

The museum is the primary site where one acquires the technique of getting the object to speak out until just before it opens its mouth and confirms what one has said in its name. The museum resembles a gigantic concert hall in which people gather to listen, through the works of art, to the transcendent law of art. This listening is performed in the framework of a wider set of practices of discourse and action, of exchange relations, and of accumulating symbolic capital. These enable all the participants in the activity in the field of art to agree that the dumb objects speak a language that in principle cannot be heard because their tongues are severed. The artist's function is to bring this language to the stage at which it appears in its inarticulateness—when it at the same time signifies both its presence and its absence. Thus the object manages not to appear too arbitrary, and it also doesn't appear to be

---

18. The emphasis is on the act of getting the work to "speak out" and not on an act of "speaking about." In art, this is usually accomplished with interpreters speaking in the name of the work or claiming that they are merely serving as a mouthpiece.

spoken of or to speak too much.[19] In effect artists are gauged by their ability to bring the object to its "authentic" state—a state that cannot be formulated verbally but cannot be said to say nothing. This intermediate state isn't of the object's essence but of the essence of the exchange relations that obtain among the different agents who contemplate the object, speak about it, and exhibit it.

Training for art, then, is the education of subjects who will be able to participate in the practice of art consumption. The educated subject will be able to confront a defined object and produce it as a bearer of meaning that can be deciphered only in connection with objects from the same family (works of art) and without this meaning exceeding the range of view, speech, and action that is permitted by the logic of museal spatialization. Thus the subject of art—the one who knows how to interpret the exhibits that signify it—turns into the guardian of the boundary, of the demarcation, of the division of labor, of the distinction between the world over there and the art world over here: over there are awful images, here the same images say something else; over there everything is serial and industrialized, here there is personal expression. And so on and so forth, the subject distinguishes a whole series of oppositions that are nothing other than the necessary conditions of the game. Whoever doesn't want to abide by the rules can go looking for another field. Without these rules, the game of art couldn't exist.

However, the game of art is but one among several games in which the visual lies at stake. This game, I have tried to show above, involves a sovereign subject (or a subject that pretends to be sovereign) and a visible object (or an object given to the gaze of a subject and posited as worthy of interpretation). That gaze and that interpretation are constrained and enabled by a set of discursive rules that guarantee the inner depth or deep interiority of both the subject and object of art and that block that inner quality's way to the surface. Among the other games in which the visual is at stake, I am preoccupied here with one in particular—the game of the photographic image. The game is partly based on the rules of the game of art: it still maintains a certain secret, an interiority that is never to be entirely exposed or uncovered, a postponement that implies that exposition is an unfinished business. At the same time, however, it is subject to another discursive regime that undermines and shakes the rules of the artistic game. This other, subversive game takes place in networks of

---

19. In *TRAining for ART: A Critique of the Museal Economy* (Azoulay, 1999a), I recalled a whole complex of patterns of behavior and exchange relations in the home of Israeli artist Rafi Lavi and tried to show how the individuals who were trained in and in connection with this place of knowledge—the Lavi home—learned how to speak like artists, how to behave like artists, how to see art, and how to speak about art.

presences in which neither the subject nor the object has a privileged position, depth is unfolded as another surface, repetition takes the place of singularity and uniqueness, and the demarcated location for the appearance of the image becomes the network's terminals and links. Intention and teleology give way to destiny and chance.[20]

The darkroom is the locus of simulation of another locus—the arena of photography, of crime, of trauma. The darkroom is the ultimate bunker to which the photographer descends to preserve the secret, to force it to reveal itself, to slowly expose it on the photographic paper. It is a secret in the first place because it preserves the unbridgeable gap between what is seen on the paper and what was seen facing the lens. This gap is unbridgeable because what is seen in the picture was there, whereas whoever sees it—including the photographer—is here. The darkroom permits the photographer to witness—for the first time, in fact—the scene revealed on the photographic paper.[21] Whoever wishes to respond to what is seen in the picture must return to "there" and go backward in time. But to act with regard to "what was there," one requires the help of a third party; one must go forward in time to the next tribunal. What is seen in the picture was there—not only in the sense coined by Roland Barthes (that is, as testimony that what is seen in the photograph was present facing the camera) but in the sense that the time lapse makes present the gap between a seemingly stabilized object seen in the photograph and the photographer's apparently external point of view. Thus, the spectator is liable to plunge into what's seen in the photograph and forget that a photographer had been there when it was taken. A few years ago I happened on a photograph of a young Palestinian woman whose hair was being pulled by two soldiers. I analyzed the photograph as part of the critical practice of press photography. I did not then doubt the moral obligation to depict the horrors of the Israeli occupation of Palestinian territories, to cast light on the dark forces of Israeli rule in the territories. Nevertheless, something about the photograph disturbed me—perhaps the visual angle, perhaps the woman's act of resistance—and I recently returned to it. I asked the photographer to reconstruct the event: "I saw young women throwing stones at soldiers. I shot a few frames. I saw two soldiers who were performing a flanking movement and who were about to catch them from behind." I asked the photographer whether the possibility didn't flash through his mind of warning the women that the soldiers were flanking them from behind. His reply was succinct: "Absolutely not. I don't change the order of things. I don't interfere."

20. In his book *Serial Killer* Zeltzer (1998) proposes a similar distinction between the modern and the postmodern based on the distinction between the concept of shock and trauma.

21. See the optical unconscious of Benjamin (1980) and my discussion of it in chapter 2.

Miki Kratzman, *Refugee Camp, Tul Karem*, 1988

The photographic paper, on the one hand, and the rhetoric of a secret that needs to be exposed and brought to light, on the other, give rise to photography as something that was there, whereas you facing it are here.

During the war in Bosnia, I read several times a horrifying story of a snipers' post and a photographers' post that were manned anew each morning, in perfect mutual equilibrium: sniper facing photographer. I tried to imagine what it would be like if one of the cameras happened to be a television camera. I imagined myself sitting at home and watching a live broadcast, devoid of any secret and outside any bunker of interpretation or critique, of the sniper sniping. Instead of seeing the photographer taking pictures, I am also sitting at his post, watching a man or woman cross the street below and be killed by snipers. The only possible interference I as a viewer can offer is to shut off the television. One interference that can be offered by the photographer who is there (if he could forget for a moment that his view belongs to and is managed by his employer) is to shoot. The sniper, of course. But in doing so, he would remove himself from a network of points of view that is, to a certain extent, immune from the snipers and would enter a network of presences that is perhaps arranging for him to become the next victim whose death I shall watch on my television screen.

The television camera during a live broadcast no longer produces signs that need be deciphered in the future. In the name of freedom of information, the public's right to know, human rights, and freedom of the press, scenes of crime are becoming transparent—so transparent, in fact, that no effort is required to imagine a point of view from which the crime can be seen committed. The photographer is no longer a messenger of light illuminating the horror, the public eye in whose wake the executive arm of the law shall appear and restore justice to its rightful place. The space is discontinuous: the eye is connected to one network, the hand to another. Only the scales of justice are still located in a defined disciplinary site, in a grand hall of homogeneous space and linear time wherein all testimonies are to be gathered. The entire public space is strewn with cameras, which even when they are points of view, are not extensions of subjectivity capable of action. They are intertwined in a network of points of view like themselves, whose presences in the network cancel each other out—like an arm-wrestling bout, like two electric minuses turning into a plus. There is no one who sees. There is no one who sees more than another sees. There is no one who doesn't see. Everyone doesn't see, just as everyone sees. We're all peeking into an arena bathed in light.

Let us return to the television camera broadcasting from Bosnia. For the photographer to be only a photographer—that neutral position that merely documents—the murderer-sniper must be only a murderer-sniper. From the moment at which the photographer is not only a photographer, he becomes a murderer or at least an accomplice to murder. And, at that very moment, the murderer becomes an accomplice to the photographic act.

The justice that can be executed only after the fact, in retrospect—when the two sides prepare for its arrival, equipped with photographic evidence of the crime—requires the photographer present at the event to bring the proofs to court. But if the witness-photographer is also an accomplice to murder, he should join the sniper in the prosecution's visual field. So, too, with regard to the other witnesses whose testimony leads to the conviction of that witness-photographer. Perhaps the Last Judgment will be the day on which the judiciary system, like photography, no longer requires a place of its own, but extends over the entire public space, is networked like communication satellites and operates in real time. It could pronounce sentence on the sniper immediately, on the spot. Then the photographer would regain his glory by illuminating this judiciary work and supervising it. On whose behalf?

Abbeele, G. Van Den. 1992. *Travel as Metaphor: From Montaigne to Rousseau.* Minneapolis: University of Minnesota Press.

Agamben, Giorgio. 1997. *Homo sacer: le pouvoir souverain et la vie nue.* Paris: Seuil.

Alon, Gideon. 1996. "Libai: No Minister of Justice will ever reduce Amir's sentence," *Ha'aretz*, March 28, p. 3a.

Azoulay, Ariella. 1992. "Photography and the Disintegration of the Public Space." *Studio* 37 (in Hebrew): 36–40.

Azoulay, Ariella. 1994. "With Open Doors: Museums and Historical Narratives in Israel's Public Space." In *Museum Culture*, edited by D. J. Sherman and I. Rogoff. Minneapolis: University of Minnesota Press.

Azoulay, Ariella. 1996. "The Archive Keepers." *Studio* no. 74 (in Hebrew): 19–21.

Azoulay, Ariella. 1997a. "Can One Make Works Which Are Not Works of Art?" *Plastika* 1. (in Hebrew): 30–33.

Azoulay, Ariella. 1997b. "Clean Hands." *Documenta\Documents* (vol. 3). Ostfildern: Cantz Verlag, (pp. 44–57).

Azoulay, Ariella. 1997c. "Un lexique." *Produire, créer, collectionner.* Paris: Hazan. 78–83.

Azoulay, Ariella. 1999a. *TRAining for ART: A Critique of the Museal Economy.* Porter Institute and Ha-Kibbutz Ha-Meuchad, Tel Aviv.

Azoulay, Ariella. 1999b. *Michal Heiman Test (M.H.T.) No. 2—Manual,* Museum Le Quartier, Quimper.

Azoulay, Ariella, and Adi Ophir. 1998. "Hello Peace, How Are You?" *Plastika* 2. (in Hebrew): 76–92.

Balibar, Etienne. 1997. *La crainte des masses.* Paris: Galilée.

Baqué, Dominique. 1993. *Les documents de la modernité.* Chambon: Editions Jacqueline.

Barel, Zvi. 1996. "Amir concluded his testimony in court," *Ha'aretz*, March 8, p. 9a.

Barthes, Roland. 1980. *La chambre claire.* Paris: Seuil.

Baudrillard, Jean. 1979. *De la seduction.* Paris: Galilée.

Baudrillard, Jean. 1981. *Simulacres et simulations.* Paris: Galilée.

Baudrillard, Jean. 1983. *Les strategies fatales.* Paris: Grasset.

Baudrillard, Jean. 1987. *Forget Foucault.* New York: Semiotext(e).

Baudrillard, Jean. 1988. *The Ecstasy of Communication.* New York: Semiotext(e).

Baudrillard, Jean. 1990. *La transparence du mal.* Paris: Galilée.

Baudrillard, Jean. 1991. *La guerre du golf n'a pas eu lieu.* Paris: Galilée.

Baudrillard, Jean. 1995. *Le crime parfait.* Paris: Galilée.

Bazin, G. 1967. *Le temps des musées.* Desoer: Liege-Bruxelles.

Benjamin, Walter. 1978. *Illuminations.* New York: Schocken Books.

Benjamin, Walter. 1979. *Reflections.* New York: Harvest/HBS Books.

Benjamin, Walter. 1980. "A Short History of Photography." In *Classic Essays on Photography.* New Haven, Conn.: Leete's Island Books.

Benjamin, Walter. 1983. *Essais* (vols. 1–2). Paris: Denöel-Gonthier.

Benjamin, Walter. 1989. *Paris Capitale du XIX Siècle-Le livre des Passages,* Les Editions du Cerf, Paris.

Benjamin, Walter. 1991. "L'oeuvre d'art à l'époque de sa reproduction mécanisée" (1936); *Écrits français.* Paris: NRF Éditions Gallimard.

Benjamin, Walter. 1996a. *Petite histoire de la photographie.* Paris: Etudes Photographiques, Société Française de Photographie.

Benjamin, Walter. 1996b. *Selected Writings.* Cambridge, Mass.: Belknap Press of Harvard University Press.

Benvenisti, Meron. 1996. *Jerusalem: A Place of Fire.* Tel Aviv: Dvir (in Hebrew).

Bishara, Azmi. 1992. "Between Place and Space: On the Palestinian Public Space." *Studio* no. 37 (in Hebrew): 6–9.

Blanchot, Maurice. 1997. "Two Versions of the Imaginary." *Documenta X: The Book,* edited by C. David and J. F. Chevrier. Ostfildern: Cantz Verlag.

Bourdieu, Pierre, and Alain Darbel. 1969. *L'amour de l'art.* Paris: Minuit.

Bourdieu, Pierre. 1979. *La distinction: critique sociale du jugement.* Paris: Minuit.

Breitberg-Semel, Sarah. 1997. "Know Yourself." *Studio* 88, 20.

Brener, Elly. 1996. "The judge: 'Heaven cries and I wonder why,'" *Davar,* p. 9.

B'tselem Reports. 1995. *Policy of Discrimination* (in Hebrew). Jerusalem: B'tselem.

B'tselem Reports. 1997. *Stop the Quiet Deportation* (in Hebrew). Jerusalem: B'tselem.

Buchloh, Benjamin. 1988. "From Factura to Factography." *October: The First Decade.* Cambridge, Mass.: MIT Press.

Buck-Morss, Susan. 1990. *The Dialectics of Seeing.* Cambridge, Mass.: MIT Press.

Buck-Morss, Susan. 1992. "Aesthetics and Anaesthetics: Walter Benjamin's Artwork Essay Reconsidered." *October* 62: 3–42.

Caruth, Cathy. 1994. *Unclaimed Experience.* Baltimore: Johns Hopkins University Press.

Caygill, Howard. 1994. "Benjamin, Heidegger and the Destruction of Tradition." In *Walter Benjamin's Philosophy,* edited by Andrew Benjamin. New York: Routledge.

Chevrier, François. 1992. "Double Lecture." *Graham/Evans.* Rotterdam: Witte de With Museum.

Crary, Jonathan. 1992. *Techniques of the Observer.* Cambridge, Mass.: MIT Press.

Crow, Thomas, E. 1985. *Painters and Public Life in Eighteenth-Century Paris.* New Haven: Yale University Press.

Daney, Serge. 1997. "Before and After the Image." In *Documenta X: The Book,* edited by C. David and J. F. Chevrier. Ostfildern: Cantz Verlag, 610–620.

De Duve, Thierry. 1989. *Au nom de l'art.* Paris: Minuit.

Deleuze, Gilles. 1968. *Différence et répétition.* Paris: Puf.

Deleuze, Gilles. 1990. *Pourpalers.* Paris: Minuit.

Deleuze, Gilles. 1992. "Postcript on the Societies of Control." *October* no. 59.

Deleuze, Gilles, and Felix Guattari. 1980. *Mille Plateaux.* Paris: Minuit.

Deleuze, Gilles, and Felix Guattari. 1997. "The Included Middle." In *Documenta X: The Book,* Ostfildern: Cantz Verlag, 466–471.

Derrida, Jacques. 1990. "Force of Law: The 'Mystical Foundation of Authority.'" In *Deconstruction and the Possibility of Justice,* edited by Drucilla Cornell, Michel Rosenfeld, and David Gray Carlson. New York: Routledge.

Derrida, Jacques. 1991. *Donner le temps.* Paris: Seuil.

Derrida, Jacques. 1995. *Mal d'archive,* Paris: Galilée.

Dower, John W. 1996. "The Bombed: Hiroshima and Nagasaki in Japanese Memory." In *Hiroshima in History and Memory,* edited by Michael J. Hogan. Cambridge: Cambridge University Press.

Duras, Marguerite. 1967. *Hiroshima mon amour.* New York: Grove Press.

Elkana, Yehuda. 1988. "The Right to Forget." *Ha'aretz* (2.3.88): p. 13.

Foster, Hal, 1996a. "The Archive without Museums." *October* no. 77: 97–119.

Foster, Hal, 1996b. "L'artiste comme ethnographe, ou la 'fin de l'histoire' signifie-t-elle le retour à l'anthropologie?" In *Face à l'histoire,* edited by Jean Paul Ameline. Paris: Centre G. Pompidou, Flammarion.

Foucault, Michel. 1963. *La naissance de la clinique.* Paris: PUF.

Foucault, Michel. 1966. *Les mots et les choses.* Paris: Gallimard.

Foucault, Michel. 1969. *L'archeologie du savoir.* Paris: Gallimard.

Foucault, Michel. 1971. *L'ordre du discours.* Paris: Gallimard.

Foucault, Michel. 1975a. *The Birth of the Clinic.* New York: Vintage Books.

Foucault, Michel. 1975b. *Surveiller et punir.* Paris: Gallimard.

Foucault, Michel. 1976. *Histoire de la sexualité* (vol. 1). Paris: Gallimard.

Foucault, Michel. 1977. *Language, Counter-memory, Practice.* New York: Cornell.

Foucault, Michel. 1978. "Qu'est-ce que la critique?" *Bulletin de la Société Française de Philosophie* 35–63.

Foucault, Michel. 1986. "Of Other Spaces." *Diacritics* 16, no. 1:7–22.

Foucault, Michel. 1989. *Resumé des cours: 1970–1982.* Paris: Julliard.

Foucault, Michel. 1994. *Dits et écrits (vols. 3–4).* Paris: Gallimard.

Friedlander, Saul. 1982. *Kitsch and Death: On the Reflection of Nazism.* Keter Press, Jerusalem, (in Hebrew).

Gaethgens, T. W. 1986. "Les musées historiques de Versailles." In *Les lieux de mémoire*, edited by P. Nora. Paris: Gallimard.

Gladman, Mordechai. 1997. "You Wake Up in the Morning and Immediately Begin to Worry." *Ha'Aretz*, November 21, p. 10.

Green, David B. 1997. "Shock Treatment." *Jerusalem Report*, December 11, p. 16.

Gurevich, David. 1997. "To Distinguish What Isn't Hell in Hell." *Ha'Aretz*, November 28, literary supplement, p. 1.

Habermas, Jürgen. 1989. *The Structural Transformation of the Public Sphere: An Inquiry into a Category of Bourgeois Society.* Cambridge, Mass.: MIT Press.

Harvey, David. 1985. *The Urbanization of Capital.* Baltimore: Johns Hopkins University Press.

Heidegger, Martin. 1971. *Poetry, Language, Thought.* New York: Harper & Row.

Heidegger, Martin. 1977. *The Question Concerning Technology and Other Essays.* New York: Harper & Row.

Heidegger, Martin. 1996. "The Age of the World Picture." *Electronic Culture*, edited by T. Druckrey. New York: Aperture.

Hogan, Michael J., ed. (1996). *Hiróshima in History and Memory.* Cambridge: Cambridge University Press.

Huberman, George Didi. 1982. *L'invention de l'hystérie.* Paris: Macula.

Kant, Immanuel. 1985. *Critique of Pure Reason.* Cambridge: Cambridge University Press.

Kant, Immanuel. 1991. *Critique of Judgment.* Oxford: Clarendon Press.

Karmi, Jadda. 1997. "One State, Two People." *Ha'aretz*, newspaper, September 10, p. 32 (in Hebrew).

Krauss, Rosalind. 1988. "The Im/Pulse to See." *Vision and Visuality*, edited by Hal Foster. Seattle: New Press.

Krauss, Rosalind. 1990. "The Cultural Logic of the Late Capitalist Museum." *October*, no. 54. pp. 3–18.

Latour, Bruno. 1994. *Nous n'avons jamais été modernes.* Paris: La Découverte.

Lyotard, Jean-François. 1979. *La condition postmoderne.* Paris: Minuit.

Lyotard, Jean-François. 1983. *Le différend.* Paris: Minuit.

Lyotard, Jean-François. 1986. *Le postmoderne expliqué aux enfants.* Paris: Galille.

Lyotard, Jean-François. 1991. *The Inhumain.* Stanford University Press.

Lyotard, Jean-François and Thébaud, Jean Loup. 1985. *Just Gaming.* Minneapolis: University of Minnesota Press.

Mansbach, Abraham. 1998. *Existence and Meaning.* Jerusalem: Magnes Press (in Hebrew).

Marx, Karl. 1936. *Capital: A Critique of Political Economy,* edited by Bennett A. Cerf and Donald S. Klopper. New York: Modern Library.

Marx, Karl, and Friedrich Engels. 1951. *On Art and Literature.* Merhavya, Israel: Sifryat Hapoalim (in Hebrew).

Meidan, Anat. 1995. "I focused on Yigal Amir because he seems to me to be a potential assassin," *Yediot Acharonot,* December 19, p. 7.

Merleau-Ponty, Maurice. 1964. *Le visible et l'invisible.* Paris: Gallimard.

Miyoshi, Masao. 1997. "A Borderless World?" In *Documenta X: The Book,* edited by C. David and J. F. Chevrier. Ostfildern: Cantz Verlag.

Nancy, Jean Luc. 1990. *La communauté desoeuvrée.* Paris: Christian Bourgois Editeur.

Nancy, Jean Luc. 1996. *Etre singulier pluriel.* Paris: Galilée.

Ophir, Adi. 1988. "Michel Foucault and the Semiotics of the Phenomenal." *Dialogue* 27, 387–415.

Ophir, Adi. 1989. "The Semiotics of Power." *Manuscrito* 12, no. 2: 9–34.

Ophir, Adi. 1987. "On Sanctifying the Holocaust: An Anti-Theological Treatise," *Tikkun* 2, no. 1 (pp. 60–67).

Ophir, Adi. 1988. "The cartography of knowledge and power: Foucault Reconsidered," in (edited by Hugh J. Silverman) *Cultural Semiosis.* New York: Routledge.

Pe'er, Edna. 1996. "Interview with Naji Nasser." *Ma'ariv,* August 9 (weekend supplement), pp. 14–15.

Perry-Lehman, Meira. 1997. "Foreword," *Live and Die as Eva Braun* (exhibition catalogue), Israel Museum, Jerusalem (pages unnumbered).

Petrova, Ada, and Peter Watson. 1996. *The Death of Hitler: The Full Story with New Evidence from Secret Russian Archives.* New York: Norton.

Portugali, Yuval. 1996. *Implicate Relations: Society and Space in the Israeli Palestinian Conflict.* Tel Aviv: Hakibbutz Hameuchad (in Hebrew).

Poulot, D. 1985. "Naissance du monument historique." *Revue d'histoire moderne et contemporaine*, no. 32.

Poulot, D. 1986. "Richard Lenoir et les musées des monuments historique."

Przyblyski, Jeannene. 1998. "History Is Photography: The Afterimage of Walter Benjamin." *Afterimage* 26, no. 2: 8–11.

Riegler, Nurit, and Tamar Trebelisi-Chadad. 1997. "Hammer to Israel Museum: Remove the Exhibition of Hitler's Mistress." *Yediot Acharonot*, November 7, p. 22.

Rosen, Roee. 1996. "The Visibility and Invisibility of the Trauma." *Studio* 76 (in Hebrew).

Rosen, Roee, and Galya Yahav. 1997. "Decent, Indecent, and What Lies Between." *Studio* 88, pp. 21–30.

Rothman, Roger. 1997. "Mourning and Mania." *Live and Die as Eva Braun* (exhibition catalogue), Israel Museum, Jerusalem.

Said, Edward W. 1993. *Culture and Imperialism.* New York: Vintage Books.

Samet, Gideon. 1997. "Holocaust and Other Denials." *Ha'Aretz*, December 5, p. B1.

Sassen, Saskia. 1997. "Global Cities and Global Value Chains." In *Documenta X: The Book*, edited by C. David and J. F. Chevrier. Ostfildern: Cantz Verlag, pp. 736–745.

Segev, Amira. 1996. "Confrontation between the Israeli Army and Palestinians in Hussan village after Sawsha funeral," *Ha'aretz*, October 30, p. 3a.

Sekulla, Allan. 1989. "The Body and the Archive." In *The Contest of Meaning*, edited by Richard Bolton. Cambridge, Mass.: MIT Press.

Shapira, Sarit. 1994. "A Camera in Limbo." In *Black Holes: The White Locus* (exhibition catalogue), Twenty-Second International Biennial of São Paolo, Israeli Ministry of Science and the Arts and Ministry of Foreign Affairs.

Sheffy, Smadar. 1997. "Defending the unstable self", *Ha'aretz*, November 13, p. 3C.

Shragay, Nadav. 1997. "Jerusalem's Deputy Mayor Demands the Removal of the Exhibition *Live and Die as Eva Braun.*" *Ha'Aretz*, November 15, p. 1B.

Smith, Adam. 1976. *An Inquiry into the Nature and Causes of the Wealth of Nations*, edited by R. H. Campbell and A. S. Skinner. London: Oxford University Press.

Steiner, George. 1981. *The Portage to San Cristobal of Adolf Hitler.* Chicago: University of Chicago Press.

Tacher, Oren. 1992. "Piaza in Ramat Aviv: the reaction to the modernist time-space structure," *Studio* 37, 40–41.

Taylor, Mark. 1987. *Altarity.* Chicago: University of Chicago Press.

Trevor-Roper, Hugh. 1947. *The Last Days of Hitler.* New York: MacMillan.

Tsippor, Asaf. 1997. "Don't Call Me a Holocaust Denier, Sweetie." *Ma'ariv*, November 28 (supp.), p. 8.

Venn, Couze. 1997. "Beyond Enlightenment?" *Theory, Culture and Society* 14, no. 3.

Virilio, Paul. 1983. *Pure War.* New York: Semiotext(e).

Virilio, Paul. 1989. *War and Cinema.* London: Verso.

Virilio, Paul. 1994. "Cyberwar, God and Television: Interview with Paul Virilio", *CTHEORY* (interviewed by Louise Wilson) pp. 1–5 (http://ctheory.aec.at).

Yahav, Galya. 1997. "Decent, Indecent, and What Lies between Them." *Studio*, (in Hebrew) no. 88: 21–30.

Yarkoni, Yoram. 1996. "Amir's father: 'my son is an idiot,'" *Yediot Acharonot*, March 8, p. 3.

Yatom, Ehud, 1996. "I killed the terrorists of Bus Line 300," *Yediot Acharonot*, July 23, p. 19.

Yosifon, Golan. 1997. "A Storm in the Wake of Exhibition Opening at Israel Museum: *Live and Die as Eva Braun.*" *Ma'ariv*, November 6, p. 12.

Zandberg, Ester. 1997. "Ulmart Won the Battle." *Ha'aretz*, June 15, p. 1B (in Hebrew).

Zeltzer, Mark. 1998. *Serial Killers.* New York: Routledge.

Ziarek, Krzyszt. 1997. "After Aesthetics: Heidegger and Benjamin on Art and Experience." *Philosophy Today*, 41 (nos. 1–4).

Zigari, Khaled. 1996. "The dump in El Azariya," *Kol Ha'ir*, July 12, p. 36.

Zizek, Slavoj. 1992. *Looking Awry.* Cambridge, Mass.: MIT Press.

Zuckerman, Moshe. 1993. "Shoah in the Sealed Room: The "Holocaust" in Israeli Press during the Gulf War" (photocopy).

Discourse, 6, 38, 61–68, 70, 78, 92–95, 98–
  100, 113, 117, 123–124, 129, 132, 134,
  136–139, 141–151, 153–158, 162, 164–
  167, 170, 172, 182–183, 185, 188, 195,
  198, 261, 268–271, 273, 275–276, 279–
  280, 282–284
Display, 15, 18, 22–28, 31–32, 59, 78, 80, 83,
  86, 101, 107, 109, 113, 129, 153, 183,
  185, 234, 268, 270–274, 278–279
Divine supervision, 135
Dönitz, Karl, 71
Duchamp, Marcel, 19, 20, 60
Duras, Marguerite, 6, 54, 58–59

East Jerusalem, 116, 125, 182–185, 191–192,
  195–197, 200, 239
Economy of violence, 220, 245
El-Aqsa Mosque, 129, 184
El-Assad, Hafez, 223
El-Azariya, 182, 188, 190–191
El-Tal, Abdallah, 187
Engels, Friedrich, 13, 29
Exchange of objects, 25
Exchange relations, 25, 59–60, 64, 66, 112,
  263, 274, 277, 279, 283–284
Exhibit, 58, 60–62, 64, 66, 79, 85, 92
Exhibition, 18, 23–24, 28, 44, 51, 62, 64–65,
  69, 109
Evans, Walker, 115
Eye, 12, 14–16, 29–30, 32, 46, 96–97, 134,
  159, 170, 172–173, 194, 200, 206, 211–
  212, 225–226, 228–229, 251–254, 260,
  274, 287
Eye contact, 171–172, 255, 258

Fantasy, 41, 53, 69, 120, 148, 251, 261–264
Fascism, 27, 31, 38, 41, 43
Fetishization, 67–68, 74
Field of art, 12, 23–24, 64, 269–270, 275–
  276, 278, 282–283

Foster, Hal, 12
Foucault, Michel, 8, 24, 93–96, 98, 101, 103,
  136–137, 139–149
Freedom of expression, 270–271, 281–282
French Revolution, 146–147, 213, 272–273
Freud, Sigmund, 18, 109
Frydlender, Barry, 6, 93, 102, 104–105, 107–
  108, 117

Gaethgens, T. W., 272
Game, 256, 276, 279–282, 284
Game of art, 78–79
Garbage, 182–190, 263
Gatekeeper, 195, 280–281
Gaze, 5–6, 14, 16, 18, 24, 26, 41, 56–59, 78,
  80, 85–86, 97, 100, 103, 109, 117, 122,
  134–137, 144, 146–149, 197, 192–193,
  234, 237, 268, 274, 284
Gazit, Shlomo, 221
Gefen, Aviv, 169
Genealogy, 93, 147, 150, 193
Ghost, 263
Gilory, Paul, 103
Governmentality, 94–96, 98, 101, 139–140,
  145, 148, 159–160, 162
Graffiti, 278–280
Graham, Dan, 115
Green Line, 116, 187, 195–196, 198–200, 216
Guattari, Felix, 50, 187, 193, 215–217
Guilleminot, Marie Ange, 6, 59, 78, 80–82,
  85–86, 88
Gunthert, André, 36

Haber, Etan, 155
Hamas, 220, 225, 249
Hand, 13–15, 29, 83, 88, 96–97, 194–195,
  199, 210–212, 217, 287
Har Homa, 125
Harodi, Erez, 176
Heidegger, 5, 17, 36, 38–47, 132